Not One of Them in Place

SUNY Series in Modern Jewish Literature and Culture
Sarah Blacher Cohen, editor

Not One of Them in Place

*Modern Poetry and
Jewish American Identity*

Norman Finkelstein

State University of New York Press

Published by
State University of New York Press, Albany

© 2001 State University of New York

For information, address State University of New York Press
90 State Street, Suite 700, Albany, New York 12207

Production by Dana Foote
Marketing by Michael Campochiaro

Library of Congress Cataloging-in-Publication Data

Finkelstein, Norman, 1954–
Not one of them in place : modern poetry and Jewish American identity /
Norman Finkelstein
p. cm.—(SUNY series in modern Jewish literature and culture)
Includes bibliographical references and index.
ISBN 0–7914–4983–1 (alk. paper)—ISBN 0–7914–4984–X (pb : alk. paper)
1. American poetry—Jewish authors—History and criticism. 2. American poetry—
20th century—History and criticism. 3. Jews—United States—Intellectual life.
4. Jews in literature. 5. Group identity in literature. I. Title. II. Series.

PS153.J4 F56 2001
811'.5098924—dc21
00–054735

10   9   8   7   6   5   4   3   2   1

The Six Hundred Thousand Letters

The day like blank paper
Being pulled from my typewriter.
With the six
Hundred thousand letters of the Law
Surrounding me,
Not one of them in place.
                                    —*Harvey Shapiro*

Contents

Acknowledgments

This book was written between 1992 and 1999, years during which my personal and professional lives went through significant changes. In 1994 I became Chair of the Xavier University English Department, which, needless to say, slowed down my research considerably. But family, friends, and colleagues were immensely supportive, and editors were gratifyingly receptive as the work gradually took shape. In addition, the University provided me with the time I needed to write. I would like to thank the Office of the Dean of Arts and Sciences for reduced teaching loads, and the Faculty Development Committee for a faculty development grant in the spring semester of 1998, when I was able to make substantial progress.

Some parts of *Not One of Them in Place* originally appeared in periodicals and critical collections. Chapter 1 appeared in *The Objectivist Nexus,* edited by Rachel Blau DuPlessis and Peter Quartermain, under the title "Tradition and Modernity, Judaism and Objectivism: The Poetry of Charles Reznikoff." Part of chapter 2 was published as "Jewish American Modernism and the Problem of Identity: *With Special Reference to the Work of Louis Zukofsky,*" in *Upper Level Music: The Writing of Louis Zukofsky,* edited by Mark Scroggins. Part of chapter 4 was published in *Contemporary Literature* as "The Messianic Ethnography of Jerome Rothenberg's *Poland/1931.*" And part of chapter 5 appeared, under the title "Looking for the Way: The Poetry of Harvey Shapiro," in *Religion and Literature.* I am grateful to the editors of these publications.

Among the friends and colleagues who shared their insights and enthusiasm while I was working on this book, I would like to thank Stephen Fredman, Ernest Fontana, Alan Golding, Burton Hatlen, Robert Rethy, Mark Scroggins, Eric Murphy Selinger, Maeera Shreiber, Henry Weinfield, and Tyrone Williams. In a car full of poets and critics between Oxford and Cincinnati, Rachel Blau DuPlessis encouraged me to consider the work of Harvey Shapiro, which proved worthwhile advice indeed. And then there are the poets themselves, with whom I have associated with the greatest pleasure: Mike Heller, my friend of many years; Hugh Seidman, who gave such a galvanic reading at Xavier; Allen Grossman, Jerome Rothenberg, and Harvey Shapiro, who have been kind enough to share their thoughts and observations in letters, e-mail, and phone calls. Armand Schwerner died in February, 1999. He had been ill while I was working on his section of the book, and I regret not being able to share it with him. Armand was a great performer of his poetry, and I was privileged to read my work on the same program with him on a number of occasions. He was a dear friend, and is sorely missed.

My children, Ann and Steven, who are now about the same age as my students and chat so knowingly about books and music and movies with me whenever they're in town, are a constant wonder to me. My stepchildren, Joie and Danny West, finally get to be mentioned in one of my books—thanks for your patience, guys. And to my wife Alice West, I can only acknowledge once again how grateful I am for your love.

—Cincinnati, Ohio

I gratefully acknowledge the following for having given me permission to quote from published work:

The Jewish Publication Society, for permission to quote from Yankev Glatshteyn, *Selected Poems of Yankev Glatshteyn,* translated by Richard J. Fein, © 1987.

Coffee House Press, for permission to quote from Michael Heller, *In the Builded Place,* © 1989.

Michael Heller, for permission to quote from Michael Heller, *Wordflow: New and Selected Poems,* © 1997.

Allen Grossman, for permission to quote from Allen Grossman, *A Harlot's Hire,* © 1961.

Black Sparrow Press, for permission to quote from Charles Reznikoff, *The Complete Poems: 1918–1975,* © 1976, and from Charles Reznikoff, *Holocaust,* © 1977.

Miami University Press, for permission to quote from Hugh Seidman, *Selected Poems: 1965–1996,* © 1995.

New Directions Publishing Corp., for permission to quote from Allen Grossman, *The Ether Dome,* © 1991; George Oppen, *Collected Poems,* © 1975; and Jerome Rothenberg, *Khurbn and Other Poems,* © 1989, and *Poland/1931,* 1974.

University Press of New England, for permission to quote from Harvey Shapiro, *Battle Report,* Wesleyan University Press, © 1966; *The Light Holds,* Wesleyan University Press, © 1984; *This World,* Wesleyan University Press, © 1971; and *Selected Poems,* Wesleyan University Press, © 1997.

The Johns Hopkins University Press, for permission to quote from Louis Zukofsky, *"A,"* © 1978; *Complete Short Poems,* © 1991.

Preface

"The highest, as the lowest, form of criticism," Oscar Wilde declares, "is a mode of autobiography" (17). I will leave it to my readers to decide whether I am writing the highest or the lowest form of criticism, but the longer I write it, the more I feel it to be a mode of autobiography. At the same time, autobiography per se tempts me more and more, as a sort of adjunct to my criticism. Some years ago, given the opportunity to revise the original edition of *The Utopian Moment*, I produced a preface that was largely autobiographical; since then, I joined twenty-nine other Jewish academics and contributed an autobiographical essay called "The Master of Turning" to *People of the Book: Thirty Scholars Reflect on Their Jewish Identity*. The writing in both instances came partly from a desire to explain my motives as a critic to myself and thus to other readers, knowing full well that in writing about "myself" I am writing fiction—and perhaps that in examining the work of other poets, I am getting closer to myself, writing autobiography as criticism. Be that as it may, I remain convinced that I write about poetry for two reasons: *as a poet* I want to explain to myself why the poetry of another is valuable to me; *as a reader* I want to convince other readers that they will find a particular body of poetry to be of value. And the same is true for writing about Jewish literature: through the work I hope to understand my Jewish self more deeply, and to convince others that the work provides insight into Jewish culture, history, and belief.

It should come as no surprise then that I regard this book, if not as the synthesis of my two earlier studies, then perhaps as the third volume of a loose and by no means preconceived trilogy. *The Utopian Moment* presents a vision of poetry by arguing for the value of a particular range of modern American poetries; *The Ritual of New Creation* presents a vision of Jewish literature by analyzing a variety of modern Jewish textual discourses. The interpretive concerns of both books inform *Not One of Them in Place*, for as readers will see, the importance of Jewish American poetry lies partly in the ways it inflects the persistant questions of mode, style, and canon formation in modern American poetry, and partly in the ways it engages equally persistant questions of modern Jewish identity. *Not One of Them in Place*, therefore, can be read as a work of literary history and of cultural studies in the broad sense of these terms. But I admit that my forte has always been close reading (the long arm of the New Criticism reaching over the decades), and in working through matters of literary ideology, canon formation, ethnicity, religious belief, and so on, I have never abandoned my faith in the category of the aesthetic, scrutinizing a great many individual poems in the hope that readers will find in them a source of pleasure. "The test of poetry," writes Louis Zukofsky, one of the most important poets under consideration here, "is the range of pleasure it affords as sight, sound, and intellection" (*Test of Poetry* vii). I have yet to find a better summary.

Although I expect that most readers of this book will have some relation to the academy, and have particular interest in Jewish studies or modern American literature, I also hope that it will catch the eye of the general reader who has some interest in the subject, and wishes to learn more. It is not a comprehensive introduction to Jewish American poetry, but it will probably serve to introduce many readers to one or more of the poets whose work I discuss. Much of that work is complex and challenging in terms of its style, its theme, and its cultural or historical context, and my prose has had to rise to the challenge. But I have tried to write in a deliberate and open style, with as little recourse as possible to a specialized critical vocabulary, that is, "jargon." The book has been composed without footnotes: everything I have to say about the subject is to be found in the text, and all quotations in the text refer to the list of works cited.

Introduction

The Traditions of Jewish American Poetry

"I do not, in fact, wish to ask or answer the question, 'What is Jewish poetry?' The poetry of a nation is whatever comes to pass in its domain in the name of poetry, and can neither succeed nor fail" (*Long Schoolroom* 159). Such is Allen Grossman's sensible disclaimer at the beginning of "Jewish Poetry Considered as a Theophoric Project" (1990), an essay which proves, ironically, to be one of our most intelligent and sophisticated articulations of the qualities unique to Jewish verse. As Grossman has known since the start of his career, the "domain" in which he has become a prominent citizen flies two flags, a situation that motivates much of his splendid work in poetics. Reviewing Allen Ginsberg's *Kaddish* in 1962, Grossman declares that for Jews writing in America, "the only significant Jewish poetry will also be a significant American poetry" (*Long Schoolroom* 158). This is not merely an observation about poetry; it is also a provocation to criticism. In what ways shall significant Jewish poetry written by Jewish Americans be understood as significant American poetry? What criteria shall be brought to bear in determining this significance? What paths through the history of Jewish culture, and through the history of American literature, lead to these determinations? As such determinations are made, is a canon of Jewish American poetry coming into being? And keeping in mind the great discursive range and complex affinities of this writing, which are commensurate with those of modern American poetry in general, can we develop a comprehensive vision of Jewish American poetry that may offer answers, however provisional, to questions such as these?

Steven J. Rubin writes in his Introduction to *Telling and Remembering: A Century of American Jewish Poetry* (1997) that "although occasional articles and critical studies have been published in the 1990s, American Jewish literary criticism remains overwhelmingly concerned with prose" (1). What Rubin does not realize, however, is that the critical neglect of Jewish American poetry may actually prove advantageous to an anthologist at work in this relatively undefined field. Every anthology participates in the conflicted process of canon formation. As Alan Golding argues in his authoritative study on canons in American poetry, "Examining the often conflicting standards that American anthologists have brought to bear on the problem of selection . . . illuminates more general issues in canon formation. It helps us understand how an anthology can reflect, expand, or redirect a period's canon; what literary and social principles regulated the poetry canon at different points in American history; and how those principles have changed over the years" (3). While it still may be too early to speak of a canon of Jewish American poetry (as one may already speak, I believe, of a canon of Jewish American fiction), we must keep in mind, as Golding tells us, that "after a selective canon has been formed, every anthologist faces the choice of maintaining or trying to change the canon" (24–25). Yet the "canon wars" that have defined much twentieth-century American poetry and have made the study of this poetry so contentious hardly seem to have had an impact on the selection of poets in *Telling and Remembering* or the American section of Howard Schwartz's *Voices within the Ark* (1980).

This is due primarily to the fact that a sophisticated criticism of Jewish American poetry, contributing to the determination of a recognizable canon, remains in a formative stage. Consider what Rubin tells us in the Introduction about the selection process for his anthology: "My purpose throughout this collection is to present the best and the most representative work of those writers who can properly be classified as American Jewish poets. I have not included those poets who, although nominally Jewish, do not deal significantly with the American Jewish experience. All the authors represented—male or female, traditionalist or experimental, modernist or postmodernist—share an interest in and a desire to explore those issues surrounding their Jewishness" (11). "Best and most representative" is part of the anthologist's standard discourse, and serves as an open invitation to argument (How, I wonder, could Rubin possibly have failed to include Grossman in this volume?). "Traditionalist or experimental" takes us closer to my concerns, but can bear a great deal of scrutiny: not only does the matter of style connect Jewish American poetry with the great debates over modern American poetry in general, but it also provides crucial insights into the particular sensibilities possessed of "a desire to explore those issues surrounding their Jewishness." What happens to "Jewishness"—which is to say, what constitutes an expression of Jewish identity—when placed in the context of American poetry? One is led to ask if any sort of theoretical perspective on either American or Jewish literature comes into play when such anthologies are constructed, or when "Jewish American poetry" as a class is invoked in a discussion of hybrid American literatures. Yet as I shall argue throughout this book, just such a perspective is crucial if one is to go beyond the casual acknowledgment of ethnic origins or the surfaces of style and theme, and understand this literature in terms of the sociohistorical and textual conditions that have shaped it and that, indeed, grant it cultural significance.

Like anthologists, all critics become more or less willing, more or less persuasive shapers of a canon. This is especially true when the poetry under discussion has not been extensively addressed, as is the case for a number of the poets here. I would be disingenuous if I did not admit that I have my preferences when it comes to Jewish American poets, and these preferences will become quite clear in what follows. But the main purpose of this book is to define and explore a particular dynamic, a historical dialectic that is still unfolding in the growing body of Jewish American poetry. This is what has determined my choice of poets, though it could also be said that my encounters with them—which were immediate, intense, challenging, and deeply gratifying— eventually coalesced into a more theoretical understanding of the field. I hope that the configurations and speculations to which I submit their work will result in the next step in the criticism of a poetry that we can recognize as both genuinely Jewish and identifiably American.

A small number of important statements serve as both the foundation of my project and, at times, the objects of my inquiry. That almost all the critics who have made important contributions to a nascent theory of Jewish American poetry are poets themselves is hardly an accident. "What is Jewish or not Jewish about certain American poems is all tied up in the vexing problem of what is poetic or not poetic about them," writes John Hollander in "The Question of American Jewish Poetry" (1988). As a rather conservative stylist with a strong investment in Anglo American Romanticism, Hollander has a definite sense of what constitutes the "poetic" in recent American verse. But when it comes to Jewishness, Hollander can be, to use his term, quite "protean" on the subject:

> I suppose that the American Jewish poet can be either blessed or cursed by whatever knowledge he or she has of Jewish history and tradition. I obviously believe in the power of the blessing, but it would be easy for any writer to be trapped in a slough of sentimentality or a homiletic bog. Literalness is the death of the poetic imagination, and all groups in the cultural community that speak for Jewishness will always be very literal about what "Jewish experience" is, as will all groups that want to speak for "American experience." Both kinds of experience are for the poet momentary aspects of the protean body of being who one is, and the analogues between American and modern Jewish identity are interesting apart from the almost exponential complications resulting from a combination of the two. These complications of the varieties of experience remain to be explored by practical criticism and cultural history. (50–51)

Hollander's fear of literalness and his reluctance to accept the authority of self-appointed spokespersons for Jewish (or American) experience indicate that the creative freeedom of the imagination, *poesis,* is of the highest priority in his evaluation of any work that falls under the rubric of Jewish American poetry. What poets *make* of their knowledge of Jewish history and tradition constitutes what Hollander calls "the power of the blessing," as in, for example, these two beautiful quatrains from his "Kinneret":

> The wind was working on the laughing waves,
>> Washing a shore that was not wholly land.
> I give life to dead letters: from their graves
>> Come leaping even X and ampersand.

Below, the dialect of the market-place
        All dark *o*'s, narrowed *i*'s and widened *e*'s.
Above, through a low gate, this silent space:
        The whitened tomb of wise Maimonides. (*Harp Lake* 4)

The free use of Jewish history and tradition that Hollander espouses is clearly represented in these lines, and the poet's imaginative freedom is counterpointed in the studied use of the form. Even a brief consideration of the text reveals the protean play of Hollander's Jewish American sensibility. "Kinneret" takes its title and setting from Lake Kinneret (*Harp Lake,* as in the title of Hollander's book), the Sea of Galilee in Israel. For the visiting American standing on the shore, this is "not wholly land," the pun on "wholly" and "holy" revealing a skepticism that is fundamental to his identity. Yet the poet remains true to his Jewish heritage: reversing the old anti-Semitic canards about the moribund nature of Jewish exis-tence, he gives "life to dead letters" in a land that the Zionist dream restored. Land and language are alive, but wait: on the shore of Lake Kinneret, in contemporary Israel, it's American English, not Hebrew, which this Jewish poet writes, part of the marketplace of languages Jews have made their own. And above this marketplace of Jewish discourse stands "this silent space:/The whitened tomb of wise Maim-onides": the richness of Jewish tradition represented as both absent and present, both silent and audible, both dead and living, by the tomb of the one of the very greatest Jewish philosophers.

Hollander's Jewish heterodoxy in his poetics and his poetry, along with his concern for the protean poetic imagination, find a parallel in an otherwise very different figure, but one who is equally important to my argument. In his indis-pensible "Pre-Face" to *Exiled in the Word* (*A Big Jewish Book* in its earlier version), Jerome Rothenberg explains that "since poetry, in the consensus of my contem-poraries, is more concerned with the 'free play of the imagination' than with doctrinal certainties *per se,* I've made no attempt to establish an 'orthodox' line or to isolate any one strain as purer or more purely Jewish than any others. Instead my assumption has been that poetry, here as elsewhere, is an inherently impure activity of individuals creating reality from all conditions & influences at hand" (9). Rothenberg would undoubtedly find Hollander's work tame, if not positively reactionary, but the strange fact remains that both of these poets from opposite ends of the contemporary American spectrum reject any orthodoxy in the deter-mination of Jewishness, stress the freedom of the imagination, and remain open to all of the possible ways in which Jewish culture and experience may be integrated into the process of poetic composition. Yet style and attitude could not be more different. Consider these lines from Rothenberg's "The Bride," in which sexual and linguistic mysticism are madly swirled together to bring us closer to the Presence:

my bride where hast thou gone then
& wherefore wherefore hast left thy milk bottles behind

thy tits will I squeeze upon for wisdom
of a milk that drops like letters
sacred alphabet soup we lap up o thou my Shekinah
do not be thus far from us in our Galician wildernesses
who scratch under our prayervests alive alive
in dreams of Shekinah's entry to the tents of God (*Poland/1931* 26)

Against the ironic equanimity of Hollander's rabbinic rationalism, we can pose the comic fervor of Rothenberg's kabbalistic messianism. Both are recognizably Jewish, and both honor the poem's free use of material drawn from the Jewish heritage. Yet the distances of Hollander's measured parables and the immediacies of Rothenberg's phantasmagorias seem to come from two very different poetic traditions. The difference is less Jewish than it is American, for it is from two different traditions in American poetry that Hollander's and Rothenberg's sensibilities are derived. And these poetic traditions relate in turn to various tendencies in modern Jewish experience, or more precisely, the historical pressures that have been brought to bear on modern Jewish culture.

Most observers agree that the defining tension in twentieth-century American poetry is to be found between two opposing aesthetics, neatly posed by Marjorie Perloff in the question that is also the title of her important essay: "Pound/Stevens: whose era?" On the one hand, the aesthetic represented by Stevens looks back to Romantic and Symbolist modes, with their emphases on a questing "visionary humanism" and the inwardness of the lyric imagination. The Poundian aesthetic, on the other hand, aggressively severs its ties with the nineteenth century and reclaims the external world by way of "collage, fragmentation, parataxis" (*Dance of the Intellect* 21, 22). Perloff's essay brilliantly catalogs the many differences between these two traditions, differences that have to do not only with technique, but with the status of the self in the poem, the view of history it presents, and the role of the poetic imagination in a social and political context. In *The Utopian Moment,* I observe, apropos of such analyses as Perloff's (or conversely, Harold Bloom's), that tradition "is always, at least to some extent, a synthetic matter; the major poet is capable of assimilating, even inventing his or her precursors. In the twentieth century, the 'tradition' of Stevens or the 'tradition' of Pound are thus critical fictions, to which active poets rarely subordinate themselves" (142). Among the Objectivists, with their strong links to Pound and Williams, George Oppen notes in his interview with L. S. Dembo that "really Blake is more important to me than Williams" and that "Wyatt's poems, and several Middle English poems, among other antiquities, mean more to me than any except one or two of the contemporary" (*Contemporary Writer* 184). Likewise, Louis Zukofsky, associated even more closely with Pound and Williams, notes late in his career that he actually felt, at least at that point, a stronger affinity to Stevens: "Reading him for the last three months I felt that my own writing, without my being aware of it, was closer to his than to that of any of my contemporaries in the last half century of life we shared together" (*Prepositions* 27).

Nevertheless, Perloff rightly insists that what is generally perceived as a division between two crucial modes of poetic discourse "is neither an idle quarrel nor a narrow sectarian war between rival academics . . . who just happen to have different literary and political allegiances. The split goes deep, and its very existence raises what I take to be the central questions about the meaning of Modernism—indeed, about the meaning of poetry itself in current literary history and theory" (2).

Given our concerns, this split also has much to do with the meaning of Jewish American poetry in current literary history and theory, for in one respect, Jewish American poetry may be understood as a peculiar fold in the larger debate. Every American poet since the beginning of the century (indeed, every poet writing in English) has had to negotiate this debate in his or her own way, for the successful negotiation of such controversies is always a necessary step in the development of an individual style. Stylistically, the most important Jewish American poets have tended toward one or the other pole, as in the cases of Hollander, whose good-humored, meditative tone owes a great deal to Stevens (as in, say, *The Man with the Blue Guitar*), and of Rothenberg, whose graphic, startling details hearken back to those of Pound's Canto XIV or Canto XLV. Here are two additional instances, the first from Grossman's "The Room," the second from Hugh Seidman's "Fabergé," from his "Collectibles":

> A man is sitting in a room made quiet by him.
> Outside, the August wind is turning the leaves of its book.
> The door is open, everything is disclosed, each leaf, all the voices.
>
> The man is resting from the making of the quiet in which he sits.
> The floor is swept, his books are laid aside open, his eyes are open.
> All the leaves and voices are outside in the restless wind. (*Ether Dome* 63)

* * *

> Royal tchotchkies: chalcedony terrier;
> gold-lipped, diamond-eyed, obsidian toad.
>
> "Bourgeoisie love coarse *cloissonné*," he said.
> The Nobels were his best non-royal patrons.
>
> Bored Edward, Wallis puffing in Regine's.
> No good, evil—just power users. (*Selected Poems* 224)

Grossman's engagement with Stevens, particularly the Stevens of such poems as "Large Red Man Reading" and "The House Was Quiet and the World Was Calm," offers him a way of recovering the Jewish devotion to the Book and its gathered voices, which in "The Room" proves analogous to the old notion of the Book of Nature and to the Mallarméan one of the Book that is the world. Stevens and Grossman are concerned with self-creation, which involves the re-creation of the exterior world through the power of the poet's interiorizing imagination. Gershom Scholem observes that in the kabbalistic tradition, God "looked into the Torah and created the world"; indeed, the Torah is regarded as God's Name, "consequently not separate from the divine essence, not created in the strict sense of the word; rather, it is something that represents the secret life of God" (*On the Kabbalah* 40, 41). According to Stevens, "We say God and the imagination are one" ("Final Soliloquy of the Interior Paramour" [524]); thus, in an uncannily kabbalistic turn, the poet sits "reading, from out of the purple tabulae,/The outlines of being and its expressings, the syllables of its law:/*Poesis, poesis,* the literal characters, the vatic lines" ("Large Red Man Reading" [424]). In Grossman's text, the poet rests after having made the room that is his world, much as God rests after the Creation: "Everything in its place is at rest inside the room./And the man is at rest, seeing each leaf, and hearing all the voices" (*Ether Dome* 63). What we have here, as Harold Bloom tells us in "The Sorrows of American Jewish Poetry," is "a blend of a devotional strain and a late Romantic visionary intensity" (260): a poetry derived equally from the tradition of Jewish textuality and the tradition of lyric inwardness that Stevens represents.

Seidman's "Fabergé" reveals a different combination of traditions. Seidman can trace his poetic lineage back to Pound through his teacher, Louis Zukofsky. Zukofsky and his colleagues both develop and revise Pound's Imagist principles (direct treatment of the material, linguistic economy, composition by way of the "musical phrase" instead of the "metronome") to derive their own Objectivist program. In Objectivism, precisely arranged detail, accurate reportage, and historical analysis take precedence over the lyric inwardness and imaginative self-making of Romanticism. Zukofsky's term, drawn from his famous "An Objective," is *sincerity*, resulting in writing "which is the detail, not mirage, of seeing, of thinking with the things as they exist, and of directing them along a line of melody" (*Prepositions* 12). "Sincerity, then," as Mark Scroggins explains, "is an attitude of absolute faithfulness both to one's perceptions and to one's language" (96). Duly followed, sincerity in writing will lead to "objectification," "the resolving of words and their ideation in structure" (*Prepositions* 13), or as Scroggins would have it, "the structural principle by which the poet's efforts of sincerity become the completed poem" (98–99).

These Objectivist values remain in Seidman's work, but as in Zukofsky's poetry, at times we find a distinctively Jewish twist. The lineage of "Fabergé" can thus be traced through the uneasy vacillations of Jewish identity in Zukofsky's "Poem beginning 'The'" back to the bitter satire of Pound's "Hugh Selwyn Mauberley." Note the startling phrase that begins the poem: "Royal tchotchkies." Many but by no means all readers will recognize the Yiddish word for knickknacks and the dismissive tone it represents. There's something of the unreconstructed ethnic in these lines, the voice of the Jewish New Yorker looking through the window of the posh midtown shop and bringing his particular view of history to bear on what he sees. The speaker in this poem is not too far removed from his working-class, immigrant roots, despite his mordantly precise language. Examining the object before him, the "gold-lipped, diamond-eyed, obsidian toad," he recognizes, with delicious irony, the essential vulgarity of his ancestral oppressors, the (gentile) aristocracy. His witheringly laconic judgment ("No good, evil—just power users") condemns a class with supposedly refined aesthetic tastes that nonetheless lacks the powers of moral discrimination that are part of the Jewish heritage. Seidman's own moral discrimination and his equally Jewish consciousness of history find a most effective poetic vehicle in the Objectivist tradition, which, although derived from (the anti-Semitic) Pound, revises his work even more dramatically than Jewish poets in the Romantic tradition revise a precursor like Stevens.

As I have been implying through these readings, style, the "what" of poetry, is related in turn to the process of poetic composition, the "how" of poetry, and to the intent of poetry, the "why." Charles Altieri distinguishes Objectivist from Symbolist procedures as follows: "Where Objectivist poets seek an artifact presenting the modality of things seen or felt as immediate structure of relations, symbolist poets typically strive to see beyond the seeing by rendering in their work a process of meditating upon what the immediate relations in their work reflect" ("Objectivist Tradition" 6). As we have seen, these distinctions in turn relate to different temporal and historical orientations. The modal and structural procedures of the Objectivist tradition lead to an analytic perspective in which historical time becomes available and manipulable to the poet through the perception and arrangement of immediate detail. By contrast, the Romantic/Symbolist motive, "to see beyond the seeing" through a process of meditation, leads to an experience of significant time that is personal and interior rather than historical. The Objectivist is concerned with the generation of historical narrative out of perceptual detail, and with the moral distinctions that subsequently arise because of our historically contingent condition. George Oppen expresses this perfectly in the opening lines of his masterpiece, *Of Being Numerous:*

> There are things
> We live among 'and to see them
> Is to know ourselves'.
>
> Occurence, a part
> Of an infinite series,
>
> The sad marvels;

Of this was told
A tale of our wickedness.
It is not our wickedness. (147)

The Symbolist, however tends to dissolve historical narrative by moving beyond detail to a point of individual vision, which betokens existential freedom. Consider what transpires in these magnificent lines from Allen Mandelbaum's "The Perfect Woman Reads a Page of Kant," in which Mandelbaum's figure of the Shekhinah meditates on the Lucretian *flammantia moenia mundi*, the "flaming walls of the world":

> . . . She reflects, as on an urn,
> upon *flammantia moenia mundi,* fallen
> walls of the world, the burning boundaries
> that held the Alps, the straining galaxies,
> and all the wind-whipped dead: the sentry house
> is cinders; border guardians, sages, friends
> are gone; her journey need not be clandestine.
> Alone, the perfect woman steps across
> the ford of air . . . (*Chelmaxioms* 97)

In a poet like Oppen, the past is alive in the details of the present, "an infinite series"; but for one like Mandelbaum, the past is gone with "all the wind-whipped dead," leaving the openness of a "ford of air." The difference, as Yosef Hayim Yerushalmi would say, is between "the historicity of the past" and "its eternal contemporaneity" (96).

Zakhor, Yerushalmi's modern classic of Jewish historiography, provides me with the means to explain why Jewish American poetry at its most significant gravitates toward either the Objectivist or Symbolist stance. In my previous study, *The Ritual of New Creation,* Yerushalmi's crucial distinction between the traditional importance of Jewish *memory* and the modern concern for Jewish *history* helped me to analyze the contemporary pressures that have been brought to bear on Jewish literary culture. The preeminent injunction for the Jewish people is *zakhor* (remember), and "It is above all God's acts of intervention in history, and man's responses to them, be they positive or negative, that must be recalled" (Yerushalmi 11). But remembrance, however much it is engaged with the past, is not historical in any modern sense; on the contrary, in its enduring power over the centuries, Jewish memory is ritualized and highly selective. It is only since the Haskalah, the Jewish Enlightenment, that "The primary intellectual encounter between Judaism and modern culture has lain precisely in a mutual preoccupation with the historicity of things" (85–86). Even today, Yerushalmi provocatively comments, "it would appear that even where Jews do not reject history out of hand, they are not prepared to confront it directly, but seem to await a new, metahistorical myth, for which the novel provides at least a temporary modern surrogate" (98). Nevertheless, as I will remind the reader frequently, what characterizes the modern Jewish sensibility is its awareness of historical rupture, leading dialectically to the reality that "history becomes what it had never been before—the faith of fallen Jews" (86).

I propose that under the conditions of modernity, those whom Yerushalmi calls "fallen Jews"—assimilated, secular, intellectual, more familiar with figures such as Shylock and Gerontion than with the sages of the *Aboth*—not only write out of these conditions, but actively seek the means to express their historical "faith." "Blest/Infinite things" writes Zukofsky in *"A,"* "So many/Which confuse imagination/Through its weakness" (231). Despite the "weakness" of the imagination confronting the infinite things of world, Jewish poets in the Objectivist tradition scrutinize those infinite things in order to make sense of the world, both in its immediacy and in its historicity. "The shock is metaphysical" declares Oppen in "Return" (26), one of the first poems he writes after his long hiatus. Empiricism never suffices for such a poet. Oppen is looking at a Sequoia seed, from which comes the gigantic tree. The "metaphysical" shock of the physical thing, in its capacity to change over time, inevitably leads him to an engagement with history, as he recalls his days as a Communist organizer, when a woman named Petra "beat/A washpan out her window gathering/A crowd like a rescue." The forces of anti-Semitism and Fascism against which Oppen and his comrades struggled remain alive in his memory, a historical lesson that loses none of its urgency years after the fact: "And how imagine it? or imagine/Coughlan in the streets,/Pelley and the Silver Shirts?" (28). The Objectivist methods provide the means to "imagine it," so that the resistance to Pelley's American Fascism and the anti-Semitic broadcasts of Father Coughlan becomes part of the historicity of Oppen's poetry, what he calls his "test of truth."

At the same time, however, the traditional force of Jewish memory remains strong, and the "new, metahistorical myth" which Yerushalmi rightly sees in the Jewish novel (as in those, for instance, of Cynthia Ozick or Steve Stern) may be found throughout Jewish literature, including poetry. Because this force, which is traditionally understood as a divine commandment of the utmost importance, coexists with the more modern faith in history, the mythologies of the prophetic self that operate in poets like Stevens prove at least as attractive as the ensemble of procedures developed by poets such as Pound. In the chapter on Hollander's *Spectral Emanations* and Mandelbaum's *Chelmaxioms* in *The Ritual of New Creation*, I argued that the quest narratives of these major Jewish American poems could be read as "symbolic substitutions for the Law that has gone beyond their grasp" (81). Poets working in this tradition are keenly aware of the problem of the covenant for the modern Jew; the struggle against the loss of the Law that binds the Jewish people to God produces a "visionary intensity," a prophetic agon that is deeply Romantic in its expression. It is a result of what Grossman calls Jewish poetry's theophoric or "God-bearing" project, which imposes a responsibility on the poet that cannot be avoided:

> And I am like the singer, among the singers I have heard:
> That great woman I once heard cry, "O Mother, I have sung
> Every word of the song that you taught me by fire and sword.
> The day is at an end, and I am out of breath. May I go out
> To play now by myself." The mother thinks a little. Then
> She says, "No, my dear. Now you must sing *The Song of the Lord.*"
> (*Ether Dome* 23)

In Grossman's "Flax," the mother may be the muse who has taught other songs, but she is above all the Shekhinah, the feminine bearer of God's Presence, who in the end will always remind the poet that "The Jew's word, strictly speaking, is One" (*Long Schoolroom* 162). The extent to which Jewish poets in the Romantic tradition can share their vision in a secular world remains an open question, for as Grossman declares,

> The song of the Lord in solitude goes up,
> Ten times enfolded, blue, and saturate
> With law to the heavens at noon of gaze,
> And down among the graves and the darker animals. (*Ether Dome* 149)

In Grossman's "Song of the Lord," "The Lord is alone"; we hear "The voice of the Lord at rest in his solitude." That solitude is the place of visionary utterance, and as in Stevens (and, for that matter, as in Whitman and Dickinson, as in Wordsworth and Keats), it is there that the Jewish poet-prophet communes with the Presence, just as the Lord, whose song is "saturate/With law," communes with Himself.

Grossman's vision of the Shekhinah, of the poet in sublime communion with the Presence, like those of Rothenberg and Mandelbaum that we glimpsed earlier, emerges from a constellation of literary, cultural, religious, and historical factors of great complexity. From the scriptural tradition of the Hebrew prophets; to its reinvention by a history of English, mostly Protestant poets that culminates with the Romantics; to its Whitmanian revision under the conditions of American newness; to American Jews in the twentieth century scrupulously attentive to shifting poetic styles: it is an uncanny set of turns and derivations. I have been arguing that the discourse of any given Jewish American poem results from dialectical determinations of Jewish history and religion as well as the equally dialectical nuances of modern American poetics. Where then is one to situate these extraordinary lines?:

> The angel of the century
> stood on the night and would be heard;
> turned to my dream of tears and sang:
> Woman, American, and Jew,
> three guardians watch over you,
> three lions of heritage
> resist the evil of your age:
> life, freedom, and memory. (Rukeyser 61)

The "three lions of heritage" that Muriel Rukeyser identifies in her poem "Bubble of Air" make for powerful equations: Woman = life; American = freedom; Jew = memory. And indeed, it could be that these heritages are sufficient for Rukeyser, who draws on their strengths to bring herself to utterance: "answer the silence of the weak:/Speak!" (61). Yet the dialectical interplay of such determinants remains to be explored, and the three tropes that Rukeyser provides can take the reader of poetry interested in compounding gender with Jewish and American identity only so far. On the one hand, this interplay is not often found in Rukeyser's own poems, which tend to articulate the experiences of a woman, an American, or a Jew without necessarily bringing them together. On the other hand, a poem such as Maxine Kumin's "Getting the Message" goes right to the heart of the problem:

> In Sunday School I shivered at God's command:
> *Take off thy shoes, thou stands't on holy ground*
> and lay awake in the hot clutch of faith
> yearning yet fearful that the Lord might speak
> to me in my bed or naked in my bath.
> I didn't know how little risk I ran
> of being asked to set my people free
> from fording some metaphorical Red Sea
> with a new-sprung Pharaoh raging at my back.
> I didn't know the patriarchy that spared me
> fame had named me chattel, handmaiden.
> God's Angels looked me over but flew by. (183–184)

The ironies are manifold. On the one hand, Kumin is absolutely right: Jewish tradition is patriarchal, and while there is a long line of assertive, confident, and heroic women in the Hebrew Scriptures, the highest forms of utterance, which we associate with both prophecy and poetry, constitute a nearly exclusive male domain. The perceptive girl attending her Jewish American "Sunday School" and caught up "in the hot clutch of faith" is bound to be disappointed once she understands the implications of the religious history to which she does and does not belong. On the other hand, as all artists quickly realize, the blocking agents of culture and identity can also act as spurs to further creative effort. *Some* force has inspired Kumin's poetry (in which Jewish, American, and female identities do indeed intermingle), even if it is not an angel of the traditional, patriarchal Jewish God. "I like to think God's talent scouts today/select for covenant without regard/ for gender," Kumin continues in "Getting the Message," and it is clear that her poetry is premised on that hope. Maintaining her belief that "divine authentication lights up truth," she holds that "Fragments of it, cryptic, fugitive/still spark the synapses that let us live." The ineluctable Jewish image of divine, sparking fragments, the kabbalistic shards, shine forth at the end of the poem.

In "Getting the Message," Kumin, as a woman poet, works her way through the issue of gender to revise and reclaim her Jewish identity. I must acknowledge, however, that this working through is not the main subject of my book, and readers will be quick to notice that all the poets I discuss at length are men. This is not to say, however, that I am adumbrating a specifically male line in Jewish American poetry, for I contend that the stylistic and cultural tensions I analyze are generally applicable to this body of literature. When the dialectic of gender does comes into play, as will be seen in a number of instances here, it usually involves the poet's use and representation of the Shekhinah. In Jewish, particularly kabbalistic, tradition, God's Presence has come to be symbolized as female. The history of the Shekhinah as mother, bride, and lover is fully detailed in Gershom Scholem's essay "Shekhinah: The Feminine Element In Divinity" (in his volume *On the Mystical Shape of the Godhead*). Two points in particular about the Shekhinah and modern (masculine) Jewish poetry are worth noting. The first is that, as we've already noted, God's Presence, gendered female, is often conflated with a figure of inspiration, a muse, likewise traditionally female. Grossman, as we shall see, devotes a great deal of his critical energy to both distinguishing and connecting muse and Shekhinah, but generally speaking, the two can be related because, as Scholem tells us, "what characterizes the *Shekhinah* is her transitional position between transcendence and immanence" ("Shekhinah" 164). This characteristic inevitably leads Jewish American poets, who are frequently even more attuned to the "Western," that is, gentile, poetic tradition than to Jewish tradition, to embrace this figure in their search for their own rhetorical stance.

The other point regarding the Shekhinah is more troubling for feminist readers. Scholem informs us that in the kabbalistic tradition, based on biblical and talmudic sources, the "*Kenesseth Yis'rael* [the Congregation of Israel] itself was understood as constituting the body of the *Shekhinah,* in which and through which the *Shekhinah* acts and suffers with the people of Israel" ("Shekhinah" 161). This notion is, in effect, the starting point of Maeera Shreiber's recent analysis of Jewish femininity as associated with "the voice of exile and return," and of the patriarchal tradition "that figures catastrophic loss of place and of collective identity as feminine" (274). Drawing on Alain Finkielkraut's *The Imaginary Jew,* Shreiber observes "a crucial gendered opposition long implicit in the dominant constructions of Jewish identity—constructions that set an idealized vision of home as whole against a view of exile-as-diaspora as perpetually broken, the feminine body figuring prominently in both cases. This binary is in dire need of dismantling . . ." (276).

Any binary that produces harmful stereotyping certainly should be dismantled (or at least unveiled), though I am increasingly convinced that such ideological deconstructions tell only part of the story. Finkielkraut sees Sophie Portnoy of *Portnoy's Complaint* as a perverse female representation of Jewish exilic loss, a figure, I would assume, comparable to that of Naomi in Ginsberg's "Kaddish." In these instances, the guilt-ridden Jewish son turns in flight from the mother; thus "in Diaspora (as typically construed) forgetting or losing a primary connection to Jewishness is as necessary as the process of individuation itself" (Shreiber 276–277). As an alternative to these admittedly monstrous yet strangely moving female figures, Shreiber offers the bilingual (Yiddish/English) poetry of Irena Klepfisz as a rather programmatically community-building project that reclaims *mame-loshn,* the mother-tongue. But if these are the choices that the dialectic of exile, gender, and Jewish identity offer us, then I prefer Ginsberg and Roth.

Fortunately, however, there are other possibilities. A poem such as Denise Levertov's "The Jacob's Ladder" is a perfect example of prophetic strength coupled with an Objectivist acceptance of the material world. In Genesis 28, Jacob's dream of the ladder assures him of God's covenant:

> And he dreamt:
> Here, a ladder was set on the earth,
> its top reaching the heavens,
> and here: messengers of God were going up and down it.
> And here:
> YHWH was standing over against him.
> He said:
> I am YHWH,
> the God of Avraham your father and the God of Yitzhak.
> The land on which you lie
> I give to you and to your seed. (Fox 130–131)

But in Levertov's midrashic revision of the dream, the ladder "is of stone,"

> A stairway of sharp angles
> angles, solidly built.
> One sees that the angels must spring
> down from one step to the next, giving a little
> lift of the wings:
> and a man climbing
> must scrape his knees, and bring

the grip of his hands into play. The cut stone
consoles his groping feet. Wings brush past him.
The poem ascends. (39)

Rather than a ladder of the spirit with its angelic messengers and the God of the patriarchs on top, Levertov's ladder is more of an earthly construction, which may scrape human knees but still has the power to console our desire for materiality. The poet sends the poem up the ladder: not only the divine, but the human as well may initiate communication between earth and heaven.

Unfortunately, Levertov rarely writes in such a centrally Jewish and midrashic fashion. The daughter of a Russian Jewish father, a descendent of the Hasidic rebbe Schneour Zalman, and a Welsh mother, a descendent of the Christian mystic Angel Jones of Mold (see her poem "Illustrious Ancestors"), Levertov grew up in England, where she was educated at home, her father having converted to Anglicanism and become a priest. Levertov herself was "converted" from British Romanticism to American Objectivism through William Carlos Williams and her association with the Black Mountain poets, and like her colleague Robert Duncan, her poems frequently destabilize Objectivist and Symbolist distinctions, often in the service of a feminist perspective. Thus the concerns of gender may be factored into the analysis of Jewish American poetry, and though in the main I do not explicitly address these concerns, I hope that what I present in this book may serve as a contribution to such investigations.

The one important exception to my observation that the major statements about Jewish American poetry have been written by poets is Harold Bloom's "The Sorrows of American Jewish Poetry" (1972), originally published in *Commentary* and reprinted in *Figures of Capable Imagination* (1976). Like his colleague John Hollander, Bloom's devotion to Anglo-American Romanticism and its modern incarnation in Wallace Stevens leads him to privilege what I regard as only one term in the dialectic of Jewish American poetry. More than twenty-five years after its appearance, Bloom's essay remains one of the clearest and most vigorous arguments for the Romantic aesthetic in Jewish American poetry, and though I take issue with it, it is still indispensable to any further consideration of the subject.

Thus chapter 1, which analyzes the work of Charles Reznikoff, begins with an extended consideration of Bloom's position, for it bears directly on the Objectivist tradition that Reznikoff represents. Chapter 2 extends this analysis to the work of Louis Zukofsky, whose codification of Objectivist practice is based on both his relation to Pound and his close reading of Reznikoff. I compare Zukofsky's program with that of his contemporaries, the Introspectivists, the one major formation of Jewish American poets to write in Yiddish rather than English. Chapter 3, at the center of the book, positions Allen Grossman both historically and theoretically. Beginning his career in the fifties, Grossman is part of the second generation of modern Jewish American poets. A major practitioner in the Romantic mode, he also writes with greater profundity on being a Jewish American poet (with equal stress on all three terms) than any other figure in the field. As an heir of Stevens and Hart Crane, his visionary Romanticism contrasts with that of the ethnopoetics project, which I consider in chapter 4. As represented by Jerome Rothenberg and Armand Schwerner, ethnopoetics offers what is in effect a synthesis of Objectivist practices with the multicultural romance of "magic, myth, & dream; earth, nature, orgy, love; the female presence the Jewish poets named Shekinah" (*Exiled in the Word* 5)—and seriously problematizes any understanding of contemporary Jewish American identity in the process. Yet a relatively unalloyed Objectivist poetry continues to be written by Jewish Americans as well, and in chapter 5 I return to New York City, where Objectivism came into being, and offer readings of Harvey Shapiro, Hugh Seidman, and Michael Heller, three of Reznikoff's and Zukofsky's most direct heirs. The Afterword of this book, more speculative than anything that comes before it, is a meditation on what may be called the Jewish difference in American poetry, or perhaps in the Western canon at large. In the Torah, the Jews are ordered by God to "choose life," yet as Wallace Stevens says, in a phrase that sums up thousands of years of poetry, "Death is the mother of beauty" (69). What does this apparent contradiction mean for modern Jewish poets, and for Jewish American poets in particular? How have these poets come to terms with such colliding cultural values? "We'll talk in slant,/American accents to code the hidden language of the Word" (*Wordflow* 89), declares Michael Heller, as conscious as any Jewish American poet of the linguistic and historical doublings that continually destabilize this growing body of work. This book is an attempt to break that code.

1

Tradition and Modernity:
Charles Reznikoff and the
Test of (Jewish) Poetry

What does it mean to be a Jewish American poet? Posed as baldly as that, the question is impossible to answer. And yet it must be posed, if only to point out that whenever critics have attempted an answer, they have found in the work of one particular poet—Charles Reznikoff—the lodestar of their speculation. Reznikoff has become the exemplary Jewish American poet; his work is crucial to our understanding of the field, whether it is constituted from the perspective of aesthetics, religion, history, ethnology, psychology, or any combination thereof. Despite his professed modesty ("not for a seat upon the dais/but at the common table" [*CP* II: 75]), Reznikoff is, as his friend Louis Zukofsky might say, the test of (Jewish American) poetry.

There is no clearer proof of this than Reznikoff's portrayal in Harold Bloom's "The Sorrows of American-Jewish Poetry" (1972), an essay that may be said to inaugurate such poetry as a distinct field of critical inquiry. Based on what was then his emerging theory of influence, Bloom's argument at first appears as an attempt to foreclose on the possibility of "strong" Jewish American poets, since poetic strength is narrowly defined according to Bloom's peculiar set of psycho-historical dynamics:

> Strong poets tend to achieve an individualized voice by first all-but-merging with a precursor and then but pulling away from him, usually by way of a complex process of fault-finding and actual misinterpretation of the precursor. All post-Enlightenment poetry in English tends to be a displaced Protestantism anyway, so that the faith in a Person easily enough is displaced into an initial devotion to a god-like precursor poet. This, to understate it, is hardly a very Jewish process, and yet something like it seems necessary if poets are to continue to be incarnated. However far from Jewish tradition they may be, something recalcitrant in the spirit of young Jewish poets prevents them from so initially wholehearted a surrender to a Gentile precursor, and indeed makes them nervous about the process itself. Displaced Judaism tends to become one or another kind of a moralism, but

not the pragmatic religion-of-poetry that young poets, for a time, must accept. (253)

If Jewish poets are to write in English, they must initially "surrender to a Gentile precursor," a process they supposedly resist, consequently becoming moralists rather than devotees of "the pragmatic religion-of-poetry." This they cannot do, presumably, because even as secular Jews they intuit that the religion of poetry demands too radical a departure from *halakah,* "the Way," obedience to a singular, demanding moral idea that in traditional Judaism is represented by the one true God of Israel.

This thesis raises a number of question that Bloom never answers: Why do Jewish poets resist giving themselves wholeheartedly to Gentile precursors, when so much else in the cultural life of modern Jews involves integration with Gentile forms and ideas? Is wholehearted surrender to the precursor really the necessary first step for Jewish, or for that matter, Gentile poets? And once Jews do attain some sort of poetic status, is their purported moralism really at odds with a genuine poetic vocation, however that may be defined? Obviously, Bloom would as soon avoid these questions, for they raise serious doubts regarding the general applicability of his influence theory and reveal his morose view of secular Jewish culture in America.

The purpose of Bloom's dubious theorizing about Gentile precursors and Jewish moralism becomes clearer when we consider his comments on individual figures. Bloom is tough on nearly all the poets he discusses, but he saves some of his harshest remarks for those Jewish Americans who "accommodate [their] vision to the metric and rhetoric of Eliot, Pound, Williams and their followers" (251). Bloom's prejudice against these modernists is a cornerstone of his criticism; it is the converse of his predilection for the British and American Romantics and their twentieth-century heirs, most notably Wallace Stevens. Marjorie Perloff, one of our best seismologists in the study of the modernist earthquake, has persuasively argued that Bloom's denial of modernism, especially Poundian modernism, indicates his preference for a post-Romantic lyric poetry that maintains a sense of organic form and an isolated speaking subject seeking a latter-day version of sacred wisdom. What Bloom calls "The Internalization of Quest Romance" becomes, for Perloff, everything that Pound and his followers sought to overthrow by creating a poetry of generic instability: dialogic, collagist, exteriorized, and self-consciously constructivist (*Dance of the Intellect* 21–23).

A major tenet of "The Sorrows of American-Jewish Poetry" is that the modernist aesthetic derived from Pound and Williams is somehow inappropriate to the "desired stance" of their Jewish "followers," including Objectivists such as Charles Reznikoff, who for Bloom "should have been the American-Jewish poet in whom younger writers could find a precursor of real strength" (251). "Why attempt to translate Yehudah Halevi into the idiom of Pound and William Carlos

Williams? Is the form of this in any way appropriate to its burden?" (251–252) asks Bloom of Reznikoff, quoting the following lines:

My heart is in the East
and I at the farthest West:
how can I taste what I eat or find it sweet
while Zion
is in the cords of Edom and I
bound by the Arab?
Beside the dust of Zion
all the good of Spain is light;
and a light thing to leave it. (*CP* II: 69)

This passage does indeed come from Reznikoff's translation of Yehudah Halevi, but just what is the "burden" of the poem to which Bloom refers? The term "burden" could be regarded as a synonym for "content" or for "theme." In music, and by extension, in poetry, the word can refer to a recurring idea or motif carried by the melody or form. But Bloom's use of the term in the context of Jewish history and culture implies another meaning as well: to be a Jew, especially an assimilating, first-generation Jew like Reznikoff, is to carry a contradictory weight of culture and literary tradition that may be too hard to bear.

But does a closer look at the poem confirm this? If "burden" refers to the exilic longing of Halevi, and by extension, of Diasporic Jewry up until the modern period, then Reznikoff's lines succeed admirably. His free verse form in this stanza is handled with great skill, as he moves from the two phrasally complete opening lines, to the troubled enjambment of the four following lines, back to the phrasally complete sigh of the last three. Bloom implies that Reznikoff's poem is flawed because of a dichotomy of content ("burden") and form, a dichotomy produced by his allegiance to what we now call an Objectivist aesthetic derived partly from Williams and Pound. Yet this is a red herring: as Michael Heller says of Reznikoff's poetry, its "shorn-down language simultaneously inhabits a number of linguistic realms at once; the datum and its meaning for the poet are so inextricably linked that the usual suspension of belief or accounting for poetic license no longer applies" (*Conviction's Net* 61).

In a footnote to his Halevi poem, Reznikoff argues against Franz Rosenzweig's insistence on translating Halevi by maintaining the rhyme and rhythm of the original. Reznikoff asserts that

the reproduction of a metre in another language does not necessarily have the same effect it had in the original: rhyme and rhythm stirring in the Hebrew may be cloying and merely tiresome in English; it may be light instead of grave and so clever as to be nothing else. And it is of interest to note that Jehuda Halevi himself said: "It is but proper that mere beauty of sound should yield to lucidity of speech."

Bloom overlooks this sensitivity to Halevi's aesthetic and simply dismisses Reznikoff's version as inappropriate, due to what he deems its Poundian idiom. Actually, Reznikoff is faithful to both Halevi and Pound. For as Perloff observes, one of Pound's greatest contributions to modern poetry is "the use of translation as the invention of a desired other" (*Poetic License* 122). That desired other, for Reznikoff, is a historically derived vision of Jewish longing and Jewish endurance; that is, an other found in Jewish history, such as Halevi, which reflects Reznikoff's modern cultural ambivalence. In the Halevi translation, as well as hundreds of his other poems derived from the Jewish past, Reznikoff finds a way to express in contemporary terms what Gershom Scholem describes as the problem produced by the messianic idea in Judaism: "in Judaism, the Messianic idea has compelled *a life lived in deferment,* in which nothing can be done, nothing can be irrevocably accomplished" (*Messianic Idea* 35).

The historical irony here (which Bloom fails to appreciate) is that in Reznikoff, and to some extent the other Jewish Objectivists, the poetic vehicle for this sensibility becomes the modernism of such figures as Pound, Eliot, and Williams. As in the case of the mostly Jewish New York Intellectuals (consider Eliot's immense influence on the verse of Delmore Schwartz), modernist poetry makes sense to the original Objectivists: the children or grandchildren of immigrants, on intimate terms with historical upheaval, they see in it a literature that acknowledges that history is accelerating to the breaking point. This modernist vision of apocalyptic history (in English, the locus classicus of this vision is the end of *The Waste Land*) resonates strongly for Jews in the late nineteenth and early twentieth centuries, for it accords with their own drastic experiences of assimilation, geographic displacement, and extreme changes in political and economic climates. In Europe—and, as we shall see, in America too—the Jewish attraction and contributions to modernism reach down to the deep pools of Jewish messianism. As Anson Rabinbach explains,

> Apocalyptic, catastrophic, utopian and pessimistic, Messianism captured a generation of Jewish intellectuals before the First World War. The Messianic impulse appears in many forms in the Jewish generation of 1914 . . . secular *and* theological, as a tradition that stands opposed to both secular rationalism and what has been called "normative Judaism." (81)

But it is not only a modernist vision of history that appeals to first-generation Jewish American writers; it is also the modernist attitude toward language. Modernism's antagonism to elaborate rhetoric and the concomitant emphasis on the direct, unadorned image, promised writers like the Objectivists a linguistic newness that was, strange as it may seem, still in keeping with certain

Jewish principles. Many of the formulations that have been used to define Objectivism—George Oppen's "test of truth," Louis Zukofsky's "thinking with the things as they exist," Reznikoff's own emphasis on "the testimony of a witness in a court of law"—not only correspond to Halevi's insistence on "lucidity of speech" but to the even older and more centrally Jewish notion: personal responsibility in the determination and judgment of truth. Objectivist attitudes toward judgment and truth may be compared to the attitude expressed in the *Pirke Aboth* (literally *Chapters* but usually translated as *Ethics of the Fathers*), the most well-known tractate of the Talmud, read for centuries as a touchstone of traditional Jewish wisdom: "By three things is the world preserved: by truth, by judgment, and by peace; as it is said, Judge ye the truth and the judgment of peace in your gates" (*Aboth* I:18). Through their emphasis on truth and judgment, cast in a direct language that tests the epistemological and ethical grounds of its utterance, the Objectivists remain in touch with a persistant Jewish stance.

In this light, Bloom's objection to Jewish "moralism" in poetry makes little sense, especially when he declares at the end of his essay that Jewish American poets can recover their covenant (and their voices) "only by somehow again walking His Way." But while Bloom admits that "persistance in seeking to recover what once our ancestors had" (262) may take many forms, Objectivism, apparently, is not one of them. Clearly, this is not because the Objectivists and the more recent poets who see them as models lack a Jewish "stance" or the means of recovering some sense of Jewish tradition. It is rather that they do not, as Bloom says of Harvey Shapiro, "speak out in a more expressionistic, highly colored, biblicizing idiom" (255). Because his style is derived from the Objectivists, Shapiro is "sadly lacking in the rhetorical resources that his insights desperately require" (256). But it is not a *lack* of rhetorical resources; rather, it is a *difference* in rhetorical resources that the Objectivist tradition demonstrates—a difference that makes a great deal of sense in a modern American context, when a "highly colored, biblicizing idiom" may not be the most effective means of expressing a Jewish sensibility. When it comes to matters of *style* (because that, after all, is what a given set of rhetorical resources produces), a complex dialectic is always at work between individual poets and the period in which they write. As Charles Altieri explains, the task here is to discern "how artists must manipulate received expectations in order to project forms of emotion they take as significant, must elaborate and interpret attitudes towards powers of sensibility which block or facilitate these emotions, and must justify treating certain emotional stances as 'authentic,' others as inviting ironic suspicion" ("Sensibility, Rhetoric, and Will" 452). Complicating matters further is the fact that Jewish American poets who wish to write *as Jews* must simultaneously negotiate modern American period styles as well as textual and cultural traditions derived from the far older history of their people. The success of any Jewish American's poetry will depend in part on that poet's ability to perform such complex negotiations, finding the personal style that is derived from the overdetermined past but that still allows for free expression.

However incoherent its critique of Reznikoff and the aesthetic tradition he represents, Bloom's essay is still acutely conscious of this situation, and indeed, points to an unresolved problem close to the heart of Reznikoff's poetry and his identity as a Jew. A number of readers have detected what appears to be a dichotomy in Reznikoff's poetry. Sometimes, as in the case of Bloom, this dichotomy is perceived to be a split between Jewish content and an incompatible (because rhetorically ineffectual) Objectivist style: a split that can be traced to a supposedly inevitable loss of poetic or cultural authority when literary assimilation takes its toll. By contrast, two other important critics find Reznikoff's Objectivist procedures relatively successful when applied to an urban, American content, but more problematic when used for Jewish material, a circumstance arising out of the poet's attempt to reconcile his Jewish and American identities. "No one," says Robert Alter of Reznikoff, "has gone farther than he in the explicit effort to be both a conscious Jewish writer and an emphatically American one" (120). Alter tends to see the work most readily identifiable as "Objectivist" (and most comparable to Williams's) as the most American, and the most successful. But Alter regards the poet's treatment of Jewish material as "a radically contradictory enterprise: to 'objectify' in poetry the impelling spirit of a body of historical experience from which he himself, standing on the other side of the chasm of modernity, is alienated" (127). The result "is no more than a rehearsal of ritual gestures, literal and stylistic, a piece of willed piety, the intervention of a kind of poetic superego rather than the expression of an integrated poetic self" (128).

Setting aside the canard of "an integrated poetic self" (more New Critical than psychoanalytic, despite Alter's "poetic superego"), we can acknowledge the presumptive split in Reznikoff between a poet of urban American immediacy and prophetic Jewish historicity, without accepting Alter's view that the Jewish poetry is "a rehearsal of ritual gestures" or "a piece of willed piety." L. S. Dembo, perhaps more sympathetic to Reznikoff's project than Alter, puts it almost in terms of a Jewish joke:

> Being himself, however, really meant not just a Jew or just an American but both and neither. When he wrote Objectivist poems, he was an Objectivist; when he wrote of "his people" he was, in a manner of speaking, a psalmist. . . . An exile, he sits down by the waters of Manhattan to weep; a wry smile comes over his face, for he realizes that he is home. And then he really weeps. (129)

Compared to those of Bloom and Alter, this is a more balanced attitude, for Dembo at least intuits the *necessity* for dialectical tension in Reznikoff's work. Dembo implies that the contradictions that arise out of being a Jew in America are sadly inevitable but must be taken in stride. Indeed, as I read Reznikoff's poetry, such contradictions are central to the work; they are textually productive, not only in Reznikoff's poetry, but whenever Jewish Americans work in an Objectivist mode. As a crucial discourse for Jewish American poetry, Objectivism is, as Derrida would say, "contradictorily coherent. And, as always, coherence in contradiction expresses the force of a desire" ("Strucute, Sign and Play" 279).

This contradictory coherence is created by and expressive of the desire to be both a Jewish poet and an American poet. Reznikoff is a first-generation American already somewhat distant from traditional Jewish religious and cultural practices; he is also a second-generation modernist who wants a poetry that is more than "fake flowers/in the streets in which I walked" and is thus attracted to "[t]he brand-new verse some Americans were beginning to write" (*CP* II: 171). The contradictory task of the Jewish American poet is to produce work that maintains both a remembrance of history and a sensitivity to the immediacies of mundane experience. The situation is further complicated by an equally powerful contradiction in the modern Jewish attitude toward the past. As Yosef Hayim Yerushalmi demonstrates in his magisterial *Zakhor,* memory and history are actually in opposition in modern Jewish culture. Collective memory is a function of the Jewish people "transmitting and recreating its past through an entire complex of interlocking social and religious institutions" (94): in other words, the tradition that more or less assimilated Jewish writers and intellectuals experience as having lost. The same forces of secularization that lead to "the unravelling of that common network of belief and praxis" (94) give rise to the Jewish consciousness of history, the attempt to understand the collective past as a problematic object of study distinct from any notion of divine providence or biblical covenant. As Yerushalmi explains,

> The modern effort to reconstruct the Jewish past begins at a time that witnesses a sharp break in the continuity of Jewish living and hence also an ever-growing decay of Jewish group memory. In this sense, if for no other, history becomes what it had never been before—the faith of fallen Jews. For the first time history, not a sacred text, becomes the arbiter of Judaism. (86)

When we think of Reznikoff's work and its relation to his cultural heritage in terms of this passage, we can better comprehend the poet's obsession with Jewish history, particularly the suffering of the Jewish people. Reznikoff's is not altogether a secular sensibility, for a strong messianic current runs through his work. But in Yerushalmi's terms, there is no question that Reznikoff could be understood as one of those "fallen" Jew for whom history, not Torah, is the arbiter of Judaism. Jewish history, not Jewish belief or tradition, is what Reznikoff draws on to maintain himself as a Jew. The treatment of Jewish history in Reznikoff's poetry is itself a product of Jewish history, and being a Jew in this historical sense is crucial to him as a poet. For Reznikoff, poetry gives meaning to history: just as history becomes the arbiter of Judaism, so poetry becomes the arbiter of history.

The secular awareness of Jewish history and the secular activity of writing poetry compensate for the loss of tradition, though they may come into being despairing of that loss.

How is this the case? On the one hand, it could be said that for Reznikoff, who is out of touch with the reality of the tradition, poetry rescues historical phenomena from mere facticity: it charges them with a vitality and existential meaning they would otherwise lack. On the other hand, poetry, particularly a modernist poetry of seriality and fragmentation, interrogates historical phenomena, rescuing them from their dangerous transformation into a reified "heritage" that becomes all too ideologically pliable. Charles Bernstein observes that "There is no poet more dedicated to foregrounding the detail and the particular than Reznikoff and no poet more averse to blending these details into a consuming or totalizing form" (204). Against which we may juxtapose this passage from Walter Benjamin:

> From what are phenomena rescued? Not just or not so much from the ill-repute and contempt in which they've fallen, but from the catastrophe when a certain form of transmission often presents them in terms of their "value as heritage." —They are rescued by exhibiting the discontinuities that exist within them. There is a kind of transmission that is a catastrophe. ("N" 63)

The rescue of phenomena through the demonstration of their discontinuities, the transmission of phenomena not as an artificially constructed heritage but as catastrophe: this production of knowledge by fragmentation and constellation is perhaps the most important strategy of messianic Jewish modernism. For such a sensibility, opposed, as we have observed, to both secular rationalism and normative Jewish belief, the inherently fragmented nature of phenomena is the sine qua non of a world always in wait of redemption.

Messianism, then, is one of the most important keys to an understanding of the instability of Reznikoff's Jewish identity and to the contradictory coherence of his poetry. In his essay "Voices Around the Text," Jonathan Boyarin defines "identity" as

> a sense of collective belonging without loss of individual consciousness. Perhaps in Judaism, the lack and the desire, along with the conviction that there is or can be a center, motivate the diverse phenomenon scholars call Messianism. Perhaps as well it is this lack and desire by which the past exercises its claim on "our *weak* Messianic power" and which ensure that the "secret agreement between past generations and the present one" [*Illuminations* 254] is fulfilled in study. (222–223)

Boyarin's reference here to Benjamin's notion of our *weak* Messianic power, which resides in the link or agreement between generations, indicates that there is hope of transmission and continuity, but that such continuity must be continually redefined. Boyarin's article is concerned with the ethnography of reading in a contemporary talmudic study group on New York's Lower East Side, the very existence of which is a sign of that *weak* Messianic power. For Boyarin, the power connecting us to the past comes into play when Jews gather around the text and form a community of readers; it is an expression of "the lack and the desire, along with the conviction that there is or can be a center"—a existential center, that is, of Jewishness. I would expand Boyarin's formulation to include modern Jewish writing as well as Jewish reading, for it is the production of new Jewish texts as well as the study of traditional ones that encode this lack, this desire, this conviction. As I have argued elsewhere, modern Jewish writing constitutes a "ritual of new creation," one in which devotion to the text—even the profane text of history rather than the sacred text of the Law—honors tradition through the very event of rupture (*Ritual* 2–3 & passim). Reznikoff is one of the best examples of this paradigm.

According to Boyarin, communal Jewish reading represents a need "to find our common ground without losing ourselves" (223). Reznikoff's contradictorily coherent poetry likewise represents this need, a need felt most acutely during periods of rapid social transformation. As much as any recent Jewish author, Reznikoff confirms Boyarin's intuition that the tense duality that we name Jewish identity constitutes a weak messianic power. But how does a Jew in increasingly assimilated circumstances such as Reznikoff's settle the messianic claims of the past? What claims does collective, messianic history have on a modern, self-consciously secular Jew? And if a poetry written in American English is to be the means through which this claim is settled, what procedures will best maintain the messianic possibility in a writing that seems to bear little resemblance to traditional textual practices?

Given such questions, Reznikoff's "Messianic," from *Separate Way* (published by the Objectivist Press in 1936), is an appropriate poem to consider. The poem is part of a sequence that includes "Depression" (drawn from contemporary anecdotes and observations of urban poverty), "The Socialists of Vienna" (based on an article in *New Masses* reporting on the 1934 Socialist revolt), and "New Land" (a montage of promise and struggle taken from early American history). Jewish messianism is therefore set in a broader international and historical context. But the sequence also focuses on the Jews as the special bearers of hope, given the account of their travail in "Palestine under the Romans" and the last poem, the magnificent "Kaddish," in which Reznikoff interpolates the traditional blessings in the prayer of mourning with images of those victimized by modern injustice.

The first stanza of "Messianic" presents an urban pastoral of the sort that Reznikoff, like Williams, had already perfected: by night "the river is brimming over/with the light/of street lights and electric signs"; by day "the sparrows will wheel about the shining twigs" (*CP* I: 174–175). But the theme of urban modernity is radically changed in the second stanza:

How far and wide
about the upper and lower bay,
along the rivers and beside the sea,
how close and evenly
the street lamps shine:
you shall know the forests of your fathers
among these posts,
and you their deserts
upon these miles of pavement
whose mica
glistens in the sunlight and the lamplight
in the heat of summer or the frost of winter,
wet with rain or white with snow.
Though your tribe is the smallest and you are the least,
you shall speak, you shall drill, you shall war:
and, dying,
wheeled away so swiftly
you see the sun
no larger than the evening star,
their boots shall carry your blood—
its corpuscles
seeds
that will grow in sandy lots,
between the cobblestones of alleys and on the pavement
    of avenues. (*CP* I: 174)

These lines quiver with the Objectivist sense of sincerity, of testimony. They are charged with intense yearning, but for the most part, that yearning is expressed indirectly. As is often the case in his poetry, Reznikoff here relies on a rhetoric of ironic conflation. Traditional Jewish identity is both renewed and undermined as ancestral forests and deserts become street lamps and pavement; the people's history is telescoped as conquerors' boots carry the "seeds" of Jewish blood to the "sandy lots," the "alleys" and "avenues" of New York. The sincere testimony in these lines is less that of a witness in a modern law court than that of a biblical prophet or psalmist who must speak an inspired truth to his people. Parallelism ("in the heat of summer or the frost of winter,/wet with rain or white with snow") and second-person repetitions ("you shall speak, you shall drill, you shall war") underscore this biblical voice.

The promise of renewal and redemption carried throughout Jewish history, as well as the emphasis on the bitter knowledge of suffering and endurance, make this poem, of course, "Messianic." The military training and violent death in the text indicate that Reznikoff may be thinking of the Jewish revolts against the Romans, especially the Bar Kochba revolt (132–135 C.E.), which was charged with messianic fervor and had the support of the religious establishment. Declared the Messiah by Rabbi Akiva, Bar Kochba ("son of a star" in Aramaic) became, in his defeat, the "evening star" of his people. In Reznikoff's presentation of the messianic scenario, apocalyptic violence gives way to a patient waiting amid the diminished but sincerely admired details of the modern urban milieu.

In Reznikoff's treatment of this milieu, he revises what we think of as Objectivist methods, bringing Jewish historical (often biblical) material to bear on contemporary life through various metaphoric or allusive procedures. A two-line poem, #40 from *Jerusalem the Golden* (1934), is a good example of such negotiations:

> Rooted among roofs, their smoke among the clouds,
> factory chimneys—our cedars of Lebanon. (*CP* I: 115)

It could almost be a poem from Pound's Imagist period, except that Pound (and for that matter, almost all of the other Imagists and Objectivists) rarely turn toward the Bible, while Reznikoff is continually attracted to it. As a rueful response to modernity, drawing on the same restrained irony found throughout the early work of Pound, Williams, Zukofsky, and Oppen, the poem could be giving voice to a thoughtful, relatively cultured urban community adjusting itself to the realities of an industrial landscape. The first-person plural appears in this context throughout the volume, as in #26 ("The twigs of our neighbors bush . . .") and #38 ("Of our visitors . . ."). As Oppen will later say in *Of Being Numerous,* "This is a language, therefore, of New York" (149); thus "our" can be read as inclusive of all urban Americans. The motivating tension in Oppen's great poem is "the shipwreck/Of the singular" (151); that is, the conflict between the "meditative man" (153) in his urban isolation and the overwhelming power of mass urban life, which continually threatens to overwhelm individual thought and expression, even among artists and intellectuals who are sympathetic to "Them, the people" (152). But in *Jerusalem the Golden,* a book with a title recalling the biblical glory of David and Solomon, "our" may mean "Jews in the American diaspora" as much as "all New Yorkers" or "all urban Americans": when factory chimneys are our cedars of Lebanon, it is specifically Jewish loss as well as the dilemma of mass American modernity that speaks. Yet discovering that factory chimneys are our cedars of Lebanon also indicates not only loss, but also the survival, even the renewal, of Jewish sensibility in the New World. It is just this sense of both loss and recovery that constitutes what I have called Reznikoff's contradictorily coherent procedure.

Jerusalem the Golden draws a great deal of its verbal energy from this conflicted sense of identity: however much the poet seems at home in New York, on intimate terms with its most common sights and unassuming details, he still claims to feel the accumulated weight of centuries of Jewish exile. What Allen Grossman observes years later about Allen Ginsberg's *Kaddish* could apply equally well to Reznikoff's work: "This mixture of nationalism and ethnicism represents

the peculiar position of the American Jewish poet who regards himself as simultaneously native and, in the special sense that always pertains to the Jew, alien" (*Long
Schoolroom* 155). Reznikoff's poems continually rehearse themes of linguistic
difference, geographic displacement and historical rupture. A lyric about autumn
in the city, for instance, is titled "Lament of the Jewish Women for Tammuz" and
given a prophetic sense of disaster:

> Now the white roses, wilted and yellowing fast,
> hang in the leaves and briers.

> Now the maple trees squander their yellow leaves;
> and the brown leaves of the oak have left Ur and
>   become wanderers.

> Now they are scattered over the pavements—
> the delicate skeletons of the leaves. (*CP* I: 115–116)

This poem is a revealing example of the way in which Reznikoff complicates
Imagist/Objectivist strategies through an infusion of biblical material. As Reznikoff notes, the title refers to the Book of Ezekiel VII:14: "Then he brought me
to the door of the gate of the Lord's house which was toward the north; and,
behold, there sat women weeping for Tammuz." The Book of Ezekiel uses its
prophetic mode to deal with the historical disaster of the Babylonian Captivity,
the first Jewish experience of diaspora. Ezekiel speaks his prophecies in exile, "in
the land of the Chaldeans by the river Chebar" (I:3). As Joel Rosenberg observes,
"So many of Ezekiel's discourses in the first half of the book—before the destruction of Jerusalem—are retrospective visions: Israel's whole pre-Exilic history is
repeatedly reviewed, as if in a kind of premature postmortem" (198). This includes the verse on which Reznikoff bases his poem: it is one of many abominations taking place in the Temple, which will be destroyed in just a few short years.
The women weeping for Tammuz are participating in a pagan ritual, for Tammuz
is the Near Eastern version of the Greek Adonis, a slain fertility god.

Autumn is the season for lamenting a dead fertility god, though one would
hardly expect to hear such lamentation in New York City in the nineteen-thirties.
(By contrast, Pound, working in Rapallo just a few years later, will draw on Frazer's
accounts of rituals commemorating the death of Tammuz/Adonis to produce
Canto XLVII, one of his most overt endorsements of the pagan mysteries.) Reznikoff is struck by the beauty of his hometown in the fall, but at the same time, he
wishes to remind himself and his readers that as a Jew, he is also in exile, and to
become too comfortable with the charms of a Gentile nation is to court disaster.
Like the women lamenting Tammuz, he may be forsaking his Jewish identity. On
the other hand, he cannot help declaring that "the brown leaves of the oak have
left Ur and become wanderers." Switching from Ezekiel to Genesis, the poet sees

the leaves as similar to that original Jewish wanderer, Abraham. Hence the lovely melancholy of the fall in this poem becomes originally Jewish, however mindful of historic rupture.

That Reznikoff's own Hebrew name was Ezekiel, a fact of which he was strongly conscious, makes the play of identity in this poem all the more poignant. As he notes years later,

> Because, the first-born, I was not redeemed,
> I belong to my Lord, not to myself or you:
> by my name, in English, I am of His house,
> one of the carles—a Charles, a churl;
> and by my name in Hebrew which is Ezekiel
> (whom God strengthened)
> my strength, such as it is, is His. (*CP* II: 80–81)

In his remarkable meditation on Reznikoff's names, Stephen Fredman calls this poem "an elegant attempt at synthesis, evincing a subtle midrashic interpretive ability, but the braiding of traditions the poet engages in unravels because he does not address the incommensurability of the social worlds of feudal England and Orthodox Judaism" (57). By playing on his Hebrew and English name(s), Reznikoff projects this acute sense of social incommensurability back on both the Jewish and the Anglo-Saxon past. This sense likewise afflicts him in "Lament of the Jewish Women for Tammuz," where his double awareness of himself as a prophet who keeps the faith and as a Jew who worships strange gods charges even the most common objects and scenes in the city around him.

This ambiguity may also be observed in "God and Messenger," from the sequence "Autobiography: New York":

> This pavement barren
> as the mountain
> on which God spoke to Moses—
> suddenly in the street
> shining against my legs
> the bumper of a motor car. (*CP* II: 30)

The same irony as in the cedars of Lebanon piece deflates the poet as urban Moses. God will not speak to him though the New York pavement is as barren as Sinai: the motor car as messenger bears God's silence in the modern world and not His voice. Or is the poet the messenger? In that case, his prophetic desire is thwarted, and his only message (to his fellow New Yorkers? to American Jews?) consists of his rueful observations of secular life.

But is this life entirely secular? Although, as I have argued, Reznikoff's Jewish identity is based in history rather than belief, that history is ineluctably charged with an awareness of Presence, a numinous quality that may be felt not by ascending Sinai but by crossing a Manhattan street. For Reznikoff, so drawn to biblical analogies, the car bumper paradoxically creates an experience of Presence: by being so resolutely secular, it dialectically creates a space for the sacred. As Walter Benjamin proposes in his uncanny "Theologico-Political Fragment":

> just as a force can, through acting, increase another that is acting in the opposite direction, so the order of the profane assists, through being profane, the coming of the Messianic Kingdom. The profane, therefore, although not itself a category of this Kingdom, is a decisive category of its quietest approach. (*Reflections* 312)

In his seminal essay on Reznikoff, Paul Auster cites "God and Messenger" just before insisting "that Reznikoff the Jew and Reznikoff the American cannot be separated from one another. Each aspect of his work must be read in relation to the oeuvre as a whole, for in the end each point of view inhabits all the others" (25). In Reznikoff's work, Judaism and Objectivism both sustain and counteract each other; as in Benjamin's formulation, they are dialectical counterforces of the sacred and the profane, and the one is continually exposed in the other. As Auster notes, "the eye is not adequate. Not even the seen can be truly seen. The human perspective, which continually thrusts us into a place where 'only the narrow present is alive,' is an exile from eternity, an exclusion from the fullness of human possibility" (25–26). Thus Judaism, which insists on the ongoing possibility of messianic redemption posed against temporality, continually asserts itself in Reznikoff's poetry. The city's pavement is never sufficient in itself; informing the poet's temporal sight is the vision of the eternal in human affairs, which for the Jew is represented by God's giving of the Law to Moses on Sinai. But conversely, the eternal vista of Presence may shrink as the car bumper looms close. Neither an ancient Hebrew nomad nor a talmudic scholar in the enclosed study house, Reznikoff is a walker in the modern city, with a sustained awareness of the present moment, the vagaries of crossing not the biblical desert nor the textual ocean but the crowded streets of New York.

In Reznikoff's work, the urban milieu becomes the site of rescue from what Benjamin would consider the "catastrophe" of modern history. We see this in the two-line poem, #69 from *Jerusalem the Golden,* so admired (though still misquoted) by George Oppen: "Among the heaps of brick and plaster lies/a girder, still itself among the rubbish" (*CP* I: 121). The poem acknowledges—indeed, it is almost a blessing on—the integrity of the girder, when all the other materials of the world have been reduced to heaps of rubbish. The girder is a made thing, a whole that was part of a larger whole now no longer intact. In this respect, it is like the poem itself, which maintains its integrity despite its fragmentary status as part of a series of more or less fragmentary texts that make up *Jerusalem the Golden*—an ironic title indeed when considered in messianic terms. Reznikoff's vision of

Jerusalem, his transmission of a Jewish worldview, is not a heritage but a catastrophe. Like Benjamin's angel of history, blown backward into the future by a storm from Paradise, Reznikoff's "face is turned toward the past. Where we perceive a chain of events, he sees one single catastrophe which keeps piling wreckage upon wreckage and hurls it in front of his feet" (*Illuminations* 257).

That Reznikoff's world is one of endless wreckage becomes all too clear in his long poems, *Testimony* and *Holocaust*. In both, "wreckage upon wreckage" are hurled at our feet. The poems, particularly *Holocaust*, could be regarded as the endpoint of Objectivism's testimonial strain, as the subjectivity and presence of the poet virtually disappears, replaced by the dispassionate court records from which the texts are drawn. Like the angel of history, we can only stare, aghast at the sight of human violence and depravity as we are blown into an ever-worsening future. Yet this is not to say, as does Robert Alter, that "this is an extended exercise in masochism conducted under the cover of an act of testimony." According to Alter,

> History, it would seem, had become a hypnotic vision of unrestrained murderous impulse for the poet: the ultimate breakdown of his whole problematic relation to the past is starkly evident in the flattened landscapes of disaster that take the place of round imagined worlds in these two long poems of his old age. (132)

Granted, Reznikoff's relation to the past is problematic, but *Holocaust* does not constitute a "breakdown." It is, I believe, a *confrontation* with history set at the limit of Reznikoff's art:

> The bodies were thrown out quickly
> for other transports were coming:
> bodies blue, wet with sweat and urine, legs covered with excrement,
> and everywhere the bodies of babies and children.
> Two dozen workers were busy
> opening the mouths of the dead with iron hooks
> and with chisels taking out teeth with golden caps;
> and elsewhere other workers were tearing open the dead
> and looking for money or jewels that might have been swallowed.
> And all the bodies were then thrown into the large pits
> dug near the gas chambers
> to be covered with sand. (*Holocaust* 46)

Holocaust offers so radical a challenge to the conventional category of poetry (or, perhaps, of the aesthetic) that in reading it, we must put aside most of our assumptions about literary texts and historical representation. Drawn entirely from records of the Nuremberg and Eichmann trials, Reznikoff's poem demands a sort of religious silence from its readers, in much the same way that witnessing the

event of the Shoah itself demands silence of those in the presence of such testimony. As George Steiner says in "Postscript" (1966), his essay on witnessing and
representing the Holocaust, "The best *now*, after so much has been set forth, is,
perhaps, to be silent; not to add the trivia of literary, sociological debate, to the
unspeakable" (163). By contrast, Steiner is critical of the dramatized, but still
largely accurate account of events in the French study *Treblinka*:

> But because that evidence is mastered by the literary talent of the writer,
> because a narrative persona full of distinct rage and stylistic force interposes
> between the insane fact and the profoundly exciting economy, hence order,
> of the book, a certain unreality obtrudes. Where it is represented with such
> skill, intricate modulations affect the hideous truth. It becomes more
> graphic, more terribly defined, but also has more acceptable, conventional
> lodging in the imagination. We believe; yet do not believe intolerably, for we
> draw breath at the recognition of a literary device, of a stylistic stroke not
> finally dissimilar from what we have met in a novel. The aesthetic makes
> endurable. (166)

In composing *Holocaust*, Reznikoff seems to intuit that "The aesthetic
makes endurable," and yet given his understanding of the testimonial role of
poetry, he is still obliged to produce a text in which what Steiner would call "a
narrative persona"—that is, the voice of the poetic subject—faintly lingers. The
order of the sections of *Holocaust* moves in a loosely chronological fashion, from
"Deportation" and "Invasion," through "Massacres," "Gas Chambers and Gas
Trucks" and "Children," to the last sections, "Marches" and "Escapes." The poem
ends with an account of the Warsaw ghetto uprising and the escape of six thousand
Danish Jews to Sweden with the help of their Gentile fellow citizens. In other
words, Reznikoff proceeds from the beginning of this *saison d'enfer*, to its darkest
moments, to the new beginning of a period of struggle, hope, and recovery.
Furthermore, a horrible irony can sometimes be heard just below the surface of the
narration, as in this last stanza from the section called "Entertainment":

> On Sundays there was no work and Jews would be placed in a row:
> each had a bottle on his head
> and the S.S. men amused themselves by shooting at the bottles.
> If a bottle was hit,
> the man lived;
> but if the bottle landed below,
> well, the man had it. (75)

The ironic resignation of that "well" in the final line can only belong to a narrative
voice that cannot lose itself entirely in the *univers concentrationnaire*.

Reading *Holocaust* throws us back on the rest of Reznikoff's poetry with a renewed sense of his cultural predicament. As we have seen, identifying with Jewish *history* means suffering the loss of Jewish *tradition*. Compelled to bear the historical burden of Jewish identity without the inner strength provided by the continuity of Jewish faith, secular Jews like Reznikoff experience the intertwined processes of secularization and assimilation as a full-blown crisis of transmission. This is certainly true for Reznikoff in comparison to his fellow Objectivists, George Oppen and Louis Zukofsky. Younger, wealthier, and much more assimilated to begin with, Oppen, after one book, embraces Marxism, itself a displacement of traditional Judaism. According to Mark Shechner, Marxism, for Jewish intellectuals of this generation, served "as a substitute Judaism, endowed with all the powers once possessed by halakhic or Orthodox Judaism for interpreting the world, dictating principles, forming character, and regulating conduct" (8). Yet Oppen probably turns to Marxism less because of ethnicity than because of class. He emerges years later as one of our greatest political poets, one for whom Jewish identity means "Burying my dogtags with H/For Hebrew in the rubble of Alsace" (211): a powerful but relatively isolated reference to his Jewishness in the late poem "Of Hours," addressed to his erstwhile mentor, Ezra Pound. In her study of Oppen and Pound, Rachel DuPlessis writes of that moment of danger in Alsace, and of "the metal tag which characterizes oneself as anathema, torturable . . . one fears one's identity because it is one's otherness" (137). For Oppen, being Jewish means claiming a kind of cultural otherness; Pound fails miserably to imaginatively identify with that otherness, despite his general sympathy with the exile and the outcast. Zukofsky, a less orthodox Marxist than Oppen but an even closer disciple of Pound, may write nostalgically of his father, Reb Pinchos, or eccentrically "translate" the opening of Job in *"A,"* but most tellingly inscribes his own ironic relation to Judaism in the early work that Pound published in *The Exile,* "Poem beginning 'The'": "Assimilation is not hard,/And once the Faith's askew/I might as well look Shagetz just as much as Jew" (*Complete Short Poetry* 17).

These are lines that Reznikoff could not have written, for even with the Faith askew, he could never regard himself as a shagetz, a Gentile male. (Nor did Pound ever reach out to Reznikoff as he did to Oppen and Zukofsky; as Charles Bernstein pointedly notes, "Pound's disinterest in Reznikoff is foundational" [205].) Instead, consider this fairly late poem from Reznikoff's *Inscriptions: 1944– 1956* (1959):

My parents were of a great company
that went together, hand in hand;
but I must make my way alone
over waves and barren land.

My grandfathers were living streams
in the channel of a broad river;

but I am a stream that must find its way
among blocking rock
and through sands and sand. (*CP* II: 80)

The subject here is the weakening of Jewish tradition and community over generations. Transmission is catastrophe, as the broad river of ancestral culture and
learning dwindles to the figure of the poet, a stream blocked by rock and sand. It is
interesting to note that when Reznikoff's anxiety over this situation is most acute,
he resorts to a more traditional *English* verse form, as if finding in rhyme and
comparatively regular meters a sense of connection to the *Jewish* (linguistically, the
Hebrew) culture that he is otherwise losing.

   Yet the images of the river and the stream have a peculiarly Jewish resonance: in rabbinic literature, the Torah (and hence those who enter into its study)
is a great river or fountain that nourishes the soul. Reznikoff's failure to master
Hebrew and become a traditional scholar weighs heavily on him all his life. As
early as *Five Groups of Verses* (1927), he writes "How difficult for me is Hebrew:/
even the Hebrew for *mother,* for *bread,* for *sun* / is foreign. How far have I been
exiled, Zion" (*CP* II: 72). And in his "Early History of a Writer," from *By the Well
of Living and Seeing* (1969), he recalls how, as a sixteen year old going to the
University of Missouri, he said farewell to his grandfather, who blessed him in a
Hebrew that the young Charles could not understand. The old man, who died
before Reznikoff could see him again, then began to weep:

   Perhaps my grandfather was in tears for other reasons:
   perhaps, because, in spite of all the learning I had acquired in high school,
   I knew not a word of the sacred text of the Torah
   and was going out into the world
   with none of the accumulated wisdom of my people to guide me . . .
                                                              (*CP* II: 167)

From the beginning to the end of his career, Reznikoff never ceases to brood on the
rupture that constitutes Jewish modernity, and how he himself is a typical product
of that rupture. Just how paradigmatic Reznikoff's situation is can be seen when
we place him in the context of other Jewish American modernists.

2

Jewish American Modernism
and the Problem of Identity
With Special Reference to the
Work of Louis Zukofsky

When we consider the aesthetic of the Jewish American modernists, whether they write in Yiddish or English, we discover that the psychosocial conflicts that beset them are both voiced and silenced in their poetic theories. Cultural identity and literary affiliation, poetic production and audience reception, tradition and rebellion: these dialectical terms form the unstable ground that these writers endlessly traverse; they constitute the historical matrix out of which their complex, volatile aesthetic is born. And as Terry Eagleton reminds us, "The aesthetic is that which speaks of historical conditions by remaining silent—inheres in them by distance and denial. . . . 'Real' history is cancelled by the text, but in the precise modes of that cancellation lies the text's most significant relation to history." Thus, we are concerned "with the specific operations whereby the ideological produces within itself that internal distantiation which is the aesthetic" (177).

If the aesthetic is, at least in part, a matter of ideological distantiation, then that process should be peculiarly visible in the statements on poetics made by the Introspectivists and Objectivists. When poets write about the goals they set for their poems—the techniques that the poems are to deploy, the subjects that they are to address, the traditions they are to oppose or continue, the aspects of human experience in which they are to ground their utterance—then we should take them at their word. A productive aesthetic stance is never "wrong" or "right," though it may be (and perhaps always is) constituted in part by ideological beliefs—in the sense of Louis Althusser's famous formulation that "ideology represents the imaginary relationship of individuals to their real conditions of existence" (162). The cultural conflicts of Jewish American poets in the twenties and thirties can be understood partly in terms of their self-representation, which was shaped in turn by their "imaginary" relationships to "real" conditions. In turning to the aesthetics of these figures, we must explore the relationship between their ambivalent psychosocial selves and their stated literary aims. In Eagleton's terms, we must consider the "specific operations" through which the ideological concern over Jewish American identity "produces within itself" that "distantiation" that is the poetics of Jewish American modernism.

In 1920, a new movement in Yiddish poetry was launched with the publication in New York City of an anthology called *In Zikh* (In Oneself). This anthology, prefaced by a crucial manifesto by Jacob Glatshteyn, A. Leyeles, and N. B. Minkov, was soon followed by a magazine, also called *In Zikh,* which was to continue publication until 1940. Self-consciously modernist in their stance, the Inzikhists, or Introspectivists, looked to their gentile contemporaries in Europe and the United States for literary models, but at the same time were deeply rooted in the secular Yiddish literature that had come into being in nineteenth-century Poland and Russia. Thus, like all Jews caught up in the process of assimilation (or perhaps to put it more accurately, the Jewish crisis of modernity), the Introspectivists were acutely aware of living between two worlds. Hence the revealing comedy of the following passage, from a discussion of gentiles and Yiddish literature, which appeared in *In Zikh* in July, 1923:

> Recently, the *In Zikh* had its own experience with Gentile colleagues.
>   The American journal, *Poetry,* got hold of an issue of *In Zikh.* And this is what the editors wrote to us:
>   "Unfortunately we cannot read your journal. We would like to know in what language it is printed. Is it Chinese?"
>   *Poetry* is published in Chicago. Several Yiddish newspapers are printed in Chicago. Yiddish periodicals, collections, books, are published there. There are certainly also Chinese laundries in Chicago, and the lady-editors of *Poetry* have probably seen a ticket from a Chinese laundry in their lifetime. And, after all that—not to mention that any intelligent person would know the difference between the way Chinese and Yiddish look—to ask whether a Yiddish journal is Chinese does not reflect very positively on the intelligence of the *Poetry* people.
>   But after all, this is not important.
>   What is important is: How long will Yiddish literature be unknown among the Gentiles? How long will they think of us—in literature—as Hotentots? (Harshav & Harshav 797–798)

Here we find the disquieting combination of verbal anxiety and verbal aggression associated with the modern Jewish passage into the dominant culture, focused, in this instance, on the matter of poetic production and reception. Outraged by the neglect and ignorance demonstrated by a gentile literary group that they ironically regard as "colleagues," the editors of *In Zikh* lash out, using terms that betray their self-conscious marginality. The gentile, English-speaking literary culture of America in the twenties is justifiably suspected of anti-Semitism.

The defensive response by these embattled Jewish modernists, with its derogatory references to Chinese laundries, Hotentots, and lady-editors, is marked by the ambivalence of an assimilating minority, as it both asserts its difference and seeks acceptance by the dominant culture. The Introspectivists anxiously remind themselves and their readers that Yiddish-speaking American Jews are full members of white, Western society, neither Chinese nor Hotentot.

These racial categories are not chosen arbitrarily. The Chinese are "Oriental," and the figure of the Jew as Oriental, and therefore as an alien other to Western culture, was a standard anti-Semitic belief. Furthermore, Yiddish was the language of the *Ostjuden,* the Jews of Eastern Europe. As Jews in Western Europe went through the process of assimilation, the *Ostjuden* came to signify the "bad" Jews, whose alien ways were a source of anxiety for Western Jews hoping to enter the European mainstream. Ironically, this image was gradually reversed: by the late nineteenth century, as the notion of self-hatred developed among assimilated Western Jews, the *Ostjuden* were romantically recast as authentic, "good" Jews. This double bind, "The Invention of the Eastern Jew," as Sander Gilman calls it, signifies "the slipperiness of the Jew's precarious position . . . Thus the splitting of the identity of the Jew into polar opposites took place in an antithetical manner that mirrored the division of the self into 'good' and 'bad' aspects" (*Jewish Self-Hatred* 270). This ambivalent splitting becomes the inheritance of the Yiddish writers of *In Zikh:* assimilated, "Western"-identified Jews born in Eastern Europe, transplanted in New York City, and insisting that neither they nor the language of which they are so proud is "Chinese."

And if they are not Chinese, they are certainly not Hotentots. The use of the term "Hotentot" evokes a tradition of racist beliefs (including scientific beliefs) that extended through the nineteenth and into the twentieth century. In his study of the Hottentot stereotype, Gilman observes that "the antithesis of European sexual mores and beauty is the black, and the essential black, the lowest exemplum of mankind on the great chain of being, is the Hottentot" (*Difference and Pathology* 83). Thus it is not merely their status in the literary sphere with which the Introspectivists are concerned; in this case, literary reputation is a metonym for their reception as Jews within American civil society. How do the genteel lady-editors of *Poetry,* holding their Chinese laundry tickets and indecipherable copies of *In Zikh,* "see" these partially assimilated Jewish writers? Against such infuriating, threatening figures, the Introspectivists feel compelled to assert their class consciousness and masculinity. But given their European origins, they also intuitively understand that

> The black and the Jew were associated not merely because they were both "outsiders" but because qualities ascribed to one became the means of defining the difference of the other. The categories of "black" and "Jew" thus became interchangeable at one point in history. The line between the

two groups vanished, and each became the definition of the other. The ultimate source of this identification was the need to externalize the anxiety generated by change in European (read Christian) middle-class society, a society under extraordinary tension during the course of the nineteenth century. The black no longer satisfactorily bore projections of anxiety. Too distanced, too controlled by the power of colonial empire, the black became part of the European world of myth. The Jew, however, daily present in society and demanding access into a bourgeois life seemingly so stable and well defined in terms of its Christian identity, was perceived as the radical par excellence. And the Jew was thus seen as one with the image of the black present in the fantasy world of European myth. (*Difference and Pathology* 35)

The Introspectivists internalize these racist myths and bring them to the New World, where the issue of assimilation remains crucial to their lives and work. As they simultaneously seek acceptance and assert their Jewish difference, they are caught in yet another double bind that we can observe in their rhetoric of literary reputation. In other words, the Introspectivists are suffering from an American Jewish version of what John Murray Cuddihy names, in the title of his enduring study of assimilation, *The Ordeal of Civility.* As Cuddihy explains,

Diaspora in the West forced a bitter choice on the emancipated Jewish intelligentsia (ultimately, also, on the Jewish "masses"): either *Yiddishkeit* lacked something and the West had something to offer, or *Yiddishkeit* had something and the West had nothing (essentially) to offer. In the former case, assimilation or conversion was in order, to acquire that "something"; in the latter case, reduction rather than conversion was indicated—that is, an essentially reductive analysis that would strip the apparently "superior" culture of its apparent superiority (thus elevating the apparently "inferior" and marginal subculture). (66)

The Introspectivists were much too far from traditional Jewish life, too heavily invested in modern Western values—but at the same time, too faithful to Yiddish—to seriously consider such a choice. Thus, theirs was the bitterness of ambivalence, a neverending ordeal. The *In Zikh* discussion concludes in a more reasonable, if not resigned manner:

A self-respecting Yiddish literature can react to this phenomenon in two ways.

First, it can ignore the external world altogether and wait until the weight, the importance and the innner value of our work forces the Gentiles to see us, to consider us and ask pardon for past misrepresentations.

Second, it can inform the non-Jewish journals that all they have printed about Yiddish thus far is false, silly misrepresentation and it can undertake the translation of the best, most characteristic Yiddish works, thus forcing them to have respect for Yiddish. (Harshav & Harshav 798)

Unfortunately, neither of these possibilities materialized. Yiddish literature, especially poetry, continued to be ignored by gentile culture in the United States; the "importance and inner value" of the work went unrecognized, and it was not until 1969, with the publication of Irving Howe's and Eliezer Greenberg's *Treasury of Yiddish Poetry* that a comprehensive body of translations became available. By then, such a book was needed as much by Jews as by gentiles, for subsequent generations of Americans Jews did not learn Yiddish. In Europe, the Yiddish-speaking community was destroyed, and with it, the extraordinary potential for a modernist poetry in a genuinely international language. But even before the Holocaust, throughout the twenties and thirties, *In Zikh* continued to lament the isolation of its poets. The responsibility for this condition, however, was gradually shifted to American Jews, who were seen as not only abandoning but repudiating Yiddish, treating it with contempt. "The pettiest Jewish scribbler in English," writes A. Leyeles in 1937, "the lowest reporter on an English newspaper feels sky-high above Yiddish—whether it's the Yiddish press or the demanding, original Yiddish literature. So many years in America, such a fine literature created here, and we remain strangers to our neighbors as if we had lived in Siam or had written in some Eskimo dialect" (Harshav & Harshav 801).

But although the Introspectivists defended Yiddish against assimilating, English-speaking Jews, they were still ambivalent about their literary forbears, especially in the early years of the movement, before it became clear that Yiddish literature in its entirety was in danger of extinction. Another column in *In Zikh* in 1923 (obviously a year for taking stock) asserts repeatedly that "We have no tradition," that "there is more direct relation between an Introspectivist and a German Expressionist or English Vorticist than between us and most Yiddish poets of the previous periods." Furthermore, this "direct relation" to "all of Modernism" sets the *In Zikh* group apart from other Yiddish writers, producing "the impression of foreignness in the eyes of those who regard Yiddish poetry merely as a part of Jewish culture, who are looking for thread-weaving, who emphasize, throughout, the word 'Jewish'" (Harshav & Harshav 794). For the Introspectivists, Jewish identity was only one thread in the Yiddish poetry they wished to produce.

The Introspectivists were not aware, as they struggled with questions of identity, audience, and artistic affiliation, that about the same time, one erstwhile "English Vorticist" was considering the vitality of Yiddish and the potential of a Jewish contribution to modernist writing:

9 Dec. 1929 Rapallo

Dear Z.

The Reznikof [*sic*] prose very good as far as I've got at breakfast. . . .
Capital in idea that new wave of literature is jewish (obviously) Bloom
casting shadow before, prophetic Jim [Joyce] etc.

also lack of prose in German due to all idiomatic energy being drawn
off into yiddish. (not concerned with the "truth" of these suggestions but
only with the dynamic.)

> yrs
> EP (*Pound/Zukofsky* 26–27)

It is a singular moment in literary history. Pound's brief speculation concerning
Yiddish "energy" is probably prompted by the novelty of a Jewish disciple, a young
man who was not only fluent in Yiddish but who had used the language to great
effect in a work that Pound admired and published, the formidable "Poem beginning 'The.'" Zukofsky, as Harold Schimmel points out, "was a born American." It
was not "his fate . . . to attend NYU Law writing free verses in Yiddish (as
Glatstein and Minkoff did)" (236). Zukofsky, unlike the European-born Introspectivists, not only admired the Anglo-American modernists, but felt secure
enough, confidently American enough, to write his poetry in their—and his
own—language. Nevertheless, he too endured the ordeal of civility, and perhaps
more painfully than any of the Introspectivists, who, despite their anxieties about
race, class, and gender, suffered mainly from neglect. Direct dealings with Ezra
Pound, however much Zukofsky sought and won his approval, had an even more
unsettling effect on the younger poet's sense of himself as a Jew.

In his reply to Pound's letter (Dec. 19, 1929), Zukofsky speaks of his article
on Reznikoff (later revised into the crucial Objectivist essay "Sincerity and Objectification") being written for *The Menorah Journal*. Anticipating its rejection (and
indeed, it was subsequently turned down), he writes: "If 'they' take it. Do I luf my
peepul? The only good Jew I know is my father: a coincidence." He then asks if he
can quote Pound's letter as an endorsement in order to convince the *Menorah*
editors to take the Reznikoff piece. Later in the same letter Zukofsky calls himself
an "antisemite" and exclaims "I hope you don't feel the Jews are roping you in"
(*Pound/Zukofsky* 27–28).

The components of this scenario must be delicately unpacked. Zukofsky,
who stands at the center of the Objectivist tradition, was then developing some of
its most important principles by applying the lessons he had learned from Pound
and Williams to the poetry of Charles Reznikoff. "Sincerity and Objectification:
With Special Reference to the Work of Charles Reznikoff" was intended for *The
Menorah Journal;* after the piece was turned down, it became part of Zukofsky's
introductory "Program" in the February, 1931 Objectivist issue of *Poetry.* (For at
least one month, that magazine had an editor who could tell Yiddish from

Chinese!) In some respects, *The Menorah Journal* would seem the appropriate venue for Zukofsky's essay. Not only did *Menorah* publish Reznikoff frequently, but, according to Alan Wald, it promoted a "particular combination of anti-assimilationism and cosmopolitanism," a spirit of "cultural pluralism" (30) in which Zukofsky's writing would appear to share.

Yet Zukofsky and the *Menorah* editors did not see eye to eye. However much Reznikoff's poems and plays on Jewish subjects represented Zukofsky's Objectivist ideals, they appealed to *Menorah* more as literary embodiments of the Jewish or "Hebraic" humanism at the heart of the *Menorah* project. As Robert Alter reports, "what is most important for *Menorah* writers is to be able to talk about Judaism in the same terms, in the same refined accents, that the secular high priests of the polite English world used to discuss their culture and history" ("Epitaph" 52). This genteel version of American Jewish intellectual life, which regarded Judaism as a "spiritual aristocracy" ("Epitaph" 52), had little in common with either Zukofsky's avant-garde modernism or his working-class roots. No wonder that in a letter to Pound written the following month (Jan. 12, 1930), he bitingly refers to the *Menorah* staff as "the Sanhedrin," anticipating by many years but also iron-ically reversing what Alter will call *Menorah*'s function as "permanent critics of the Jewish Establishment, almost a kind of shadow rabbinate" (54). In the same letter, Zukofsky expresses regret over his desire for acceptance by their "'thoughtful' heads," and notes that he had already criticized the *Menorah* group in *"A"*-4 (*Pound/Zukofsky* 32). He is probably referring to these mordantly senescent lines:

> Wherever we put our hats is our home
> Our aged heads are our homes,
> Eyes wink to their own phosphorescence,
> No feast lights of Venice or The Last Supper light
> Our beards' familiars; His
> Stars of Deuteronomy are with us,
> Always with us,
> We had a Speech, our children have
>   evolved a jargon. (12)

Here Zukofsky appropriates the elegiac falling rhythms of *The Cantos* to give voice to the aged, exilic Jewish consciousness. Separated from the aesthetic treasures of the Christian West, these old Jews cling instead to the beauties of the Torah. Their complaint would have been familiar to Zukofsky from an early age, for the terms "Speech" and "jargon" refer to the debate between advocates of Hebrew and Yiddish that had raged ever since the mid-nineteenth century, when Yiddish (often called "zhargon," and not only by its detractors) became the language of a secular Jewish literature. For these old men, Hebrew is *loshen kodesh*, the Holy Tongue, the only proper language of Jewish textuality. Its biblical gran-deur and purity are meant solely for religious purposes, as opposed to the vernacular use to which Zionist settlers were putting it in Palestine. This was as much a modern aberration as secular literature in Yiddish: "If the speech has subsided into a jargon studded with alien expressions, as they [the old men] fear, then it no longer transmits the ancient traditions" (Ahearn 52). Zukofsky, of course, disagrees, which is why translated verses from Yehoash (famous for his Yiddish rendering of the Hebrew Bible) appear later in *"A"*-4.

Yet if the voice of the elders is also meant as a jab at the *Menorah* "Sanhedrin," then Zukofsky is setting up a sly analogy: the genteel Jewish humanism of *Menorah* is to Hebrew grandeur as Zukofsky's modernism is to lively, upstart Yiddish literature. Jewish culture cannot remain mired in tradition: just as Yehoash can "make it new" through his Yiddish poetry and translations, so Zukofsky can challenge the high-minded Arnoldians of the Jewish American intellectual elite. The Jewish difference in *Menorah*'s humanism may have been intended to offer "the intellectual an invaluable critical perspective on the Western world" ("Epitaph" 53), but for the young poet, this perspective was not critical enough: compared to the Poundian springs from which Zukofsky was imbibing, the *Menorah* perspective probably tasted stalely Victorian. As the old men say in *"A"*-4 (sounding more like Eliot than Pound), "Even the Death has gone out of us—we are void" (13).

But while it was a high-spirited gesture to defy one's Jewish humanist elders, it was quite another matter to turn and embrace Pound's cultural agenda instead. As John Tomas says of Zukofsky in his essay on "Poem beginning 'The'":

> Like so many other Jews, he has adopted the ways of the secular culture that surrounds him, but he has refused to ignore the consequences of his choice. He has emphasized that his rebellion is inevitably linked to his other revolts: political, artistic, and cultural. Yet he admits his discomfort with his position. He has not chosen to write in Yiddish, as had many of his contemporaries, and his choice of English as a medium for verse means that he has committed himself to preserving and extending that poetic tradition, a tradition that has been essentially hostile to Jews. (61)

It remains difficult to determine the extent to which Zukofsky ever reconciled these contradictions, especially around the figure of Pound, who, for the younger poet, always represented the tradition's cutting edge. We know that in the early years of their friendship, their correspondence is strewn with references to Pound as father, Zukofsky as son, sometimes in terms of literary parentage, sometimes as a parody of God the Father's relation to Christ (*Pound/Zukofsky* xix). These joking references point to what the friendship meant to both men, not only as poets involved in a project of literary renewal, but as anti-Semite and Jew, a dyad that cannot be neglected in any narrative of modernism.

In his encyclopedic study of Pound's fascism and anti-Semitism, Robert Casillo argues that

Pound's constant attacks on the despised Jews actually reveal his high and fearful estimation of their power and that of their patriarchal god. However much Pound claims access to the divine, Judaism and the Jews remain his most formidable enemy, rival, and obstacle. In these terms, one might view Pound's anti-Semitism as in part a revolt against the punitive parental rival and superego, a conflict between the religion of the forbidding father Jehovah and that of the messianic son. (28/)

Pound saw himself as a messianic son of the father-religion, an oedipal antagonist whose attempt to restore a pagan worldview would ultimately lead to his sacrifice at the hands of the vengeful Jews. At the same time, Pound's anti-Semitism "marks a curious fascination and even emulation" (Casillo 298) of the Jews, a fascination related in turn to his repressed beliefs that he might be Jewish and that the Jews have rejected his messianic claim. The ritualistic violence of anti-Semitism that Pound eventually espouses is thus a form of psychological projection; by projecting "repressed wishes, instincts, and desires" onto an other, "the individual feels free to attack his projected and distorted self-image in other human beings" (Casillo 207). As Casillo makes clear, Pound's scapegoating of Jews "is most likely to appear where his need for definition is as great as his ambivalence, where his distinctions collapse and his terms hover in uncertainty. For the sacrificial crisis is signalled by a failure of distinctions, the inability to clarify cultural values and boundaries" (210).

The first part of Pound's correspondence with Zukofsky begins in the late twenties and extends through the thirties, a period during which Pound became increasingly isolated from American politics and culture, while his fascism and anti-Semitism grew more extreme. Given his obsession with father-religions and son-religions, the idea of a young Jewish American disciple must have been immensely gratifying: here was at least one Jew who recognized his paternal authority and was willing to spread the Word. As Pound's "Deerly [*sic*] beloved son" (*Pound/Zukofsky* 101), Zukofsky was a convert, a self-declared "shagetz" for whom Judaism meant little compared to the new modernist faith. Yet at the same time, friendship with Zukofsky stirred Pound's repressed fascination with matters Jewish, and his letters to Zukofsky are filled with ambivalent emulation in the form of his mock-Yiddish discourse.

The psychology of Zukofsky's filial role in this relationship, while having none of the vicious implications of Pound's "fatherhood," is nearly as vexed. Zukofsky's guilt at abandoning his own father's orthodoxy must have been acute; hence the bitter irony when he declares in "Poem beginning 'The,'" "Assimilation is not hard,/And once the Faith's askew/I might as well look Shagetz just as much as Jew" (*Complete Short Poetry* 17). Although Zukofsky's first important work focuses on his mother, what the poet calls the "Residue of Oedipus-faced wrecks" (*Complete Short Poetry* 9) continues to cling to him throughout the Thirties. Zukofsky's typical strategy in writing about his father—and his father's faith—

involves what I have identified elsewhere as a strategic use of nostalgia for an unbroken cultural tradition, which in itself is the mark of rupture (*Ritual* 130–131). In Zukofsky's case, orthodox Judaism, the figure of the rabbi or sage, and especially the figure of Reb Pinchos Zukofsky, are cast in a gentle, melancholy light (see, e.g., *"A"* 150–159), despite Zukofsky's insistence, as we have seen in his relations with *The Menorah Journal*, that modern Jewish writing depends on breaking from tradition in order to maintain its vitality. This doubleness appears throughout *"A"* and partly accounts for Zukofsky's lifelong fascination with one of the earliest in a long line of rebellious Jewish intellectuals, Baruch Spinoza.

An especially poignant instance of Zukofsky's filial dilemma occurs in an exchange of letters with Pound in 1936. Inevitably drawn into a tangled debate with his mentor over politics and economics, Zukofsky was particularly concerned that Pound's association with Italian and American fascists would destroy his already waning reputation. He continually warned Pound that his attempts to determine the Jewish role in the development of capitalism would lead to accusations of anti-Semitism, from which Zukofsky always tried to shield him. As Zukofsky bluntly tells Pound in March, 1936, "If you're dead set on completely losing whatever readers you still have in America, keep it up" (*Pound/Zukofsky* 177). Three months later, Pound actually enlisted the help of Pinchos Zukofsky in his campaign by having Louis ask his father to explicate the prohibitions against usury in Leviticus 25. This is especially ironic given Pound's peculiar obsession with the Hebrew word for usury, *neschek* (literally "the bite"), related in turn to his anti-Semitic oral aggression, a behavior he projected on the Jews themselves (Casillo 57–59). Zukofsky consulted his father, who offered a literal explanation of Leviticus 25:36–37, emphasizing that although in the Diaspora, the religious laws against usury are relaxed, "it is a crime to make any distinctions" (*Pound/Zukofsky* 183) between Jews and gentiles in collecting interest. As Zukofsky writes to Pound about his father, "his natural & sweet conscience troubl[es] him wherever he runs across an explicit difference, or what may possibly be interpreted as an implicit difference, btwn the rights of yid & goy" (*Pound/Zukofsky* 182).

Later in the letter, however, Zukofsky revealingly lashes out at both his fathers, setting his own faith in Marxism against Pinchos's Judaism and Pound's fascism:

> Where he's Messianic he's as antiquated as you sunk in an absolute which has no useful relation to the present, or a bettering of the present. Strikes me in trying to isolate the root-idea of the reprehensibility of usury—which is what you seem to be doing?—you forget that even roots grow in a soil, & that soil changes with the times. You're both suffering from cart-before-the-horseness. Serves you right for not making any effort to understand Marx's criticism of Proudhon: "the economic forms in which men produce, consume, exchange are *transitory* and *historical* . . ." (*Pound/Zukofsky* 183)

In this passage, the gentle, outdated natural father and the fierce, modernist poetic father receive equally harsh treatment by the rebellious son. Zukofsky could hardly have expected Reb Pinchos to embrace Marxism after a lifetime of Talmud and strict Jewish observance. But he always posed Marxist economics against Pound's advocacy of Social Credit, and insisted that Pound, given his literary genius and political concern, ought to recognize the failings of his right-wing stance.

By accusing both fathers of being "Messianic" and "antiquated" in failing to grasp the material historicity of economic (and hence social) forms, Zukofsky asserts his intellectual and cultural independence. Pinchos may long for the Messiah while Pound idolizes Mussolini, but they are equally obtuse *idealists;* they suffer from "cart-before-the-horseness" because they cannot grasp the basic Marxist principle that the material conditions of society produce systems of thought and belief. In the previous chapter, we observed that Marxism, for Jews of Zukofsky's generation, served "as a substitute Judaism, endowed with all the powers once possessed by halakhic or Orthodox Judaism for interpreting the world, dictating principles, forming character, and regulating conduct" (Shechner 8). Caught between traditional Judaism and fascist modernism, Zukofsky negotiated his oedipal crisis and his ordeal of civility through recourse to Marxism, a Jewish modernism that provided an answer to both Pinchos and Pound.

But what does such an answer sound like when shaped into poetry? Here is one example:

> . . . Broken
> Mentors, unspoken wealth labor produces,
> Now loom as causes disposing our loci,
> The foci of production: things reflected
> As wills subjected; formed in the division
> Of labor, labor takes on our imprecision—
> Bought, induced by gold at no gain, though close eye
> And gross sigh fixed upon gain have effected
> Value erected on labor, prevision
> Or surplus value, disparate decision. (*"A"* 106–107)

Or perhaps more simply,

> Arrived mostly with bedding in a sheet
> Samovar, with tall pitcher of pink glass,
> With copper mugs, with a beard,
> Without shaving mug—
> To America's land of the pilgrim Jews?
> To buy, after 20 years in a railroad flat,
> A living room suite of varnished

Mahagony framed chairs and
Blue leather upholstery,
To be like everybody, with what
        is about us. (*"A"* 83)

Whether writing in the extravagant canzone form of the first half of *"A"*-9 (1938–1940) or the more straightforward free verse of *"A"*-8 (1935–1937), Zukofsky's goal in regard to Jewish identity is a poetry wholly open to the forces of modernity, including, paradoxically, the force of "Broken Mentors" in diaspora, "the pilgrim Jews" who both resisted and accommodated themselves to the New World. And as Mark Scroggins observes in his definitive study of Zukofsky, "By the time Zukofsky comes to write 'A'-12 (at around age 46 [1950–1951]), he has resolved some of the conflicts between the religion and nationality of his (literal) fathers and the poetics (cultural and literary) of his (Bloomian) forbears" (135).

The question of resistance and accommodation to American culture among the Jewish American modernists can be examined further if we consider two of their most significant statements on poetics, and some of the poems related to these statements. Of crucial importance for the Yiddish poets is the Introspectivism manifesto of Glatshteyn, Leyeles, and Minkov, written in 1919 and published as a preface to the *In Zikh* anthology in 1920; of comparable value for the poets writing in English is Zukofsky's "Program: 'Objectivists' 1931," which appeared in the Objectivist issue of *Poetry* and was revised later as "An Objective." Both documents are unsettling combinations of abstract theory and up-to-the-minute polemic, highly conscious of the tradition of the manifesto which had already played a large part in the history of earlier avant-garde movements. Only the Introspectivism manifesto deals explicitly with Jewish matters, though as we have seen, the Introspectivists insisted that their links to international modernism were at least as strong as their relation to Jewish life. As the manifesto states:

> We are "Jewish poets" simply because we are Jews and write in Yiddish. No matter what a Yiddish poet writes in Yiddish, it is ipso facto Jewish. One does not need any particular "Jewish themes." . . . It is not the poet's task to seek and show his Jewishness. Whoever is interested in this endeavor is welcome to it, and whoever looks for Jewishness in Yiddish poets will find it. (Harshav & Harshav 780)

For the Introspectivists, writing in Yiddish naturally meant writing as a Jew, and in the manifesto, they insist that Yiddish is "a fully mature, ripe, independent, particular, and unique language"—though Yiddish poetry is "merely a part of the general European-American culture." Again we see the Introspectivists' desire both to assert their Yiddish particularity and to identify that particularity with the dubious construction of "general European-American culture," a unified entity that exists mainly in the imagination of a marginalized group.

Thus the Introspectivists raise as many questions as they answer, especially in comparison to English writers like Zukofsky or Reznikoff. If a poem written in Yiddish is ipso facto a Jewish poem regardless of its theme, can the same be said for a poem written in English by a Jewish poet? In the latter case, theme cannot be so easily discounted, since English is not a Jewish language in the way that Yiddish (or Hebrew) is. It would appear that poems written by Jews in English which do not deal with Jewish matters are not Jewish poems, but are rather works that belong solely to the "general European-American culture." For what other criteria, apart from language and theme, can apply to a "Jewish" poem? Critics often speak of a "Jewish sensibility" informing a work of art; likewise, the great "metanarratives" of modernity, such as Marxism and psychoanalysis, have been extensively analyzed as ideological displacements of traditional Jewish thought or as partaking of a peculiarly Jewish "intellectual grammar." How are such intellectual and aesthetic reformulations at work as Jewish American poets forge their modernist aesthetic?

One crucial reformulation of the Jewish sensibility in its confrontation with modernist poetics involves the notion of sincerity. In their manifesto, the Introspectivists insist

> that the poet must really listen to his inner voice, observe his internal panorama—kaleidoscopic, contradictory, unclear or confused as it may be. From these sources, he must create poetry which is the result of both the fusion of the poet's soul with the phenomenon he expresses and the individual image, or cluster of images, that he sees *within himself* at that moment.
> (Harshav & Harshav 774–775)

Readers familiar with the various strains of modernism, including Objectivism, will recognize the Introspectivist emphasis on the "fusion" of soul (the Yiddish word *zel* can also mean "psyche") and phenomenon or image, as this fusion occurs at one particular moment. For the Introspectivists, the true poem is one that refuses the task of attaining "universal, or, in a more traditional term, *eternal*, value." What counts is the external phenomenon as the poet perceives and responds to it: hence the insistence on the world being "in oneself." (Again, the English "introspective" from *in zikh* may carry a sense of sustained, meditative duration that the Yiddish phrase does not.) "We Introspectivists," the manifesto declares, "want first of all to present life—the true, the sincere, and the precise—as it is mirrored in ourselves, as it merges with us" (775). And that "us" is, as we have observed, a cosmopolitan American "us," just as "life" is cosmopolitan American life—though both are also ineluctably Jewish.

Sincerity, precision, and a uniquely Jewish American sensibility are all to be found in Glatshteyn's "The Shoeshine Boy, the Bird, the God," from his collection *Free Verse* (1926):

The spring sun strays like a love-song in his head.
His grimy hand fondles a mute black shoe.
The black shoe has eyes, a blond head, and a stocking
            of black silk.
He is young. The day is fair. The street is bright.
The floor is stone. The cramped workshop is cool.
The cool shoeshine thrones gleam with polished brass
            and marble disdain.
The worm doesn't crawl on the dusty box,
but in the wide blue eye of the boy.
An idea meanders under his red hair—
how pleasant it would be if instead of a worm
a bird hopped in today,
a gold-green bird with gorgeous beak.
This modest spring-thought climbs
up the workshop's green and branching ladder to the young man's god,
climbs and clings with pudgy hands to the neck of the god.
The young man's god—a sweet greybeard—kisses his thought and nurtures
            it.
Blasé New Yorkers won't believe
that the young man really saw the golden-green bird
collecting scraps with his gorgeous beak on the stone floor.
The young man's heart swells with pleasure, his eyes are moist.
This is no rapt Sinbad rubbing a wishing ring.

In the cramped workshop a grimy hand pets and fondles
a mute black shoe. (Glatshteyn 21)

Glatshteyn's control over his volatile material is masterful. The shoeshine boy, whose red hair marks him as a typical Polish Jew, is caught in the midst of a masturbatory fantasy, as the shoe he fondles becomes the blond in silk stockings, an erotic image from the bourgeois, gentile world of elegant New York streets. Though he is alone in a cool, calm, bright moment, he still feels the disdain of the "shoeshine thrones," so often occupied by others from that forbidden world who literally and figuratively look down on him as he works. His sexual fantasy is a worm, with its connotations of corruption and death, yet this "modest spring-thought" is transformed into a "green-gold bird" (probably a peacock), a symbol of fulfillment and peace in much Yiddish folk music and literature. Furthermore, his thought climbs up "the workshop's green and branching ladder" to be kissed and nurtured by the young man's god, "a sweet greybeard." As his "heart swells with pleasure," the shoeshine boy's moment of erotic fulfillment, however vexed by his class consciousness and sense of cultural inferiority, is transformed into a visionary experience, beyond the comprehension of "blasé New Yorkers."

But what is the significance of these metamorphoses, this vacillation between sacred and profane, acceptance and repugnance? It would appear that for Glatshteyn, in accordance with Introspectivist principles, the task of the poet consists in finding just such moments of transformation, moments when sincere, precise representations of ordinary modern events merge with the poet's own sensibility to produce poems that partake equally in inner and outer life. The ambivalence of the Jewish shoeshine boy to his experience in New York is also the poet's ambivalence, and no doubt that ambivalence struck a chord in Glatshteyn's readers who first encountered the poem in Yiddish in 1926. As poetic values, sincerity and precision allowed—indeed, necessitated—a direct, unabashed treatment of Jewish American life. In poems like "The Shoeshine Boy, the Bird, the God," however, sincerity and precision also meant facing the torn sensibility of a generation of newcomers, often in impoverished circumstances, full of energy and longing but caught between conflicting ideologies and cultures. The Introspectivists' generation found no lasting resolutions to these conflicts, but Introspectivism itself provided the means to render them into an enduring poetic legacy.

Twelve years after the Introspectivist manifesto, in the Objectivist issue of *Poetry*, Zukofsky also presents the poetry of Charles Reznikoff as a model of "sincerity," a literary characteristic that Zukofsky regards a prerequisite for the ultimate desideratum of poetry, "objectification" or "rested totality." Zukofsky implies that these are qualities, however rare, which any writer may achieve through sufficient attention to craft and detail, "thinking with the things as they exist" ("Program" 381). The sincerity and objectification of Reznikoff's work is partly due to the fact that, for Zukofsky, the poet "looked about him (in the boroughs of New York) and wrote verse that is definitely his own and thus *sincerely* contemporary" ("Program" 385). This assertion is followed by Reznikoff's poem about the Jewish shoemaker (*CP* I: 63–64), cited as an example of objectification (or precision, as the Introspectivists would say), in which images of poverty, industriousness, piety, and simple pleasures do indeed combine to form a rested totality. Sincerity and objectification are best achieved through the local and the familiar, which includes, in Reznikoff's case (though Zukofsky never states this explicitly), an unabashed consideration of Jewish New York's immigrant working class:

> The shoemaker sat in the cellar's dusk beside his bench and sewing-
> machine, his large blackened hands, finger tips flattened and
> broad, busy.
> Through the grating in the sidewalk over his window, paper and dust were
> falling year by year.
>
> At evening Passover would begin. The sunny street was crowded. The
> shoemaker could see the feet of those who walked over the
> grating.

He had one pair of shoes to finish and he would be through.
His friend came in, a man with a long black beard, in shabby dirty clothes,
        but with shoes newly cobbled and blacked.
"Beautiful outside, really the world is beautiful."
A pot of fish was boiling on the stove. Sometimes the water bubbled over
        and hissed. The smell of fish filled the cellar.
"It must be beautiful in the park now. After our fish we'll take a walk in
        the park." The shoemaker nodded.
The shoemaker hurried his work on the last shoe. The pot on the stove
        bubbled and hissed. His friend walked up and down the cellar
        in shoes newly cobbled and blacked.

This poem, though not nearly as psychologically vexed as "The Shoeshine Boy, the Bird, the God," is written from the same cosmopolitan perspective of the Jewish New Yorker, and offers the same controlled, matter-of-fact presentation of urban, working-class Jewish life. From the appearance and remarks of the shoemaker's friend, it would appear that these two Jews are Hassidim, whose orthodoxy extends to an appreciation of all of God's creation, including the beauty and holiness of the natural world, which in other modes of Jewish belief is hardly stressed at all. As they anticipate their simple meal and a walk in the park (and at the end of the day, presumably, the Passover seder), the two are at peace with themselves and their modern American milieu.

    Yet the problematic nature of modern Jewish identity continually hovers over Zukofsky's examination of Reznikoff's work, as is appropriate for a piece originally intended for *The Menorah Journal*. In contrast to the shoemaker poem is "Hellenist," which Zukofsky offers as another example of objectification. Written in accordance with the formal principles of Imagism, it revealingly turns the tables on the Imagist fascination with matters Greek:

As I, barbarian, at last, although slowly, could read Greek,
At "blue-eyed Athena"
I greeted her picture that had long been on the wall:
The head slightly bent forward under the heavy helmet,
As if to listen; the beautiful lips slightly scornful. (*CP* I: 107)

From a Greek (and a genteel, educated, Christian) perspective, Reznikoff is a "barbarian," though he manages to learn enough of the language of civilization to read to the image of "blue-eyed Athena." But the severe idol in its "heavy helmet" only regards the upstart Jewish worshiper with scorn. For the ironically named Hellenist, no genuine Greek, it is an objectified moment of anxiety, religious, cultural, even erotic in nature: the meek, poorly schooled, Jewish barbarian before the warlike, blue-eyed pagan goddess. As L. S. Dembo wryly observes, "False God, graven image, *shikse,* Athena, Goddess of Western Wisdom, is the very epitome of blandishment and menace to young romantic Jews" (*Monological Jew* 125). Given Zukofsky's own anxieties, Reznikoff's brief poem must have spoken volumes, and it is not for aesthetic reasons alone that it appears in Zukofsky's seminal essay on poetics.

Among his remarks on "Hellenist," Zukofsky curiously states that "The mind may conceivably prefer one object to another—the energy of the heat which is Aten to the benignness of the light which is Athena. But this is matter of preference rather than an invalidation of the object not preferred" ("Program" 382). Objectification, as Zukofsky and his colleagues tell us, is a formal process, a process of linguistic composition that begins with the sincerity of the writer in addressing the object, the "thing," the material of the poem. The object itself is, as Zukofsky says here, "a matter of preference"; what counts is the sincerity of that preference and the production of "word combinations" that are "concomitants" of the writer's encounter with the thing, a process of composition that may eventually yield a "rested totality." The choice of Aten or Athena as the object of the poem does not invalidate the object not preferred—though in Reznikoff's poem, it is as if Athena does not prefer to be the object, at least not the object of this barbarian poet. Would the poet have been better off writing about Aten? And why does Zukofsky invoke Aten in opposition to Athena?

Aten, god of the sun, was the deity which the pharaoh Akhenaton imposed on the Egyptians, leading to what some scholars believe was one of the first versions of monotheism—a notion that another Jewish author would exploit some years after Zukofsky's essay in a "historical novel" called *Moses and Monotheism.* Freud's ordeal of civility as expressed in his last book is far more extravagant than Zukofsky's, but the appearance of Aten in Zukofsky's discussion of Reznikoff's poem is still quite intriguing. If Aten is a code word here for monotheism—that is, Judaism—then Jewish materials, as we have seen, make for successful poems, at least as much as does Athena, goddess of classical wisdom and gentile culture. In modern poetry, the preference for a Jewish object over a gentile object does not invalidate the gentile object—and vice versa.

Yet the negative encounter of the barbarian poet with "benign" Athena has also produced the objectification that Zukofsky associates with a successful poem. The Jewish poet should not shrink from an encounter with gentile culture, even a conflicted encounter (as in "Poem beginning 'The'"), so long as the encounter can be sincerely addressed. For Zukofsky, Reznikoff is an exemplary poet because he can objectify the Jewish American experience, including the ordeal of civility, and still maintain a sincere sense of his identity, a secure sense of himself.

It must be noted, however, that Reznikoff himself questioned the uses to which Zukofsky put his work, though it took over fifty years for him acknowledge this. As he says in his 1968 interview with L. S. Dembo, "I was not displeased, of course, but I confess I could not follow all that Zukofsky had to say about 'objectification' or, for that matter, 'sincerity'" (*Contemporary Writer* 210). Indeed, however richly interpretable Zukofsky's formulations may be, Reznikoff's own attempts to define Objectivism have the advantages of elegance, simplicity, and brevity. Quoting from the introduction to an anthology of ancient Chinese verse, Reznikoff offers this: "Poetry presents the thing in order to convey the feeling. It should be precise about the thing and reticent about the feeling" (206). And drawing on his own vocational experience, he states:

> By the term 'objectivist' I suppose a writer may be meant who does not write directly about his feelings but about what he sees and hears; who is restricted almost to the testimony of a witness in a court of law; and who expresses his feelings indirectly by the selection of his subject-matter and, if he writes in verse, by its music. (207–208)

Compared to his colleague Zukofsky, Reznikoff is winningly direct here, and one would suppose the same would be true on the subject of the writer's Jewish identity. But despite the fact that Reznikoff writes about Jewish culture and history from the beginning to the end of his career, his comments in this same retrospective are as disturbingly ambivalent as Zukofsky's more veiled remarks so many years before. As Reznikoff puts it, "The tendency is, on the one hand, to be assimilated and, on the other, to be yourself. Some people accentuate one or the other, but assimilation has historically been common among Jews. It's in one's nature to become part of the surrounding community" (212).

The tension here between the individual and the community stems from being both a Jew in diaspora *and* an American in one's native land, for although assimilation is a concept that is usually associated with a minority group facing a dominant culture, the desire "to be yourself" produces an agon that is as American as it is Jewish. American ideology valorizes both individualism and group identification, standing apart from and being one with the people, a powerful dialectic in American poetry from Whitman on. We should not think it odd then that in a book like *Jerusalem the Golden* we find not only some of Reznikoff's most characteristically Jewish utterances, but some of his most Whitmanian as well: "Feast, you who cross the bridge/this cold twilight/on these honeycombs of light, the buildings of Manhattan" (*CP* I: 116). Between Jew and American, between individual and group identity, Reznikoff and his colleagues try to make their way, confronted by contradictions which, as the century goes on, prove increasingly insurmountable—but out of which will come great poetry. As Oppen declares in *Of Being Numerous* (1968), " 'Whether, as the intensity of seeing increases, one's distance from Them, the people, does not also increase'/I know, of course I know, I can enter no other place" (153). Perhaps this is why, at about the same time, when asked to respond to the comment that "in your poetry . . . Judaism is a state of mind rather than a faith," Reznikoff replies: "I think it's a kind of discipline too. One may not accept all aspects of that discipline, but the one he must accept is that he be himself, although he may conform to his environment in minor ways.

These are the Jews who survive as Jews" (*Contemporary Writer* 213). Like Objectivism itself, Judaism becomes a discipline, a way of being, a way of acting—and a way of writing—in the world. Traditionally, Judaism calls for the identification of the individual with the people, the Law, and the God of Israel, a concept, as we shall see, that will return with greater strength in the next generation of Jewish American poets. But for Reznikoff, as for the other Jewish modernists, one need not fully accept this covenanted relationship to remain a Jew. "The Jews who survive as Jews" will have taken from Judaism what they need to be themselves and to participate, fully but uneasily, in American life. To use Reznikoff's terms, American Jews must be disciplined indeed to survive these difficult negotiations of identity and produce a poetry that attests to that survival.

3

Allen Grossman's Theophoric Poetics

Allen Ginsberg's *Kaddish and Other Poems* was published by City Lights Books in 1961. It was Ginsberg's second book. The appearance of *Howl* five years previously had made Ginsberg into a countercultural icon, a symbol of the Beat movement, and a persistent source of controversy that would extend far beyond the question of poetic value into wider debates over social mores and political beliefs. Mark Shechner calls Ginsberg "a power poet: a poet for whom the word is not only a medium of emotional power but a claimant to other forms of power as well. . . . Neither the Milton nor the Blake of our age, he has nonetheless, more than any other American writer since the war, crossed the border from sensibility to power and left his mark upon the events of his time" (181). Shechner's brief chapter on Ginsberg in *After the Revolution,* which remains one of our best studies of the modern Jewish American imagination, is provocative insofar as it is devoted almost entirely to the poet as a cultural figure. Shechner is quite frank in this regard: while "*Howl* and *Kaddish* rank as great modern poems" and "perhaps a dozen others . . . reward rereading," the fact is that "the *Collected Poems, 1947–1980* is less the record of sustained creative achievement than a hectic *tsimmes* of landscapes, dreams, jeremiads, exorcisms, anathemas, and prophecies, some of them violent and electric, many of them excruciatingly dull. . . . In Ginsberg's case, it is the example of the life, and the myth that surrounds it, that is destined to last, while the greater part of the poetry is likely to retain only documentary interest" (181).

No doubt many would agree with Shechner's assessment. Yet if *Howl* and *Kaddish* are great modern poems, and Shechner's concern is with Jewish American literary achievement, why does he choose not to consider *Kaddish* at least in some way as a categorically Jewish poem? Shechner regards Ginsberg as a "convert," a man who transforms himself, through Blake and Buddhism, from a middle-class Jewish boy with an "unpromising life script" to "that mythic American, the self-made man. . . . a man on his way down who was saved by poetry" (184). Be that as it may, Ginsberg never disavows his Jewish roots, and at least in *Kaddish,* attempts to integrate some aspects of his Jewish identity with his syncretic vision-ary concerns. The manner in which this has been acknowledged (and passed over) reveals as much about the situation of contemporary Jewish American poetry— and its readers—as it does about the poem itself.

Kaddish and Other Poems was widely reviewed when it first appeared, hardly surprising given Ginsberg's notoriety, and Jewish poets and critics certainly had their say. In one of his very few prose texts, George Oppen, writing in *Poetry*, considered the book along with works by Charles Olson and Michael McClure, two other highly visible avant-garde figures of the time. Oppen notes favorably how the title poem "moves in its final sections through the heavy bars of the traditional Hebrew prayer. It is a poem of very great power, of very great 'mass.' It is also a poem of great visual acuity, and often startling verbal precision, avoiding nothing in its path. It is not, to say again, a poem which could easily be forgotten" ("Three Poets" 329). Given Oppen's relative lack of Jewish literacy, it is not surprising that he assimilates "the traditional Hebrew prayer" to matters of form and technique. For the arch-Objectivist, who had himself only recently returned to poetry after a thirty-year hiatus, phrases such as "great visual acuity" and "startling verbal precision" are terms of high praise. Two other Jewish poets with Objectivist affinities found the poem an even greater achievement. David Ignatow in the *The New Leader* acknowledges the religious dimension of *Kaddish,* calling it "an act of purification, an expression of the need to be accepted, understood and loved." Like Oppen, Ignatow is impressed by the sheer verbal power of the text: "it succeeds, not by any rule of religion or poetics, but simply because it has form and mass and drives forward into the day. This poem, I believe, will be read many years from now as one of the great modern acts of faith, rising classically out of the extremes of human life" (24). Harvey Shapiro reviewed *Kaddish* in the Jewish publication *Midstream* with equal enthusiasm. Shapiro's review begins with an English translation of the opening line of the traditional prayer ("Exalted and hallowed be God's great name in this world of His Creation"), but for him, the significance of the poem as a Jewish work of literature lies less in its religious dimension than its psychological, social, and historical documentation. Ginsberg's achievement is to be found in his ability "to capture a story and a period of American-Jewish life, a fat novel-full, in verse that never slides under the material it has to carry while it keeps the long breath that is his signature and the pure impulse that is his gift" ("Exalted Lament" 95). But perhaps even more important, what Ginsberg represents to Shapiro is the figure whose work, more than that of any other contemporary, demands a reconsideration of schools and styles of *American* poetry. Through his claim to visionary inspiration and his popularity among "the young, the college kids, the Village girls and boys" (98), he takes poetry out of the hands of the quarterlies and the academics, in effect reopening the debates over open and closed forms and the social value of modern verse.

Harold Bloom, of course, demurred. Bloom's piece in the *Yale Review,* which he reprinted ten years later as "Poetic Misprision: Three Cases" in *The Ringers in the Tower* (the other two cases are those of Auden and Borges), acknowledges Ginsberg "as a legitimate though querulous follower of the main Romantic tradition in poetry, the line that in English runs from Blake and Wordsworth to *The Broken Tower* of Crane. But his major efforts, *Howl* and *Kaddish,* are certainly failures, and *Kaddish* a pathetic one" (213–214). Misprision eventually becomes a highly charged word for Bloom, which can connote productive misreading as well as disabling misalignment. In Ginsberg's case, "he has read the displaced religious poetry of Romanticism with some technical profit," but "The sadness is that his content, and not his form, is largely and increasingly out of control" (214). And as regards this content, including the specifically Jewish content of *Kaddish*, "Ginsberg is ruined poetically by his wilful addiction to a voluntaristic chaos, by a childish social dialectic as pernicious as any he seeks to escape. The ruin is very evident in *Kaddish*, a poem that is a prayer for the death anniversary of Ginsberg's mother, and also (as the title implies) an attempt at a sanctification of the name of God." To use Shechner's term, *Kaddish*, as much as Ginsberg's *Collected Poems*, is a *tsimmes*, and not a very appealing one at that. Skeptical of Ginsberg's revolutionary enthusiasms and already moving toward his idiosyncratic, but happily, un-doctrinaire cultural conservatism, Bloom cannot accept the poem's claim to be a genuine act of sanctification. Playing on one of Ginsberg's last lines ("Lord Lord O Grinder of giant Beyonds my voice in a boundless field in Sheol" [227]), Bloom judges that "Ginsberg's voice, which seemed to have possibilities of relevance, will at this rate soon enough constitute a boundless field of Sheol" (215). And indeed, in "The Sorrows of American-Jewish Poetry," it is to a cultural Sheol that Bloom consigns Ginsberg, declaring that he has "been raised to that bad eminence where every fresh failure is certain of acclaim as an event, something that has happened and so is news, like floods, fires, and other stimulating disasters. The genuine painfulness of reading through *Kaddish* is not an *imaginative* suffering for the reader, but is precisely akin to the agony we sustain when we are compelled to watch the hysteria of strangers" (260).

Considering these responses, it would appear that *Kaddish* is something of a test case for Jewish American poets and critics. Whether regarded as a success or a failure, it is acknowledged to be a poem born largely out of the modern Jewish urge toward self-transformation, a intense declaration of a post-Jewish, American sensibility that would both cling to and break from its cultural as well as its poetic history. The pathetic content of Naomi Ginsberg's life that it so graphically displays, the traditional religious beliefs toward which it so dramatically gestures, and of course, Ginsberg's persistently prophetic mode of utterace, makes *Kaddish* an automatic example of "Jewish American poetry." But as Bloom's Yale colleague and Ginsberg's Columbia classmate, John Hollander, observes, "What is Jewish or not Jewish about certain American poems is all tied up in the vexing problem of what is poetic or not poetic about them" (40). Wrestling with these matters in "The Question of American Jewish Poetry" (1988), Hollander finds both form and content to be of limited help in perceiving a poem's Jewish dimensions; rather, in considering the poets discussed in Richard Howard's *Alone with America*, "it might be better to ask . . . 'Can you tell from their poems that these poets are Jews? And, when you can, how does each poet's work reveal or conceal or ignore that fact in its own way?'" (38). Drawn inevitably to *Kaddish*, Hollander calls the poem "turgid"—so much for form and content!—and then proceeds with what may be the only sustained attack on the work using distinctly religious categories:

> Whether or not one admires this poem, one must recognize that it ignores the meaning—the nature, structure, liturgical function—of the prayer after which it takes its title. The litany of Aramaic predicates of sanctification, conjoined with Hebrew afterthoughts; the fact that its recitation by mourners is only one special occasion of its frequent reappearance throughout the synagogue service; the fact that the text on that occasion does not refer to its use as a prayer for mourners—as if *thereby* (that is, by having those mourners, instead of lamenting in public, intone sanctifications of God's name) it were being deeply, rather than trivially, appropriate: Of none of these facts is the poem's allusion in the title aware. It is as if the poem thought that "kaddish" meant only a public plaint or dirge for the bereaved. Furthermore, there is nothing in Ginsberg's *Kaddish* to suggest that he somehow knows all this and is deliberately making his "kaddish"—his poetic revision of the prose, as it were, of public ritual—into a metaphoric antisanctification: No matter how blasphemous that may sound, it might have made a true poem, and more truly interestingly Jewish in an antinomian way. (39)

When Hollander accuses as famous a work as *Kaddish* of misunderstanding a basic part of the liturgy and the theological concept which underwrites it, he is in effect declaring that the most highly visible American poet of the postwar decades, a poet whose Jewish background ostensibly informs at least some of his most important work, has failed to maintain the possibilities for a genuinely *Jewish-* American poetry. Furthermore, he implies that knowledge of the sort Ginsberg lacks is crucial to the production of such poetry, that a mere amalgam of historical references (what Shapiro much more sympathetically calls the poem's "fat novel-full" of Jewish life) and imprecise allusions is insufficient compared to the richness of the Jewish religious tradition, even in an attenuated American context. By the time Hollander writes "The Question of American Jewish Poetry," he has already published his own "avowedly Judaic and American poem" (51), the magnificent quest allegory, *Spectral Emanations*. Richly inventive in its use of Jewish lore, stately in its procedures, and measured in its passions, *Spectral Emanations* is as remote from Ginsberg's Beat aesthetic as can be imagined, and not merely because of its "academic" pedigree. A rabbinic impulse runs throughout Hollander's poetry, and is nowhere more evident than in this poem about the Second Temple's lost menorah, a poem that in its aggadic figurations follows the Talmudic injunction to put a hedge around the truth of the Law. Hollander speculates that *Kaddish* could have been "more truly interestingly Jewish in an antinomian way," but my guess is that he actually does see the poem as a crude example of antinomianism, a betrayal of the Jewish sanctification of the Name and not merely a "turgid" work of art.

Hollander's critique appears a long time after *Kaddish* is published, and that in itself is also significant. Critical thought devoted to Jewish American literature has changed in recent years, as somewhat less attention is paid to the work as a purely sociological phenomenon and more is given to matters of genre, form, intertextuality, and that not altogether definable set of religious and philosophical structures that Cynthia Ozick calls "the Jewish Idea." This is not to say that critics would no longer consider matters, say, of culture shock and assimilation in Ginsberg's presentation of Naomi as a "little girl—from Russia, eating the first poisonous tomatoes of America" (209): on the contrary, based on such a line of poetry, the reexamination of identity taking place under the ethnographical aegis of the "new Jewish cultural studies" could generate a "thick description" of immigrant life that would take us a great deal further than the older form of criticism that simply examines images of Jews in American society. But it seems to have taken some time to read a poem like *Kaddish* (even, as does Hollander, in a negative light), and not only ask about the social nature of Jewish identity, but raise questions about liturgical genres and religious concepts as well. This shift in critical perspective parallels the move in Jewish American literature, which Irving Howe describes as "a transition from *Jewishness as experience* to *Jewishness as essence*," the latter term indicating concern with "a religious or metaphysical content" as opposed to outward circumstances and social milieu ("Response" 70). In the span of time represented by this shift, Jews have become even more assimilated, more comfortable with their place in American society, have developed a more powerful economic and political base—and have turned inward to reflect on what they have gained and lost in terms of culture, tradition, and belief.

We have come once again, by way of *Kaddish* and its readers, to the same set of problems that will always be posed by modern Jewish literature, whether the work comes from Israel or the diaspora, and regardless of its content, its form, or its particular cultural matrix. Every major critic of this literature has struggled with questions of definition, for Jewish writing is ultimately a reflection of Jewish identity, and Jewish identity, especially under modern conditions, is notoriously difficult to define. Social and historical analysis has vied with religious and philosophical interpretation, and while the former has been the more direct and obvious path to take, the latter has presented the greater challenge. Perhaps this is due to the possibility that "in the twentieth century art has finally begun, by divorcing itself from the pagan aesthetic of nature and from the Christian aesthetic of incarnation, to catch up with the aboriginal Jewish aesthetic (for Jews and Gentiles alike) of a phenomenal world in eternal pursuit of the ideal, divine, or at least messianic world" (Schwarzschild 5–6). But in modern Jewish literature, the rich textures of Jewish life, of the ways in which Jews place their particular stamp on the "phenomenal world," cannot be easily dismissed—and this is as true for poetry as it is for prose fiction, since it is the compelling power of narrative art that still comes most often to mind when Jewish literature is invoked. The greatest task for the critic of Jewish literature is to articulate the relationship between the sociohistorical dimensions of a work and its elusive play of Jewish ideas. It is in that relationship that the inscription of Jewish identity may be seen.

The same year that *Kaddish* appeared, a rather different book by a Jewish American poet was published. *A Harlot's Hire* was Allen Grossman's first collection of poems. At twenty-nine, Grossman was six years younger than Ginsberg. Born in Minneapolis, he went to Harvard, and was soon to begin what would be a long career teaching at Brandeis and writing, in addition to his poetry, critical studies on such figures as Yeats, Lowell, and Crane. But despite his resemblance to academics like Hollander and Bloom (and indeed, Bloom is now one of the champions of Grossman's work), Grossman regarded Ginsberg as a kinsman, not in terms of literary style or demeanor, but in terms of cultural situation. His response to *Kaddish*, which appeared in the magazine *Judaism* in 1962, is revealingly called "The Jew as an American Poet: The Instance of Ginsberg," indicating that Ginsberg's situation in writing *Kaddish* is paradigmatic: according to Grossman, "Ginsberg has had the sense to perceive that the only significant Jewish poetry will also be a significant American poetry" (*Long Schoolroom* 158). As we shall see, this review of *Kaddish* is as much a meditation on the instance of Grossman as that of Ginsberg. But it is also an unusually prescient essay, for it approaches Ginsberg and his poem, as Howe would say, in terms of both Jewish experience and Jewish essence, comprehending the subject historically as a sociological and religious dialectic. In other words, Grossman's understanding of *Kaddish* is based on both ethnicity in relation to *American* history and religious belief in relation to *Jewish* history.

Grossman seeks to account for the emergence of the Jews into American literary prominence, which he regards as analogous to the Irish emergence into English letters in the late nineteenth century. The Irishman then and the Jew now "presents himself as the type of the sufferer in history" (151). As Grossman explains the situation, "The characteristic literary posture of the postwar poet in America is that of the survivor—a man who is not quite certain that he is not in fact dead. It is here that the Jew as a symbolic figure takes on his true centrality. . . . Ginsberg's poetry is the poetry of *a terminal cultural situation*. It is a Jewish poetry because the Jew is a symbolic representation of man overthrown by history" (153). The Holocaust as the epitome of Jewish suffering provides, however, only the most dramatic instance of the Jews' historical relevance to America. The fact of the Holocaust brings home to America the fact of Jewish difference, and by extension, the problem of ethnic difference in the American social fabric. Grossman describes "Ginsberg's Jewish protagonist" as an ethnic version of the outsider as a recognizable American type, "the apotheosis of the young radical Jewish intellectual, possessing now neither social nor political status. Having exhausted all the strategms of personal identity, sexual and ethnic, he is nonetheless determined to celebrate his state of being and his moment in history" (153).

This determination is an American quality, and Grossman notes that Ginsberg "regards himself as the heir of the American transcendentalist rhetoric" (155). The result is a "mixture of nationalism and ethnicism" that "represents the peculiar position of the American Jewish poet who regards himself as simultaneously native, and, in the special sense that always pertains to the Jew, alien" (155).

Grossman is aware that this mixture is highly unstable, especially in as volatile a work as *Kaddish,* and it is from this awareness that his most important insights are derived. In effect, *Kaddish* documents the dissolution of Jewish ethnicity through the death of Naomi, the "Jewish mother" at the heart of popular representations of Jewish social being. As Grossman puts it, "The death of the Jewish mother in Ginsberg's *Kaddish,* and the succession of cultural generations implied in the burden of identity laid by the mother on the son, is unquestionably the most momentous record in English of the problem of the passing of the older sociology and meaning of the Jewish family-centered culture in America" (157). But Grossman also sees Naomi as "the Shechinah, the wandering soul of Israel herself" (154); thus "Ginsberg attempts simultaneously to document the death of history itself, of which the Jewish people personfied by Naomi is the symbol, and to erect a new ground of being beyond history, of which his own poetry is the type and of which the symbol is the mother, or Israel, transformed as (gentile) muse" (155). The attempt to move beyond history may transform the mother from Shechinah to gentile muse, but it also connects Ginsberg with the tradition of Jewish mysticism, in which "the gnostic attitude represents the attempt of the Jewish mind to reconstitute itself outside of history" (154). And this is true not only in terms of historical content but form as well: "Like the Jewish Kabbalist, Ginsberg regards his words and indeed the letters of which they are composed as living things that in their form represent the recreation of 'the syntax and measure of poor human prose'" (156).

Kaddish, then, turns out to be precisely the kind of antinomian poem that Hollander claims it could have been if Ginsberg had a greater knowledge of religious tradition. The American experiences of Naomi and her son represent Jewish history and Jewish identity pushed to the breaking point, after which only a literature beyond history and beyond ethnicity is possible. "For Ginsberg," Grossman concludes, "the poetic identity must supersede the ethnic identity if the poet is to survive" (156). And with great dialectical irony, Grossman notes that "Jewish symbology becomes available in American poetry just at the point at which the Jewish poet finds it necessary to document the death of the Jewish cultural fact" (157). Thus "Ginsberg can entertain the Jewish subject matter only as it is in the process of being transformed into something else. . . . The death of the mother in *Kaddish* represents the death of parochial culture, and the poem emerges at the point when it is necessary to lament that loss and refound identity. Ginsberg represents a brilliant though uncertain invasion of the American literary community by the Jewish sensibility in the process of transcending parochial limits" (158).

It is a compelling analysis, and one that is altogether worthy of a young Jewish poet with great rhetorical ambitions of his own. Even today, what Grossman calls the "parochial limits" of ethnicity continue to set the boundaries for much Jewish American literature. But Grossman, steeped in the Romanticism of Blake, Shelley, Yeats, of Whitman, Crane, and Stevens, not only identifies with what he sees as Ginsberg's cultural and poetic situation, but to some extent makes that situation over so that it more closely resembles his own. Ginsberg's visionary proclivity is actually modified by his connection to Objectivism. A disciple of Williams (who wrote introductions to *Howl* and *Empty Mirror*) and an admirer of Reznikoff, Ginsberg is one of a number of important midcentury figures whose work represents a rapprochement of modernist and Romantic tendencies. Like Robert Creeley, Robert Duncan, Denise Levertov, Frank O'Hara, John Ashbery— indeed, many of the poets who appear in Donald Allen's *New American Poetry*— Ginsberg often finds the source of his vision in mundane events. For Grossman, *Kaddish* may represent the dissolution of ethnicity, but it is still grounded in the details of Jewish American life, of Naomi "with the YPSL's hitch-hiking thru Pennsylvania, in black baggy gym skirts pants, photograph of 4 girls holding each other round the waste [*sic*], and laughing eye, too coy, virginal solitude of 1920" (210). As David Ignatow notes in his review of *Kaddish,* the poem gives us "a very recognizable world, with houses, streets, bedrooms, kitchens, food, poverty, ideals and ambitions, all distorted in the face of a mad mother and issuing in the frightful voice of her son as poet" (24). Grossman's aesthetic, from his earliest work on, is much less involved with exterior reality, though like all poetry in the Romantic visionary tradition, it is certainly responsive to historical conditions, particularly those of Jewish history. It may be that for Grossman, rather than Ginsberg, "the poetic identity must supersede the ethnic identity if the poet is to survive."

Grossman's understanding of himself as a Jewish American poet is, in fact, unique, in terms of the literary and cultural debates that shape the terms of this book. As his review of *Kaddish* indicates, Grossman sees "the Jew as an American Poet," especially after the Shoah, at a critical impasse. As he explains to Mark Halliday in *Against Our Vanishing,* "I was ten years old in 1942. The most persuasive public experience that I can bring to mind from that time is the experience of helpless spectatorship of an historical drama of mutilation and the extinction of persons. The 'I' of my poetry derives from a sense of the self as obliterated, surviving only by accident. My most fundamental impulses are toward recovery, the securing once again of selfhood in something that lies invulnerably beyond history, something which promises enormous, inhuman felicity" (*Sighted Singer* 40–41). The urgent need to secure that sense of lost selfhood, to speak for the dead (and "at that moment, all the dead were Jews" [51]), is connected to what Grossman calls his need to establish a "lineage," an authoritative understanding of the self's origins, both as a poet and as a member of a particular culture. But the assertion of ethnic identity through poetry, even in the face of genocide, is highly problematic: "It is my feeling that the enterprise of this way [of] establishing a poetic lineage—that is to say, at the intersection of the ethnic and the cultural—is a failed enterprise. At the same time, much of the thinness and arbitrariness of poetry in the present time arises from the deliberate separation of these two elements" (51). In effect, to establish and validate his lineage as both a poet and a Jew, Grossman must accept the obligation to write poetry as a Jew, while at the same time sensing the inadequacy and parochialism of what would ordinarily be understood as Jewish poetry. The problem that ethnicity poses is quite clear: "Ethnicity, and Judaism is an ethnicity, is also merely another violent phantasm, out of scale with human life, which drives us against one another in conflicts so dangerous as to be unimaginable as a desirable state of affairs" (*Sighted Singer* 121). But ethnicity is also an ineluctable reality, which Grossman recognizes in "the proliferation of Jewish poetry and, indeed, parochially sponsored poetry of all sorts" (121). Throughout his career, Grossman wrestles with the possibility of writing an ethically responsible, identifiably Jewish poetry that cannot be reduced to "another violent phantasm."

Grossman's dissatisfaction with what he frequently labels "parochialism" stems from an impulse that can be understood as both vocational (poetic) and cultural (Jewish). Consider this statement, which follows immediately after his attack on ethnicity:

> My poems are addressed to some state of the persons around me other than that which they currently find themselves in. My poems should be addressed, are intended to be addressed, not to the present powers, but to the future powers of my readers. I believe that poems should not be addressed to the already possessed states of consciousness of the persons who read them. Poems should have an empowering strangeness about them which summons its audience rather than receives its audience. (122)

Utopian, universal, even messianic in his conception of poetry, Grossman is certainly faithful to his Romantic and his Jewish lineage. The prophetic tradition informs all of his work, as it does the work of every poet who believes himself to be "a person whom a poetic voice has found" (*Sighted Singer* 80). The "empowering strangeness" of that voice, its ability to summon an audience to a state of consciousness hitherto unexperienced, is simultaneously restorative; its defamiliarizing obscurity can, paradoxically, reconstruct—as in the kabbalistic sense of *tikkun*—what Grossman calls the "shattered or exploded countenance." Thus, "The highest form which poetic ambition, in my mind, can take is to join together oracular profundity with the whole, intact, harmonious, and socially-addressed countenance" (*Sighted Singer* 97–98).

The rhetorical correlative to this ideal is Grossman's embrace of the high style, and his insistence that poets make full and unrestrained use of the verbal resources at their disposal. "I have been astonished, throughout my life," he announces, "at the poverty of the utterance of those people who call themselves poets, their unwillingness, in the language of Yeats, to open their throats, to speak both directly and with a full sense of the privilege of the art that they practice" (*Sighted Singer* 54). Unlike other Jewish poets of his generation, Grossman cannot see the Objectivist mode as a viable option, and his critique poses a severe challenge to Objectivism's rhetorical stance:

> The subject matter of poetry, whatever its means may be, however vast a net it throws over the world of objects, is always, in my view, the person. For poetry there is no sky which is different from the unknown inwardness of other selves, the knowledge of which will construct selves as persons. I see for poetry no possibility and, indeed, no need consistent with its nature or its purpose in the world to make any offering whatsover toward a world which is not the person. The idea of Objectivist verse seems to me simply a premature conclusion about the function or nature of a particular kind of poetry, which addresses the self without giving it its proper name—in effect, an evasion. The most remote thing that can come to mind is the inwardness and very being of another, and it is only that that the telescope properly focused can see. Poetry is the lens by which that thing is seen and in this age may be the only such lens. (*Sighted Singer* 63–64)

Grossman may be accused of having a reductionistic view of Objectivism's methods and goals, but his radical humanism—his belief that in poetry, the object world must in the end lead to the person—is certainly consistent with his understanding of the poetic vocation and of his cultural lineage. In chapters 1 and 2, I attempted to relate Objectivist principles and practices of sincerity, precision, and testimony to certain formations in Jewish history and thought; in Grossman's overriding concern for "the unknown inwardness of other selves," we see the other pole of this dialectic. Objectivist poetry is an evasion insofar as it looks on the object world (including the human figure) in and of itself, without seeing beyond it. Objectivism's rhetorical scrupulousness and exteriority of content cannot restore an "intact, harmonious, and socially-addressed countenance," which only an prophetic *vision* of another's interiority can provide.

Grossman's references to poetry as lens or telescope are based on his early poem "In My Observatory Withdrawn," which he is discusses with Mark Halliday just prior to his remarks on Objectivism. In that poem, all human contact is authorized by "the transcendental Beloved," and it is on this figure that all poetic observations of inwardness in another are ultimately focused. Thus, poetry is an ocular instrument that leads to a transcendental knowledge of the Other. Consciously or not, Grossman revises Zukofsky's "An Objective," which begins with an optical definition of "Objective" as "*The lens bringing the rays from an object to a focus. That which is aimed at*" and is then extended as the "*Desire for what is objectively perfect, inextricably the direction of historic and contemporary particulars*"

(*Prepositions* 12). Zukofsky's conception of objectification as "rested totality" involves the ordering of particulars, of material details cast as verbal structures. The poem is a lens that focuses and organizes worldly experience. But Grossman, like Blake, seeks the "Human Form Divine" in all things; vision means inner vision, and its only object can be the countenance of the Other.

Furthermore, Grossman views the Jewish poet's relationship to the world, to Creation, as mediated by language, to be distinctively different from that of the non-Jewish poet. Unlike the gentile poet, whose reference is to the world, the Jewish poet's reference is to God. In "Jewish Poetry Considered as a Theophoric Project" (1990), a densely argued essay that first appeared in *Tikkun*, Grossman seeks an understanding of Jewish poetry by elaborating the distinction between the fictive or poetic, and the sacred: "Poetry in the usage of Western language may sometimes be called 'divine' or sacred; but for the Jew *there is always a sense* (a profound understanding beneath all other understandings) *that the category of the sacred and the category of the poetic repel one another*—because the poetic defers the sacred, which is, nonetheless, the destination of all things" (*Long Schoolroom* 161). Both the poetic and the sacred begin with a summoning from above: in the former case, Hesiod meets the Muses, the daughters of Mnemosyne, descending Mt. Helicon; in the latter, Abraham is called by God, the first time to leave the land of his birth, the second time to sacrifice Isaac. Poetry, authorized by Memory, reproduces the world through language; "Things and persons so reproduced become part of cultural memory. They die as things and persons and are reborn as signs" (160). But the sacred "has no representational correlative and no existence but Presence, its own term and explanation" (161). Grossman then summarizes the distinction:

> The gentile poet is called by language in all the openness—the ontological problematicity, as it is—of language's relation to the world. The Jewish poet (the Jew's *great* poet whom I wish speculatively to summon to mind) is called monologically by Presence itself. The correlative but severely contrastive figure in traditional Jewish narrative to the gentile muse (daughter of Memory) is the Shechinah, whose name means *dwelling*—the dwelling of the name in the world: the Jew's place to be. (163)

Linguistically, the gentile poet speaks to and of the world, utters a multiplicity of names. The Jewish poet speaks to and of Presence, utters a single Name. Jewish poetry, therefore, is theophoric ("God-bearing") poetry; what Grossman calls its "representational logic" is different from that of all other poetry: "The Jew's word, strictly speaking, is One (holy, sacred, *Kadosh*), and is unlike all other words in that it does not signify by difference but rather serves the Master who is difference—which is to say, existence itself" (162).

The implications of Grossman's comparison are of the utmost importance. Jewish poetry is not to be primarily understood in terms of ethnicity; it is related to the Jewish people as an ethnic group only insofar as Jewish culture has been shaped by its sacred history. God's covenant with the Jews, His calling them into His Presence and His continued insistence that they maintain His standards of holiness, distinguishes Jewish poetry as it distinguishes the Jewish people itself. Grossman's analysis, developed over a period of at least thirty years, represents the most sustained attempt to understand Jewish poetry as a work of the religious imagination. It returns Jewish poetry to an originary moment, the moment at which Jewish history begins and which may be renewed on each occasion a Jewish poet sets out to write a poem:

> The Jewish poet who invokes the Shechinah has an obligation to construct the place "where Light and Law are manifest," to which the nations may come because it is where they are. The obligation is the same as the obligation to the intelligibility of experience, the covenant. And the place of holiness is the ground—neither heaven nor earth—upon which the paradigms of experience (the adequacy of the constructive mind to history) can be restored, where loss is given back as meaning and where the People and the peoples are equally at home. (166)

The redemptive power of this prophetic vision is mitigated, however, by what Grossman insists is the speculative nature of his remarks. Whether Jewish poetry of this sort has ever been written—whether it can be written—remains an unanswered question, given the radical demands on the poet who enters into the culture of holiness. Following traditional Jewish belief, Grossman notes that the "dwelling" signified by the figure of the Shechinah "is precisely *the homelessness or placelessness of the word,* existence itself and only that" (166). The ontological homelessness of the Shechinah, which of course finds its correlative in the exilic conditions of Jewish history, as well as the textual homelessness that distinguishes Jewish writing, is "the contradiction of representation" (166). In his essay "Holiness," Grossman observes that the *kedusha* prayer "performs the continuous exchange of experience for holiness by which the world is maintained: the voluntary concession of the meaning of the world to its source obligatory upon the Jew, as the transactive reciprocation of the creation and as responsive to the free act of God by which the Jew was 'chosen from the among the peoples'" (*Long Schoolroom* 184). But poetry, finally, is not prayer. *As poets,* even devout Jews may not be able to enter fully into the culture of holiness through this concession of worldly meaning. It could be that all poets, including the Jewish poets who recognize their obligation to Presence, must still partake, at least to some extent, in the culture of representation. The utopian vision of a Jewish poetry of "Light and Law" giving itself to all the nations emerges out of a contradiction, for as Grossman himself tells us, the sacred repels the poetic; its utterance "intends to withdraw the world into its source in Divinity" (161). "What can be *done?*" cries the poet in "Out of the Blue," perhaps his greatest enactment of Jewish poetry's dilemma: "The meaning of the world/Is being made in defiance of the Jew" (*Ether Dome* 48). The poems that Grossman writes that draw on Jewish themes would prepare a *makom,* a place for Presence in the world. But because this place is of the world, because it comes into being out of representational language, these poems can never partake fully in the condition of holiness.

As his review of *Kaddish* indicates, Grossman is preoccupied with the possibilities for a Jewish American poetry during the early stage of his career. *A Harlot's Hire,* which, according to the poet, "collected poems that were written as early as my teens" (*Sighted Singer* 49), also contains more overtly Jewish poems than any of Grossman's subsequent collections. Its title comes from Deuteronomy 23:19, and Grossman uses the verse (but does not identify the source) as the book's epigraph: *Thou shalt not bring the hire of a whore, or the price of a dog, into the house of the Lord thy God for any vow: for even both of these are abominations unto the Lord thy God.* "Dog" is a pejorative term for a male prostitute, and the entire verse is found in a section of Deuteronomy presenting "various civil and criminal laws which, as always, aim at raising the level of the people's communal and individual purity. . . . together they are the basis for making Israel a fit partner in God's covenant" (Plaut 1492). The problem of holiness, distinguishing the pure from the impure, thus is set out in radical terms even at the beginning of Grossman's work. On the one hand, in declaring his first gathering of poems to be the hire of a whore, Grossman implies that he is unworthy of entering into the holy congregation of Israel. His trafficking in the worldly culture of representation, from which is derived his very identity as a poet, precludes him from the sacred rites and throws into question his identity as a Jew. On the other hand, the title and epigraph can also be read more ironically: even these poems, as devout and observant as they may be, still are as a harlot's hire when compared to the sanctity of the Lord's house and the purity of those who would maintain God's covenant. The poet, then, acknowledges the impossibility of a sacred Jewish poetry and the contradictions inherent in his own self-conception.

When he reprints some poems from *A Harlot's Hire* in *Of the Great House* (1982), Grossman calls one in particular, "The Sands of Paran," "the beginning of my work." Paran, the scene of the poem, "is imagined to be the desert around Sinai" (*Great House* 87), as the speaker casts himself back into the life of Moses in an attempt to imagine the nature of the primal Jewish experience, the personal encounter with the deity in whose image we are said to be made. Having "questioned them all, Miriam and Aaron/And many who hated him more, of what he saw/Those days and nights of storm" (*Harlot's Hire* 3), the poet, contemplating Moses on Sinai, wonders about prophetic election and the uncanny meeting of the human with the divine. In Harold Bloom's view, Moses, God's prophet, the instrument of Israel's liberation, and the giver of the Law to the people, "is not particularly inspired, though he is certainly used, and even ill-used, by Yahweh. Reluctant at first, and then doggedly stubborn, Moses plods along in J, loyally

trying to make up in zeal what he lacks in zest" (*Book of J* 285). Grossman may be
drawn to Moses in this early poem because of the very pathos of his uninspired
situation. "My mind is in the wilderness with Moses" he declares, for the wilderness is the place of confrontation and testing, of purification and of the Law. Here
are the final two stanzas of the poem:

> I seek the wilderness again, and the light
> Falling in flights of arrows; the long
> Way round, and the imminence of the mountain where
> The plough-share hardly serves as an adequate weapon.
> I would recover, not the dream,
> But the confrontation, not the nice complement
> Of olive and cedar, but the complex face
> That talked with Moses there, and spoke on stone.
>
> I am not the remnant, and I lack
> The hatred of my people. Yet in some dawn,
> Usurping the hierarchy of the birds,
> When I have climbed up there to where he stood
> I shall in my own voice speak of my need. (*Harlot's Hire* 3)

Longing for poetic authority, Grossman would recover "the confrontation,"
the sublime intercourse of humanity with divinity, however much it may expose
his utter inadequacy before God's "complex face," which we are forbidden to see.
The term is a reminder of the kabbalistic view of God's multiple countenances and
of the complicated interactions of divine attributes within the Godhead. Yet even
before such immensity, the poet insists on his election. His need *is* to speak in his
own voice, and in a condition of impossible earliness, to speak his own word on
stone. This is an act of usurpation, which as Bloom would tell us, is always
necessary when a young poet first breaks forth into strong utterance. Grossman
acknowledges that he is "not the remnant," referring to the *she'erit Yisrael*, "the
concept, especially cultivated by the biblical prophets, that a defeat of Israel will
never be total or irreversible; a remnant will always remain and allow a new epoch
to unfold" (Glatzer 779). Visionary inspiration in some respects separates him
from the surviving faithful; like other Romantic poet-prophets, Grossman imagines himself to be cast out from the community for daring to act like Moses,
climbing "up there to where he stood." But given his aspirations, he finds no other
course acceptable.

The strength of Grossman's prophetic aspirations is even more apparent in
"The Voiceless Star," a poem which, in retrospect, confirms both the Bloomian
understanding of the ephebe's agon with his precursors, and Grossman's sense of
himself as a young poet called into utterance after the devastation of World War II
and the Shoah, who must somehow speak for the dead. The first stanza turns on

the word "everything," which can refer to poetry, to Jewish life, and to civilization itself:

> Having been born when everything was ended
> Or almost over
> And nurtured in a pauper's dream of riches
> Which, when gotten, no longer were desired
> And educated by the dead
> In a vague dream of unheroic combat
> Which transpired elsewhere, and yet changed my life,
> I now turn round and round declaring, "My God
> Is faceless, and I am made in His strange likeness." (*Harlot's Hire* 14)

Lineage, to use Grossman's term, counts for everything here: poetic lineage, ethnic lineage, and cultural lineage are inextricably intertwined. The fate of poetry, which is to say the attitude that the young poet takes toward his "pauper's dream of riches," is dependent on his education by the dead, who may be understood as both his precursors and all who have recently died in the war and in the Holocaust. But however belated and distant from the historical events and literary texts that have changed his life, he is still aware of a living God that he acknowledges and feels obliged to comprehend. "The Sands of Paran" stresses the intimate encounter on Sinai between God and prophet, and the connection between the divine and human image through "the complex face/That talked to Moses there." "The Voiceless Star" is concerned with the more vexing paradox of God's unrepresentability, his facelessness that is still somehow the model for the human image "made in His strange likeness." Remote and imageless, God cannot be known by one who experiences election; the poet cannot rely on the enigmatic knowledge that he is made in His likeness to aid him in his terrible task. That task, now that everything is "almost over," is revealed in the last stanza:

> Therefore it is my meaning
> To find out still places, and rehearse
> All rites of purity that ever served
> To clean the murderer, or to solicit
> The prophetic dream. For I was born
> To purify the cry, and I shall weep,
> First of all men,
> In the strange language of the voiceless star,
> Child of a quiet time yet hearing voices,
> Prophet and diplomat of the void. (*Harlot's Hire* 14)

The pathos of these lines is deeply moving, but there is something disquieting about them too. Grossman's understanding of his poetic vocation, which develops in the first stanza out of negation, out of human loss and divine absence, takes on a positive sense of mission at the end of the poem. Yet this sense of mission may be incommensurate with the task at hand, which is, arguably, beyond the scope of human agency, including that of art. This is not to subscribe to cultural pessimism and respond to Grossman with Adorno's notorious statement that "To write poetry after Auschwitz is barbaric" (Adorno 34). On the contrary, Grossman correctly recognizes the absolute necessity of poetry after Auschwitz. As the traditional vehicle for comprehending the dialectic of truth and beauty (I am assuming that, given Grossman's Romantic lineage, such terminology is appropriate in this discussion), poetry is one of the few resources left that may help us understand the Shoah, along with the other catastrophes of the twentieth century. But Grossman is not merely asserting the necessity of poetry in the wake of the Holocaust. Rather, by casting himself as "Prophet and diplomat of the void," he declares that the poet, even though he has not personally experienced the disaster which has "transpired elsewhere," is still that figure who can "purify the cry" of those who have been lost, and even "clean the murderer" through the performance of the proper "rites of purity." Unlike other American poets, such as Reznikoff in *Holocaust* (in which the poet becomes a sort of court reporter) or Rothenberg in *Khurbn* (where the poet is possessed by "the dibbiks who had died before their time" [*Khurbn* 3]), Grossman insists on the prophetic imagination's transformative power, even in the face of the very worst historical circumstances, the virtually complete collapse of the moral dimension of human life.

The risk that Grossman takes in "The Voiceless Star" depends on his rhetorical power, his ability to convince the reader of the poet's positive moral authority despite a faceless God and the wreckage of the social order. As he insists in "A Poem for Statesmen," after "so long an agony of ignorance/And the dying of so many thousand deaths/ . . . I am still a poet/With power to make you beautiful and free" (*Harlot's Hire* 42). Once again, Grossman's youthful audacity results in a prophetic flamboyance, produced by the very gravity of the situation he would address:

> . . . Hear me and I shall open
> The ghetto of ghosts
> And give back to the nation the beauty of her dead
> And they will walk beside the living, and make them free. (*Harlot's Hire* 42)

This hyperbolic view of the poet is certainly questionable, going to the heart of the debate about artistic representations of the Holocaust, one side of which is summed up, as we have seen in chapter 1, in George Steiner's statement that "The aesthetic makes endurable." For Grossman, on the other hand, the redemptive force of poetry (especially Jewish poetry, given what he regards as its theophoric potential) is equal to the greatest of human evils. Mark Halliday, in discussing "A Poem for Statesmen" with its author, remarks in a dry understatement that "It strikes me as a rather bold way to talk to statesmen." Grossman, aware of his sublime *chutzpah,* answers that

> It was indeed not such a bold way to talk to statesmen, for statesmen were not listening. It strikes me as an arrogant way to define human enterprise. It was, however, an effort, which I still affirm, to take into my hands as a man the particular powers which the poet administers and to use those powers for the ends of poetry; that is to say, to make others both beautiful and also (what is from the point of view of the poem the same thing) free in a specific way. (*Sighted Singer* 53)

In Grossman's view, beauty and freedom constitute goods in and of themselves, and however arrogant the poet may appear, it seems that such goods *must* be administered through poetry, even when reality points toward the impossibility of their fulfillment. Referring to the end of the war in the second part of "A Poem for Statesmen," Grossman declares that

> Victory beguiles some other and more innocent weariness;
> For us there are no victories in war.
> Out of the ovens, out of the unnumbered chambers
> Of mutilation and the long memories of hurt children
> Who were not present at the horror of their making
> What triumph comes of which to make a song?
>
> What peace is possible among such multitudes
> So broken? What image lives in the minds of men
> So beautiful that it can gather to its breasts
> Such mutilation and such loss and still be beautiful? (*Harlot's Hire* 43)

Grossman depends here on an old poetic strategy, in which the possibility of beauty is called into question in a lyric utterance that is simultaneously intended to embody that beauty. Only in the poem can beauty, freedom, and peace be realized; poetry is thus the necessary confirmation of lived experience, for the virtues it addresses come to life, as it were, in the lyric utterance. Likewise, in the last lines of that section, the poet says that "We live in the silence after speech,/And the silence before speech begins," knowing full well that the poem uttered in the present lays the past to rest (if that is possible in such an extreme instance) and creates the unfolding future.

"I am certainly a high-style writer," Grossman tells Mark Halliday in their discussion of *A Harlot's Hire;* "I was then and I am now" (*Sighted Singer* 50). "The high style is the style of high hope," he adds (*Sighted Singer* 60). In *A Harlot's Hire,* the triumphal extravagance of Grossman's rhetoric is a direct result of the way he views his poetic mission. As a voice of "high hope," a figure appointed to "give back to the nation the beauty of her dead" (and "nation" may be read as both America and the Jewish people), Grossman must pitch his writing in a very high style indeed. History places an immense burden on him as he comes into consciousness as a poet and a Jew, for as he says of the "ghetto of ghosts" passage in "A Poem for Statesmen," "the system of representation available to mind in Western civilization has become inadequate to the representation of the major fact of history, of which the Holocaust is now the sign" (*Sighted Singer* 55). This anxiety of representation affects many of the poems in Grossman's first book, including those that do not deal with the Holocaust, but rather with the fragmentation of Jewish religious and cultural heritage. These poems, although cast in the "high style," are less hopeful. Brooding over Jewish loss and exile, they appear to be written under the sign of historical disaster; and in their ghostly dialogue of past and present, they represent a crisis of transmission of the sort that both constitutes and produces a modern Jewish understanding of Jewish existence in history. As theorized in the work of such writers as Benjamin, Scholem, Yerushalmi, and Bloom, transmission *is* catastrophe, and tradition means rupture as much as continuity. Grossman, seeking a rhetoric that is commensurate with this experience, understands the violence that is inherent in any attempt at its representation. Loss can produce only further loss, and yet the poet must engage in the work of representation, must somehow acknowledge and transcend the discontinuities that are his inheritance.

The greatest of these discontinuities is the Jew's relation to "The Law," which becomes the subject and title of one of Grossman's most beautiful early poems. Drawing on some of the oldest tropes in the lyric and spiritual traditions, the poet declares his "deep desire to be wise," and proceeds to describe his vision of "the woman Wisdom." She is

> A whore but very beautiful, standing undressed
> Almost knee-deep in weeds in the garden
> Early in the morning. She is a girl,
> Younger at least
> Than any woman I have ever known;
> A Jewess, her hair as dark as night;
> And we are of a single race, but she
> Is beautiful. (*Harlot's Hire* 4)

There is much to unpack in this passage, beginning with the vexing assertion that Wisdom (who by the end of the poem will be equated with the Law) is a whore. We are led back to the title of the volume, but in this case, rather than the work of the poet being judged a harlot's hire, it is the poet's desire, the object of the work, Wisdom as the Beloved, who is regarded as having been prostituted. If the poems are a harlot's hire then they may not enter the precincts of the sacred, but if Wisdom or the Law itself is a whore, then the very category of the sacred is called into question. The sacred and the profane cannot be distinguished, at least through verbal representation, for they are embodied in the same seductive figure.

The desire for Wisdom is to be understood as a form of eros (here the poem is as Platonic as it is Jewish), and though the poet calls her a whore, there is much about her that also resembles the Beloved of the Song of Songs. She is, after all, a young, dark-haired Jewess, waiting like a bride for the poet: "And we are of a single race." Does the degradation of the Beloved indicate that the Lover has been degraded as well? This leads us to a further question: what is the precise nature of this wisdom the poet so desires? If we follow Grossman's distinctions in his essay on theophoric poetry, we can say that Jewish wisdom as it is embodied in poetry differs from that of non-Jewish poetry in its closer connection to the sacred, just as the Shechinah differs from the muses who met Hesiod on Mt. Helicon. At a number of points in his exhaustive essay on the Shechinah, Gershom Scholem links this figure with that of Sophia (see "Shekinah" 142–144, 168, 185). Is Grossman's "woman Wisdom" a muse, or is she the Shechinah? Here is Harold Bloom on the subject of the (gentile) muse as whore:

> Poetic anxiety implores the Muse for aid in divination, which means to foretell and put off as long as possible the poet's own death, as poet and (perhaps secondarily) as man. . . . His word is not his own word only, and his Muse has whored with many before him. He has come late in the story, but she has always been central in it, and he rightly fears that his impending catastrophe is only another in her litany of sorrows. . . . The poet thinks he loves the Muse out of his longing for divination, which will guarantee him time enough for fulfillment, but his only longing is a homesickness for a house as large as his spirit, and so he doesn't love the Muse at all. (*Anxiety of Influence* 61)

This passage is useful in that its truth is diametrically opposed to that of "The Law." The wisdom that the poet in Grossman's poem desires is not to be achieved through divination, which is expressly forbidden by the Mosaic code. What the poet of "The Law" seeks is not the knowledge of his death, which is to say his fate in the eternal passing away of all things in the natural world, the world of representation that is the concern, according to Grossman, of gentile poetry. Rather, the Jewish poet in this poem seeks the assurance of God's eternal Presence, of his possession by the Shechinah, in whom the Jew finds his only dwelling in his wandering among the nations. According to kabbalistic tradition, the Shechinah accompanies the Jewish people into exile; her place in the Godhead (including her frankly sexual relation to other aspects of divinity) will only be restored in the messianic age. Until then, the Shechinah is in a "fallen" state, and at her worst, as Scholem observes, "actually comes under the sway of the Other Side, which penetrates and becomes entrenched within her, with disastrous consequences for Israel and for the entire world" ("Shekinah" 189). The situation of the Jews is thus symbolized through the Shechinah; even in exile, she remains the expression of Jewish hope, as is abundantly clear in the poem's magnificent final stanza:

> You will awaken with the dignity
> Of beauty still upon you, and go forth
> Like one who has not long since worshipped.
> It will be like some mysterious Sabbath
> When the Book was taken from the Arc,
> The crown, the breastplate with its wreath of bells,
> And all the royalty that hides the Law
> Opened and laid aside, and you knew the words,
> As a man knows a woman who is raven haired
> And odorous.
> You will be as infinite as your desire
> Knowing the Law is young and beautiful
> When you awake one morning in your cold hotel
> After a night of vision. (*Harlot's Hire* 5)

The text lovingly modulates from the erotic to the liturgical and back again to the erotic. The ritual "undressing" of the Torah and the reading of the Law on the Sabbath is equated with the poet's desire for the Beloved, and to know the words of the Law is to know the Shechinah, just as it is actually considered a *mitzvah* for a Jewish couple to have sexual intercourse during the Sabbath, for it helps to restore the Shechinah to her rightful place in the Godhead. Yet full restoration cannot take place: the last two lines of the poem (which sound like Hart Crane, one of Grossman's most important precursors) remind us that the Jews are still in exile. The poet awakens in his "cold hotel," and though his vision of the Law grants him a dignity that transcends his immediate circumstances, no true reading has taken place. The poet's love of the Law is both dream and reality; he is alone with his desire, but with neither Book nor Beloved.

Grossman's anxiety over the possession of the Law as a desirable woman is dramatized to an even greater extent in "The Discourse of Shemaiah and Abtalion," based on a Talmudic legend. Hillel, perhaps the greatest of the rabbis in the Talmud, was originally a poor man who could not always find the necessary fee to study with his teachers, Shemaiah and Abtalion. On one such occasion, Hillel climbed onto the roof of the synagogue to hear the discourse going on inside, and stayed all night, despite a snow storm. Rescued the next morning by his teachers, Hillel was rewarded for his devotion to Torah by being allowed to study without charge from then on. In Grossman's version of the legend, told from Hillel's point of view, knowledge or ignorance of the Law is explicitly equated with sexual privilege, as well as with warmth and cold, inside and outside:

I cannot hear the words. The thing
That I was born to know
Is hidden by the winds and by the snow;
The winter of the Law
Has made me ice. I die of awe.

It is my bride they fondle in the night,
Aged and awkward exegetes of my delight,
Usurpers of the rich unseeded womb,
Huddled by the fire in a darkening room
Sick with desire and powerless to know
While I was worn with watching and with the snow. (*Harlot's Hire* 34)

Although Hillel indignantly calls the old men "usurpers," their intimate
knowledge of the Law gives them access to "the rich unseeded womb" that the
younger man cannot as yet possess. "What gloss applies to the unwritten page?" he
asks, for he has not yet been inscribed with such knowledge, and though he may
"die of awe" when confronted by the Law, it is an awe born of a condition of
relative ignorance. Lacking "The sweating intimacy of the Book," the future sage
wonders "What will be born in such great cold?" and answers himself as follows:

Not love,
(Love that is on us like a plague of blood)
But rather some far simpler thing,
Some thing one man can tell another
Something one man can tell his brother
While standing on one foot, about to fall,
Saying, "To know this is to know, and this is all."

And when this has been spoken all will rise
And see spring come in one another's eyes
And I will walk among them in my pride
Telling of the splendour of my bride. (*Harlot's Hire* 35)

The reference here is to a later event in Hillel's career, said to summarize
both the Jewish understanding of ethics and the Jewish attitude toward study: the
heathen's challenge to Hillel to teach him the entire Torah while standing on one
foot, and Hillel's reply, "That which is hateful to you, do not do to your neighbor.
This is the entire Torah; the rest is commentary—go and learn it" (Holtz 11). Yet
this "far simpler thing," as the poem would have it, is not, in true Talmudic
fashion, all that simple. Compared to Shammai, Hillel's great rival, who in righteous indignation drives the heathen away when he poses his question, Hillel "may
be a more generous sort—perhaps a bit of a soft touch in fact." Be that as it may,

"The rest is commentary, but the commentary cannot be ignored. When both feet are finally resting on the ground, then the task really begins—'go and learn it'" (Holtz 12). Thus, Hillel's recognition of the essential truth of the Law may bring spring after winter and the bride to her rightful groom, but like the heathen converted by his answer, his task—and by implication, that of the poet—has only begun. The poem ends at the threshold; we still face "the coming of a new age," in which the fate of a generation in relation to its heritage, the fate, as it were, of the bridegroom and the bride, remains to be determined.

Years after *A Harlot's Hire,* in a revealing poem called "The Loss of the Beloved Companion," Grossman declares that "in the void/Mirror of my early art, it comes to this—/Sex and the imagination are one" (*Ether Dome* 77). This statement does not merely confirm the erotic dimension of poems like "The Law" and "The Discourse of Shemaiah and Abtalion"; it verifies the manner in which the erotic and the religious overlap to express a problematic sense of poetic and cultural identity. For Grossman's statement echoes that of Wallace Stevens in one of his eerily kabbalistic poems, the very late "Final Soliloquy of the Interior Paramour": "We say God and the imagination are one." In Stevens's poem, the poet and his muse (or is it the Shechinah?) "make a dwelling in the evening air,/In which being there together is enough" (524). Grossman, however, especially at the beginning of his career, cannot so easily join sex and divinity together and, in the supreme confidence of a master, enfold the Beloved and make a dwelling in his own godlike imagination. Rather, in *A Harlot's Hire,* it is anxiety over sexuality, over religious tradition, and over poetic authority that run together. We see this not only in those poems uttered in a male voice, but in two pieces in which Grossman assumes a female persona, one tragically human, the other demonic but equally tragic in the end.

"The Secret Religionist" is spoken by a Jewish daughter deeply frustrated by her father, who has shirked his responsibility to his people and to her personally by failing to secure a suitable husband for her. The title points to a situation such as that of the Marranos after the Expulsion from Spain, but the father "leans against the doorpost in a derby hat" and the daughter, thinking back to the destruction of the Temple, exclaims at the end of the poem that "Ashes drifting down two thousand years/Darken my hair, and eyes, and all my laughter" (*Harlot's Hire* 45). These ashes may be those of the burning Temple itself or of the sacrifices that took place there before its destruction, especially the sacrifice of the "red heifer" which "bellows from the cold altar." The ashes of the red heifer were used in rites of purification, as described in Numbers 19, but these ashes seem to have the opposite effect. Drifting ashes also carry a more contemporary significance, that of the Shoah. The poem thus presents a metonymic chain of Jewish catastrophes through history, and part of its appalling modernity lies in its implication that all Jews have somehow become "secret religionists." By this I mean that in the logic of the poem, Jews, although they may appear to blend in with the surrounding society, are the bearers of a tragic hidden identity, distilled age by age from a worsening sequence of historical disasters until nothing is left to them but reverie, stagnation, and ruin. As the daughter puts it,

> Woe to the house when the eldest son dreams.
> My father has no wares to sell. No price,
> Now that the Temple's gone, will buy
> Doves for sacrifice.
> And dreaming is best done at home at ease;
> Dreaming is labor in the fields of peace.
> My father's skin is sweet. He does not sow
> But reaps continually where strange flowers grow.
> His house is ruinous. Who will dower me
> To a husband if my father cannot? (*Harlot's Hire* 45)

In the modern discourse of anti-Semitism, Jews are the bearers of physical disease, social malaise, cultural decadence, and economic corruption. One need look no further than T. S. Eliot's "Gerontion": "My house is a decayed house,/And the jew squats on the window sill, the owner,/Spawned in some estaminet in Antwerp,/Blistered in Brussels, patched and peeled in London" (21). Anthony Julius, in his meticulous reading of "Gerontion," calls the poem "a condensed instance of all these anti-Semitic themes"; the "jew" is "kept apart because he is unclean, unwelcome even in the house that he owns, wretched yet monied" (49). Grossman's "Secret Religionist" answers "Gerontion" point for point. Rootlessness is hardly a natural characteristic of Jewish "spawn"; it is the result of the Jews having been driven from place to place for centuries. This Jew is no slumlord; his own house (meaning both physical dwelling and family line) is "ruinous" and he is impoverished, having "no wares to sell." Furthermore, his "skin is sweet," not "blistered . . . patched and peeled." Both Julius and Sander Gilman discuss the commonly held anti-Semitic notion that Jews have diseased skin, variously attributed to syphillis, leprosy, and "divine displeasure": "The pathognomic sign of the Jew is written on the skin; it is evident to all to see" (*Jew's Body* 100–101). And rather than an unwanted intruder, the father in Grossman's poem keeps to himself, idling at home.

This, however, is the real problem in "The Secret Religionist." Although the poem responds forcefully to anti-Semitic stereotypes of Jewish threat, it does so by drawing on a set of images and beliefs connected to Jewish passivity. A history of defeat, exile, and victimization has turned the Jewish father into an ineffectual dreamer, which is related in turn to the *fin-de-siecle* tone and atmosphere of the text. He has neither the economic resources nor the strength of will to find a husband for his daughter, although she tells him that "I love a man and he has asked for me." He is responsible for the ruin of his own house; and his daughter, who longs to "walk white out of my virgin tower,/And carry to my husband one strange flower,/And lay upon the altar an unblemished dove" becomes a variation on the theme of the "tragic Jewess," a sexualized figure with a long history in both anti- and philo-Semitic literature (Julius 87–90). Although still faithful to her father and her people, the daughter is caught between Jewish and gentile cultures, and given the image of the flower and the dove, it could be argued that the man she loves is a Christian, or even Christ himself. She may already be a "secret religionist" of a different sort, keeping that secret from her Jewish father. Thus, Jewish identity is certainly in crisis in this poem, however slow and dreamy its movement. At best, Judaism has fallen into a historical trance, a victim of cultural lethargy that seems doomed to total stasis. At worst, as Christianity contended for centuries, it is a superannuated religion that has become incapable of providing for any of its own needs. Nevertheless, the Law of the Father—patriarchal faith and divine authority—remains strong, strong enough to frustrate the desire for personal fulfillment. The resulting pathos resonates throughout the poem. This is the tragic aspect of Grossman's theophoric vision: the Jews may protest, but their word is "One" and still serves "the Master who is difference."

Grossman delves deeper into the nature of this struggle in another equally urgent protest, one that emerges from Jewish lore rather than Jewish history. "Lilith" gives voice to "the first made woman" (*Harlot's Hire* 22), who according to kabbalistic legend, "was created from the earth at the same time as Adam, and who, unwilling to forgo her equality, disputed with him the manner of their intercourse" (*Kabbalah* 357). Transformed in her rebelliousness into a force of demonic female sexuality, Lilith strangles infants, threatens women giving birth, and seduces men sleeping alone, "from whose nocturnal emissions she bears an infinite number of demonic sons" (*Kabbalah* 357). But in Grossman's poem, she is a far more sympathetic figure who "first wept/Alone in the changed light of evening in a chamber/For love." Enamoured of the glories of nature, she is filled with regret over the her loss of status as first woman and Adam's equal, declaring that:

I cannot say what I could have been:
The plenitude
Meted to his emptiness
The heat of which he dreams in the cold night
And the light
All lost. (*Harlot's Hire* 22)

Lilith implies that she was the complement of Adam, plenitude to his emptiness, heat to his cold. But the balance of male and female principles is gone, and with it, the perfection of nature and the cosmos. Now she is "Lilith, the unmarried,/Whom three strong angels could not haul/Back to Eden./Let Adam howl like a whipped child/The loss was my loss." The loss of Eden which she, and subsequently Adam, have endured, can never be restored, and it could be that Lilith understands and feels the pain of these circumstances more deeply than

Adam and his children. Lilith, after all, can hold no hope of redemption; she is part of the *sitra ahra* (the "other side"), "the domain of dark emanations and demonic powers . . . no longer an organic part of the World of Holiness and the *Sefirot*. Though it emerged from one of the attributes of God, it cannot be an essential part of Him" (*Kabbalah* 123). Yet she concludes her monologue with the same pathos we hear in the daughter's speech in "The Secret Religionist," gesturing in a way one would ordinarily associate with her divine opposite, the Shechinah: "Let exiles and altarless men worship me/As night without stars./I spread my hair over them." It is an image of both threat and comfort, terror and consolation. Scholem observes that the Kabbalah, especially the *Zohar*, "does not even recoil from such obviously paradoxical changes as attributing characteristics of Lilith to the *Shekhinah* ("Shekhinah" 191). And as we saw in our discussion of "The Law," in the fallen condition of exile, due to human error and sin, "the *Shekhinah* actually comes under the sway of the Other Side" ("Shekhinah" 189). In Grossman's vision, the shifting polarity of the divine and the demonic in the figure of the supernatural female is one of the most consistent symbols of historical rupture and spiritual loss.

Although Grossman's awareness of a crisis in the transmission of Jewish culture and belief permeates many of his early poems, it is worth noting that most of these make only the slightest reference to the details of daily Jewish life in either the past or the present. As should be clear by now, Grossman's poetic imagination is fundamentally mythopoeic; in this respect, he not only differs from Objectivists like Reznikoff or Zukofsky, but also phantasmagoric poets like Ginsberg or Rothenberg, who, because of the influence of Objectivism, tend to weave numerous mundane details into the fabric of their extravagant visionary utterances. In Grossman's case, although he may deal with specific historical moments or place a poem in a contemporary context, he tends toward a symbolic rhetoric that draws on traditional, virtually archetypal figures such as the Shechinah, the Book, the Talmudic sage, and so on. Even a poem like "The Breaking of the Law," occasioned by his son's circumcision, moves quickly to a thunderous consideration of primal Jewish fatherhood: "For you the hurricane is rising fast;/I feel the horns of Moses on my head,/And Law wrenched again from the dead/Hand of deity, and I descend out of the blast to you" (*Harlot's Hire* 46). Looming above his infant son, the poet becomes Michelangelo's Moses bearing "the rage/That broke the Law upon you like a rain of stone." The mythic force of deity descends on the poet himself in much the same way, and though it rarely carries the explicitly biblical charge after *A Harlot's Hire,* Grossman's work remains cast in the high style, through which a visionary conception of Jewish life and belief manifests itself in increasingly uncanny lyric circumstances.

This is the case because as the poet matures, his understanding of Judaism's relation to his vocation becomes more complex and problematic. We have noted that in Grossman's thought, the Jewish concepts of holiness and of Israel's covenant with God produce a counterforce to the "bitter logic" of poetic representation as it has been practiced in the West. A bold theorist of poetry's oracular power, Grossman understands the poetic tradition as born out of the "violence of representation," whether derived from the female "painstory" of Philomela, "which engages the contest of describers at the point of threat to individual self-invention" or from the narrative of Orpheus, "the cosmic singer, the male epic-master *alienated to the above*, the technician of the social order" (*Long Schoolroom* 35–36). But male or female in its original moment, "song arises punctually at the moment after loss has become inconsolable, and the destination of the self irretrievable by other means, at the moment when there is no recourse other than song" (31–32). This is why "In the gentile world as we now receive it, the champion on the human part is the poet" (23).

The operative term, of course, is "gentile": it is in gentile culture that poetic representation finds "its power to defer the violence that it also requires" (38). By contrast, "the text of the Jewish God (fundamentally inimical to representation) is perhaps the most persuasive model of a solution to the fatality of representation that civilization in the West presents" (13). The countervailing pressures that this situation places on Grossman produce, in the seven volumes that he has published since *A Harlot's Hire*, one of the most unique trajectories in recent American poetry. The task of the Jewish poet, "prophet and diplomat of the void," as adumbrated in his first book, is never to be forgotten. But as an important heir to the Anglo American visionary tradition, Grossman also reads deeply, as he tells us in "The Book of Father Dust," from "the cobalt tower text/Of Hart Crane; spinster Stevens' intricate/Book of needles; oracular Yeats,/Unkind" (*Ether Dome* 64). In this poem, dedicated to his father, Louis, and full of the echoes of poetic fathers, Grossman becomes the voice of the "Bright morning,/when all the gifts of the lineage/Were set down, as from/A spectral truck or vast galleon, warped/ Silently in, out of the infinite, circling, high/Oceanic roads" (65). The "spectral" powers of the tradition are transformed into lyric "gifts of the lineage" in another moment of impossible poetic earliness, "this still/Morning of outcome" in which the poet declares "I marry Louis,/My author—the dust" (66). Again and again in Grossman's poems, he seeks the circumstances from which such fatal victories may be secured. At the same time, however, he also seeks those circumstances in which such fatality may be thwarted, to allow for the theophoric utterance that is his responsibility as a Jew.

Another poem from the same volume as "The Book of Father Dust" (*The Woman on the Bridge Over the Chicago River*, 1979) makes this dialectical tendency quite explicit. It is called "Victory," and as in some of the stories and essays of Cynthia Ozick, it appears to revive the old debate between Hebraism and Hellenism over the related issues of nature, fate, and death. As the poem begins, the poet is in bed, surrounded by "a radiance," in a house "filled with unborn children" (*Ether Dome* 88). As in "The Book of Father Dust," the morning is illuminated by what seems to be the poet's potential (hence the unborn children, the poems he may yet compose), but rather than rising and going forward, he sleeps, "reading/The bright day backward like a Hebrew book." The image is troubling, for only a gentile, as it were, would see a Hebrew book as one that must be read "backward." And as is gradually revealed, this is a gentile poem indeed, deeply implicated in "the fatality of representation that civilization in the West presents." It is not a poem of potential and birth, but of the fulfillment of fate and the coming of death. In his dream, the poet sees "the whole body of ocean/From a hill." We move to a familiar *topos* of the Romantic sublime:

> The bed is a mountain, and the light is
> The magnanimity of the mountain,
> In the still space of the room where I sleep.
> On the mountain we met a young hunter
> Who asked the way of us, and did not wait
> But strode off without the answer in another
> Direction.—We climbed the iced flume
> Carrying the answer to the grim rage
> Of the top, where the whole earth stands, in the
> Peril of high seeing—bed and abyss: (*Ether Dome* 88–89)

The poet seeks the place of high seeing, which is the place of his fate. The "young hunter" asking the way is another poet-quester, but each must find the way for himself. The poet also awaits "a woman I knew" but at the summit he does not find her, thinking "She will/Never come. Not to him, not to me—alone of men." Upon this realization of loss, the poem moves to its climax:

> And so if I bind on Apollo's phylacteries
> I do it now to tell the plain truth.
> Come, I will stop this talking. That is what
> This voice inside you I am saying means.
> Let us draw the black ship down to the divine sea—
> Set the purple sail to the great death winds
> Of the South, and empty
> Out of the burden of our singing, you and I.
> This is the whole ocean. Also the end. (*Ether Dome* 89)

There is little that is Jewish in these lines: the love of fate that culminates in the oceanic return to oblivion is securely "bound" to the primal wisdom of Western or gentile poetry going back at least as far as the Greeks. Yet this moment of revealed truth, which appears so frequently in the Anglo American tradition, comes to Grossman when he "bind[s] on Apollo's *phylacteries*," indicating that there must be a Jewish dimension to this fatal wisdom. The image is both scandalous and strangely comic; it points to the way in which Grossman tries to understand, if not fully reconcile, his dual identity as poet (in the Western sense) and Jew.

In his conversation with Mark Halliday, Grossman offers a lengthy explanation of another poem that first appeared in *The Woman on the Bridge Over the Chicago River,* called "The Thrush Relinquished," which includes the crucial line "No poetry tonight. Death tonight." What he has to say about death in that poem has an equal bearing on the ending of "Victory." Invoking Stevens's "Death is the mother of beauty" and "death's outlet song" of Whitman, Grossman explains that:

> I'm summoning these traditional implications of death as they have always been summoned as a challenge or, even more specifically, as an affront to your conceptions of sociability. . . . The term that in this poem I offer is the term "death," both empty and very full, the point at which the other disappears as the self disappears. The value of the person arises in the space of that disappearance, unqualified by the contingencies of reference, or even of hope as it is constrained by possibility. (*Sighted Singer* 75)

Death, then, is not only the mother of beauty, but also the guarantor of human value. When self and other have entered oblivion, what remains is human value, inscribed on absence. In this formulation, poetry depends on death, and death casts meaning upon life through poetry.

This traditional poetic wisdom may well be an affront to conventional notions of sociability, but it is unquestionably an affront to the Jewish worldview, as Grossman himself knows. In "Holiness," Grossman argues that "the nature of the Hebrew culture of holiness—in accord with the the strict monotheism that founds it—is peculiarly severe, admitting, as in the Kaddish, no affirmation less than total even in the face of death. The refusal of the will to accept God's description of the one world is the refusal of being. There is no space, as in Greek culture, for example, for the valorization of the oppositional self, and therefore, in the modern sense of things, no space for the self" (*Long Schoolroom* 186). If this is the case, then death is of no value whatsoever, for value is derived solely from the manifestation of God in human experience. Death is not a negation that dialectically bestows positive worth to the human, as in the poetic economy of the gentile West; death is "pollution" to be cleansed by sanctifying prayer. It is "the disease of a will that can no longer praise the Name, that can no longer by words of sanctification on its own behalf return the world to its maker" (186). These two views of death's relation to human value produce as stark a contrast as can be found between the Hebraic and Hellenic worldviews.

Let us return "Apollo's phylacteries," an oxymoron that can only figure, but in no way reconcile Grossman's double bind. Once the poet has been vouchsafed his vision of the "divine sea," the poem must end in death. All the tropes that have been introduced fall into place: the book of the "bright day" that had been "read backward" is revealed to be "a book about dying," and the poet dies as "the woman Victroy/Unbound the strap from his forehead/And the other strap from his arm, and laid/Them by" (*Ether Dome* 89–90). Presumably, in the poetic economy, the muse/mother/lover who finally arrives in death is also a goddess of Victory because the poet and his other have died, leaving the realization of human value in their now vacant place. Yet somehow this must be a Jewish act of sanctification as well. The book read backward and the phylacteries reverently removed from the poet's body by a pagan goddess are reminders that even when faced with the absence of death, God's Presence cannot be dismissed from the human experience of creation, though natural wisdom may seem sufficient to human needs.

The place of the Jew and the function of the Jewish poet in the created world is the subject of "Out of the Blue," one of a set of poems remarkable for their visionary clarity and breadth called *Pastorals of Our Other Hours in the Millennium*, the new work in Grossman's retrospective volume *The Ether Dome* (1991). In the blurb that appears on the back of this volume, Richard Howard notes "the paradoxical situation of [Grossman's] poetry as *original ritual*," certainly an apt description of this particular poem. As a ritual, the poem seeks the reconciliation of the Jew, who lives under the sign of the holy, with what Grossman calls in the "Holiness" essay "the long and precious inventory of human concerns" toward which the "culture of holiness" is "absolutely destructive" (*Long Schoolroom* 186). In other words, "Out of the Blue" attempts to resolve the problem that a poem like "Victory" could only pose and describe, and in this respect, it takes us to the furthest boundary of Grossman's work as a Jewish poet.

The subtitle of "Out of the Blue" is "a river doggerel" and its German epigraph reads "*Nur in dem Fluss der Gedanken und des Lebens haben die Wörter Bedeutung*" ("Only in the flow [flux or stream] of thoughts and of life do words have meaning"). Our expectation then is of a poem of natural processes, an Orphic poem like the one that immediately precedes it in *The Ether Dome*, "Mrs. O'Leary's Cat," which ends with the image of "the weary lutanist" in Ur of the Chaldees (the city from which Abraham departs in order to enter into God's covenant), "summoning his slaves to the Orphic mill" (*Ether Dome* 44). The first lines of "Out of the Blue," which sound like both Whitman and Rilke, continue the Orphic theme by enacting the idea adumbrated in the epigraph, the task of the gentile poet—to mediate, through language, the currents of creation with those of the soul:

> Out of the blue! A lyre of seven languages!
> Or more! What? Is it the soul? I see it.
> Like steel or ocean (our universal destination)
> It flows in its own direction, in several
> Motions at our feet, as thinking is urgent
> And sometimes quick but for the most part slow. (*Ether Dome* 45)

Yet Grossman immediately complicates this vision of flux by introducing the Jewish dimension of the poem, represented by R. Tarfon's lines from the *Pirke*

Aboth (II:20–21), in the context of "grave waters" (both serious and deadly) that power a Blakean "prophetic mill":

> Out of the well below, the blue throne of
> The marshland, grave waters rise, swell, and then
> Go down—to turn a prophetic mill by falling
> In its arms: "It is not your duty to complete
> The work. Neither are you free to desist
> From it." It says, "O soul! The time is short,
>
> The work is great. The laborers weary. The master
> Of the house is urgent"—like thought. Look up!
> The day lights of the mill dim, flicker and go out.
> The looms fake, falter, and stop. The threads
> Tangle and break, because the flow of the stream
> Is blocked by a corpse on the grate. (*Ether Dome* 45)

R. Tarfon's sayings are understood to refer to work in the service of God, especially the study of Torah, the labor that is celebrated throughout the *Pirke Aboth*. In "Out of the Blue," it is the "loom of prophecy,/Dream of the Jew" (48) which performs this sacred work, weaving human fate, "the sentence/Of the soul" (47), in what seems to be both a mechanized and Hebraized version of the Three Fates. But a corpse at the grate has stopped the waters that power the mill, the corpse of a "woman in her tears under the throne" who was "swept down, in the hour before dawn,/And drowned in the great flood out of the blue" (47). A weeping woman beneath the throne usually signifies the Shechinah, who both mourns for and consoles Israel in its exile. But in Grossman's new myth, her corpse must be cleared away in order for the work to resume, for "The mastery must be (as I have said elsewhere)/In the continuation" (48). In effect, it is the death and removal of the traditional symbol of the Jewish exilic condition that will allow the theophoric project to continue.

The removal of the corpse is the task of "gigantic boatmen," Blakean figures like the mill they would repair. One clears the grate and starts the loom, the other, a "noble messenger," heads "upstream," having "power/With the Lord of the throne, the throne secure" (47). Using a discourse reminiscent of the rabbis in the *Aboth,* they call to each other and to the poet, a bystander whose helplessness is the subject of their mockery:

> "Yo, phantom! What does he fear?" "The hardness
> Of the work" is the reply (out of the blue),
> "The impending war, the darkening hour,
> And the Godforsakenness of the Jew." (46)

Ironically, it is the Jew who is called "Godforsaken," apparently because he is reluctant to enter into a condition of worldliness or engagement with creation. What Grossman demands, then, is a change in our understanding of holiness, at least in terms of the work of the Jewish poet. To restore the meaning of the world and restart the loom of prophecy, the Jewish poet cannot withhold himself, as he learns in the climax of the poem:

> What can be *done?* The meaning of the world
> Is being made in defiance of the Jew.
> The boatman lifts the corpse, the wreckage of the storm.
> The day lights of the mill flicker and re-illume.
> The rivers flow. Nor can I much detain
>
> Them as they pass under the sower's hand,
> The windy rain. Night falls. "Yo, Jew, revoke
> Thy *tristia*. Here comes the capacious ship
> Of light—on time—out of the blue. Look!
> The orchestra on deck strikes up a song,
> 'The Meaning of the World.' The mother tongue!" (48)

The Jew must revoke his *tristia*, which I take to mean his condition of existential sadness, the mournfulness of exile. Only then will he appreciate—and participate in—the meaning of the world through the "mother tongue." Grossman's recent work, both in poetry and poetics, is filled with complex references to mother tongue and father tongue, as well as mythopoeic visions of his own mother and father, as in the uncanny sequence *Poland of Death*. In his conversation with Mark Halliday, he describes the speech of the mother as "the speech not of the self, but of the other as mother, as maternal source, source of the world, the deep source of art, the point of intersection between nothing and something; both for myself as an individual, as the mother is, and myself as a member of a cosmos which did itself have a beginning" (*Sighted Singer* 61–62). Likewise, in the *Summa Lyrica,* the father tongue is fictional or representational, while the mother tongue "is associated with the nonfictional (not with prose but with the actual, by contrast to the represented) as also with the nonvoluntary and compelled aspects of the natural" (*Sighted Singer* 357). Be that as it may, "poetic knowledge is knowledge of the mother tongue" (360). Thus for the Jewish poet to speak the mother tongue is actually to move him closer to the Source of holiness, to make him, in effect, more Jewish. For the father tongue is the speech of representation, but as we have seen, the Jewish poet must always turn to that which is beyond all representation. And it is here, "the point of intersection between nothing and something," that the meaning of the world is to be found and the Jewish poet is to do his work. But this may be apprehended only through the ritual of disaster and restoration enacted in

"Out of the Blue." The ending of the poem grandly proclaims this knowledge, securing Grossman's place as one of the most ambitious poets of our time:

> What do I know? The body on the grate
> That stops the loom, and breaks the thread,
> Puts out the light of prophecy, and blocks
> The flow of the *mother tongue* . . . is the dead
> End of the imagination ("Adore
> The throne, and clear the grate. Work, Jew, while it
> Is light!"),—and the beginning of all song. (*Ether Dome* 49)

4

Between Poland and Sumer: The Ethnopoetics of Jerome Rothenberg and Armand Schwerner

In 1981, Jerome Rothenberg published "Harold Bloom: The Critic as Exterminating Angel," a scathing attack focused particularly on what Rothenberg himself calls "the Jewish question" in Bloom's theory of influence. Not as well known as Cynthia Ozick's "Literature as Idol: Harold Bloom" (1979), Rothenberg's essay is even more severe: whereas Ozick sees Bloom as "sometimes purifying like Abraham, more often conjuring like Terach" (199), Rothenberg finds Bloom, despite all his Jewish concerns and rhetorical practices, as totally at odds with a Jewish sensibility. He is, for Rothenberg, the exact opposite of a Jewish writer—he is a critical version of Dr. Josef Mengele, the exterminating angel of Auschwitz, who looked over the Jews as they entered the camp, sending them either to the barracks or the gas chamber. Aware of "the hyperbole, even the absurdity involved in setting Bloom beside Mengele," Rothenberg still insists that Bloom's obsession with "the killing-off of poets" makes the comparison valid: "it seems unlikely to me that as 'Jewish' a critic as Bloom would not, in making his assertion of a 'you live/you die' function for criticism, have been struck by the image of Mengele, in much the same way that as 'Jewish' a poet as myself immediately felt its presence" (5).

Rothenberg's critique is as detailed and exacting as Ozick's, and like Ozick's, it reflects his own vision of Jewish literary culture. If Jewish culture for Ozick stands for moral discrimination as opposed to the idolatry of aestheticism (hence Bloom as Terach betrays his Jewish heritage), Jewish culture for Rothenberg is heterodox and inclusive in ways that go far beyond the normative. Rothenberg recognizes that in works such as *Kabbalah and Criticism,* Bloom makes use of "uncanonized traditional material," and intersects "with a referential network that touches as well on Jewish orthodoxy and gnostic heterodoxy—non-canonical also from a Western/Christian point of view. It's my feeling that if Bloom had allowed this network to expand, he could have made an extraordinary synthesizing contribution to our concepts of *poesis*" (16). But Bloom, unfortunately, is too caught up in his vision of poetic competition to see the creative opportunities that such a synthetic network of cultural references can offer. Instead, Rothenberg senses that Bloom, especially when considering the ostensible anxiety felt by Jewish poets in the face of gentile precursors, "feels himself cut off from poetry, and that he projects this deprivation onto other Jews. . . . This self-projection—& I have no other way of describing it—is then translated into a 'double belatedness' for modern Jewish poets, 'coming after the virtues and sufferings of their ancestors, and also after the main sequence of Western poetry has worked itself through and perhaps out'" (21, 22).

Rothenberg regards the double dilemma that Bloom projects on Jewish poets as "a neurotic distortion of what the real work is all about" (23). The real work, "set in the framework of a special culture or tradition"—in this instance, Jewish culture or tradition—is "the work of rewriting ourselves within a real but collapsed tradition of language-centeredness & resistance to oppression. . . . But this 'Jewish instance' itself, for all its particularities, is part of a larger work of human striving" (22). Bloom, in effect, misses the boat: the rich traditions of poetic and religious writings that he explores with such passion and invention lead him to a vision of literary strangulation and cultural decline, rather than to the creative opportunities that Rothenberg celebrates. These opportunities become all the more apparent through the historical spasms of modernity and postmodernity, which for Bloom, caught in the trammels of his Romantic agon (as opposed to Rothenberg's equally Romantic sense of freedom), are only signs of the continual waning of tradition.

To compound the irony, Rothenberg later reveals, in response to Sherman Paul's troubled concern over the Jewish poet's *ad hominem* attack on the Jewish critic, that Bloom himself had at one point acknowledged how close they were in their understanding of the Jewish literary imagination. Rothenberg quotes from a letter he received from Bloom after "The Sorrows of American-Jewish Poetry" and before "The Critic as Exterminating Angel": "we are much in the same stance & place, except for (to me) 'mere' stylistics. Pound & Olson are not my poets; Stevens & Hart Crane are. But your vision & mine are *very* close. It is a puzzle to me—I read Ashbery & Rothenberg—his language ravishes me more (though yours is, to me, the strongest in your tradition) but your substance & drive are where I find myself" (*In Search of the Primitive* 175). Yet despite such intuited affinities, Bloom continues to publically castigate most Jewish, and particularly Jewish American poetry, this time in an even more gloomy than usual piece in The *New York Times Book Review* on Howard Schwartz's and Anthony Rudolph's anthology, *Voices within the Ark* (Jan. 4, 1981). "American Jewish poetry has no tradition," Bloom asserts baldly, "and its practitioners work in the thematically irrelevant stylistic modes of Pound and Eliot, W. C. Williams and Charles Olson, or even of Stevens" ("Heavy Burden of the Past" 5). Furthermore, "Jewish history, almost always catastrophic, is now so immensely burdensome to a sensitive consciousness that any poet willing to be open to it risks immediate flooding and drowning" (24). It is at this point that Bloom becomes, for Rothenberg, a figure "that I thought it worth speaking out against . . . & from a situation close enough to his own (as he wrote of it) that he would less likely treat it with indifference" (*In Search of the Primitive* 176).

This sparring match reveals, as both participants seem to understand, the extent of the common ground held by those given to thinking through the issues of Jewish American poetry and Jewish American identity. Such poetry seems capable of encompassing the normative and the heretical, the historical and the religious, within a sweeping vision of Jewish culture. But at the same time, it is also important to note that term "'mere' stylistics" in Bloom's letter to Rothenberg, related to Pound and Olson on the one hand, Stevens and Crane on the other. A similar phrase, "thematically irrelevant stylistic modes," appears in Bloom's *Times* review. Once again we see how matters of style—not "mere" at all—determine the variables in the equation of Jewish American poetry. Bloom may find Rothenberg's Jewish "substance & drive" attractive, but his stylistic affinities and literary historical assumptions ultimately do not meet Bloom's stringent requirements for strong poetry. Likewise, Rothenberg's notion of Jewish heterodoxy, set in the broader context of his ethnopoetics project, may resonate to some extent with Bloom's gnostic stance. Yet Rothenberg is too much the advocate of American modernism and of the European avant-garde—too much the champion of cross-cultural dialogue—to accept the grim necessities built into Bloom's theories. For Rothenberg, when Jewish poets open themselves to their cultural heritage among all others, "flooding and drowning" ceases to be an option.

"The word 'ethnopoetics' suggested itself, almost too easily, on the basis of such earlier terms as ethnohistory, ethnomusicology, ethnolinguistics, ethnopharmacology, and so on" (xi). So writes Rothenberg in the "Pre-Face" to his definitive anthology of ethnopoetics, *Symposium of the Whole*. There is a certain offhanded charm to this remark, perhaps even something of the archetypal trickster or ironist in the self-deprecating "almost too easily." Poet, performance artist, translator, editor, and anthologist, Rothenberg, as one of the figures most closely associated with the ethnopoetics movement, has labored mightily for over forty years in the field that he named. Not merely a development in the arts, and certainly not confined to the academy, ethnopoetics, as Rothenberg understands it, is a complex set of processes, activities, and engagements:

> On the one hand, this discourse explored an ongoing "intersection between poetry and anthropology," in Nathaniel Tarn's words, and on the other hand, between contemporary poets as the "marginal" defenders of an endangered human diversity and poets of other times and places who represented that diversity itself and many of the values being uncovered and recovered in the new poetic enterprises. The discourse opened as well to include what Richard Schechner called the "poetics of performance" across the spectrum of the arts, and it also tied in with movements of self-

definition and cultural liberation among third-world ethnic groups in the United States and elsewhere. (*Symposium* xv)

Rothenberg's goal, which he shares with his colleagues in the arts and social sciences, has always been "a redefinition of poetry in terms of cultural specifics, with an emphasis on those alternative traditions to which the West gave names like 'pagan,' 'gentile,' 'tribal,' 'oral,' and 'ethnic'" (*Symposium* xi). This is, to say the least, an intriguing set of concerns for the New York son of Polish-Jewish immigrants originally from an orthodox milieu. Yet the connection between Judaism and ethnopoetics is certainly no accident. As a young man, Rothenberg was urged by the poet Robert Duncan (who had a lifelong interest in kabbalah) to explore his own previously suppressed ancestral "world of Jewish mystics, thieves, & madmen" (*Exiled* 4). Rothenberg went on to edit a series of anthologies that brought together mythic, religious, and magical texts from numerous cultures under a poetic rubric, all the while writing a poetry that reflected these same multicultural interests. Eventually, Rothenberg recognized that his own ethnopoetics must consist "of some supreme yiddish surrealist vaudeville" (*Exiled* 4), a phrase he took from another colleague, David Meltzer. The result was *Exiled in the Word* (in its original version called *A Big Jewish Book* [1978]), the anthology of "Poems & Other Visions of the Jews from Tribal Times to the Present," which Rothenberg edited with Harris Lenowitz, as well as Rothenberg's own collection, *Poland/1931* (1974), one of the most important works of the ethnopoetics movement and one of the most extraordinary achievements in the canon of Jewish American poetry.

The "Pre-Face" to *Exiled In the Word* begins with the poet's account of a dream that he came to regard as "central to my life, an event & mystery that has dogged me from the start" (3). In the dream, Rothenberg and all his friends find themselves in "THE HOUSE OF JEWS," facing a room that is "more like a great black hole in space." Rothenberg, as a Jew, must lead his companions into that room, but can do so only by naming it. As he says, "I strained my eyes & body to get near the room, where I could feel, as though a voice was whispering to me, creation going on inside it. And I said that it was called CREATION" (3). In the analysis that follows this recitation, Rothenberg connects "CREATION—*poesis* writ large"—with his identity as a Jew, which is to say that Rothenberg discovers that in his case, being a Jew and being a poet are bound together inextricably.

How is this the case? First, Rothenberg himself points out the Kafkan sense of reluctance that imbues the dream, noting its resemblance to both "Before the Law," with its ferocious guardian of a door "made just for you," and to the diary entry in which Kafka asks "What have I in common with the Jews? I have hardly anything in common with myself" (3–4). I would relate this reluctance to a remark Rothenberg makes later in the Pre-Face: "For many Jewish poets & artists, working within a Jewish context came to mean the surrender of claims to the sinister & dangerous sides of existence or to the fullest range of historical human experience" (7). In other words, the modern Jew tends to dissociate Jewishness from "CREATION," due to the conservative traditions of moral rectitude and cautious behavior that obtain in normative Judaism. Furthermore, the modern process of Jewish assimilation leads to what John Murray Cuddihy calls "the ordeal of civility." As Cuddihy wryly observes, "'Niceness' is as good a name as any for the informally yet pervasively institutionalized civility expected—indeed, required—of members (and of aspirant members) of that societal community called the civic culture" (13). Civility or "niceness" is "a dimension of the threat posed by modernization to a traditionary subculture . . . the danger that the prospect of being 'gentled' posed to an 'underdeveloped' subculture indigenous to the West" (Cuddihy 14). For Rothenberg, only a profound, archetypal, visionary experience can realign a Jewish sense of the self with the primal processes of *poesis* readily seen in other cultures, so that one can enter into the creativity of Jewish tradition and recall "that the actual history of the Jews was as rich in powers & contradictions as that of the surrounding nations" (*Exiled* 7). Kafka, writing out of one of the most conflicted and dangerous moments of Jewish history, transforms his ambivalence into an oblique, hermetic art of the highest order. Rothenberg, writing in a very different milieu, one perhaps a little too comfortable for the Jewish artist longing for the "sinister & dangerous sides of existence," needs a more direct and thorough confrontation with the repressed dimensions of Jewish tradition.

This leads us to the second aspect of the dream: that creativity involves a confrontation with repressed material. In this respect, the dream, or Rothenberg's rehearsal of the dream, is patently, self-consciously "psychoanalytic" in nature. The dark, the unconscious, the abyss, the unknown, the mysterious, the forbidden . . . and the Jewish. In Rothenberg's analysis (invoking Duncan), the Jews take their place "among the 'old excluded orders'" (4) and share with other peoples the mythic and ritualistic proclivities through which humanity represents to itself the sense of its material and spiritual being: "No minor channel, it is the poetic *mainstream* that he [the poet] finds here: magic, myth, & dream; earth, nature, orgy, love; the female presence the Jewish poets named Shekinah" (5). And lest this room in the House of Jews become too portentous, let us recall Rothenberg's use of the term "vaudeville": the all-encompassing poetic mainstream, perpetually transgressing and contradicting itself there in the female dark, is fundamentally comic in its performance of the orders of being. Thus the specifically Jewish material that Rothenberg uncovers and puts to poetic use is playful in all senses of the word, embodying processes of cultural and textual transformation and exchange that resist stabilization, orthodoxy, and canonization: "the framing, raising of an endless, truly Jewish 'book of questions'" (7).

This openness of Jewish verbal and cultural experience to what Rothenberg calls "the human" is the third crucial feature of his dream. The poet says of his friends in the House of Jews that "[w]hether they were Jews or not was unimportant: I was & because I was I had to lead them through it" (3). Here Rothenberg addresses the issue of exclusivism and universalism that has been at the center of

Jewish experience since of the beginning of Jewish history. Rothenberg's notion of ethnopoetics is certainly one of the more recent representations of the universalizing strain in Judaism, though paradoxically, its universalism opposes "the reduction of particulars to what has become the monoculture" (6). The particulars of every culture must remain intact: only then can we perceive the parallels and similarities among them, while at the same time acknowledging the volatile but always creative conflicts between the orthodox and the heterodox that obtain among cultures and within each of them. In Rothenberg's understanding, poetry "is an inherently impure activity of individuals creating reality from all conditions & influences at hand" (9). Ethnopoetics is the discursive practice that both enables us to study this activity and to participate in it.

The poems in *Poland/1931* must be read in these "impure" terms. As intersections of poetry and anthropology, they appropriate the materials of Eastern European Jewish culture, and through sophisticated verbal techniques, transform them into contemporary linguistic artifacts. Yet these materials are not treated in an antiquarian fashion; rather, they are composed with a sense of immediacy and urgency that creates a sense of presence. That which is distant in terms of time, space, and culture, is brought near. It becomes available for performance, not as an actor performs, but as Rothenberg explains, through "a lack of separation between the maker & his work, & of a virtual innocence of any means of performance beyond the ones immediately to hand" (*Pre-Faces* 132). This lack of separation extends to the relation of the contemporary poet with "poets of other times and places" whose recovered values the contemporary poet represents and defends: hence the political dimension of the ethnopoetic project.

But in *Poland/1931,* unlike Rothenberg's treatments of Native American or Asian ethnographic material, the contemporary poet/anthropologist belongs to the same culture as the one he would understand. A special poignance and irony obtains here, as in the case of Jewish ethnography generally. As Daniel and Jonathan Boyarin note, "a disproportionate number of North American ethnographers, both in the 'founding' generations at the turn of this century and more recently, have come from Jewish backgrounds"—yet "Jews as an ethnographic specialty have long been marginalized. . . . Much work in Jewish ethnography is therefore done by scholars who have established themselves through research on non-Jews and later turned to Jewish ethnography" ("Introduction" xii). Like the Jewish anthropologists for whom Jewish life finally becomes the object of their professional studies, *Poland/1931* is a sort of autoethnography, in which the poet performs a reclaimed vision of his own previously occluded culture and history.

Looking at the book as a whole, we can observe an ironic doubleness of intent and of effect, on which depends much of its power. As a poetic rendering of ethnographic or historiographic material, it presents itself, to use the titles of two of its sections, as "A Book of Testimony," "A Book of Histories." In other words, it is a writing after the fact, a phantasmagoric representation of the cultural past of

Rothenberg's people. But it is also a poetry of immediate enactment, influenced, on the one hand, by writing practices such as those of Gertrude Stein, Charles Olson, and the Objectivists; and on the other hand, by Jewish kabbalistic and magical traditions. It is therefore a book of inscribed "events," a book in which inscription constitutes event. In this respect, it is not only a work that represents the past, but one that exists in a timeless present, an eternal "Poland/1931" of "amulets," "dreams," "visions" and "circumstances." The situation of the writing bears a marked resemblance to Paul de Man's description in "Literary History and Literary Modernity": "the writer's language is to some degree the product of his own action; he is both the historian and the agent of his own language. The ambivalence of writing is such that it can be considered both an act and an interpretative process that follows after an act with which it cannot coincide" (152).

The temporal binarism that I am positing in Rothenberg's book, in which the consciousness of past and present uneasily coexist, is not one to be reconciled or synthesized (nor, for that matter, to be fully deconstructed), for the impact of the poetry depends on its remaining in this continuous state of ambivalence or tension, as if it were nostalgic for itself even as it comes into being. In this respect, Rothenberg's sensibility in *Poland/1931*, for all its raucous sensuality, is akin to that of Walter Benjamin in his melancholy "Theses on the Philosophy of History." Both Rothenberg and Benjamin are engaged in messianic projects in which the writer, as Benjamin says, "grasps the constellation which his own era has formed with a definite earlier one. Thus he establishes a conception of the present as the 'time of the now' which is shot through with chips of Messianic time" (*Illuminations* 263).

The poetry that forms such a constellation is an inherently unstable, volatile, indeterminant linguistic entity, and the ground of its utterance is constantly shifting. Because the poet is the historian and the agent of his own language (or the native living or "performing" a culture and the ethnographer observing, recording, and interpreting it), the reader is led to ask who or what is speaking, from where does this speech come, and in what time frame is it being articulated. In *Poland/1931*, these questions are inextricably linked to content, to what the poem is "about."

"[T]here is still someone to write the jewish poem" (12) declares the poet of *Poland/1931*, and that is the point. In Rothenberg's book, the Jewish poem endures; it grows strong and flourishes in even the most adverse conditions; nourished and sustained by the streams of "an alternative tradition or series of traditions hidden sometimes at the heart of the established order" (*Exiled* 5). Given the inherent "impurity" of poesis (and consider the importance of distinguishing between the pure and the impure in normative Judaism), it seems impossible to define the Jewish poem or fix the identity of the poet who writes one.

In the Pre-Face to *Exiled in the Word*, Rothenberg cites the well-known dictum of Marina Tsvetayeva, "all poets are Jews" (7). And yet, like the lady in Rothenberg's poem, the reader is still called on to become "The Connoisseur of Jews":

> the first jew to come to you is mad
> the train pulls into lodz
> he calls you
> by your polish name
> then he tells the passengers a story
> there are jews and alphabets
> he tells them
> but there are also jewish alphabets
> just as there are jewish locomotives
> & jewish hair
> & just as there are some with jewish fingers
> such men are jews
> just as other men are not jews
> not mad
> don't call you by your polish name
> or ride the train to lodz (*Poland/1931* 12)

The play of identity, the representation of self and other in the utterance of the poem, is well worth considering. One of Rothenberg's most important rhetorical strategies in *Poland/1931* consists of a flamboyant revalorization of the physical, psychic, and cultural qualities stereotypically regarded as "Jewish" (by both non-Jews and Jews) in the nineteenth and early twentieth centuries. Rothenberg's "mystics, thieves, and madmen," like those of I. B. Singer (the fourth poem in *Poland/1931* is an homage to Singer called "Satan in Goray"), become positive models of a "genuine" Jewishness, in contrast to the bourgeois civility of assimilated Jews who seek acceptance in gentile society. The stage for this revalorization is "Poland/1931," which is, as I have observed, a timeless present, a mythic phantasmagoria of Eastern European Jewish culture both in its place of origin and in America, to which the primal Jewish couple, Leo Levy and Esther K., will emigrate in the latter part of the book. Yet this "timeless" domain bears a date, 1931, the year of Rothenberg's birth, which symbolically reminds us of the incipient destruction of that culture, implacably historical in its reality, however fraught with mythic violence. And by "us" I mean Rothenberg's American audience of civil poetry readers and comfortably assimilated Jews, who can use a good dose of Jewish madness.

Then again, it could be that all Jews are mad, however they may resemble "other men [who] are not jews/not mad." The predisposition of Jews to various forms of mental illness was an accepted fact in the milieu about which Rothenberg writes, in both the popular mind and that of the scientific establishment. Just as the Jew's body was seen as particularly susceptible to various diseases and deformations, so too "Jewish mental illness was the result of the sexual practices of the Jew, such as inbreeding, which created the predisposition for disease, and the pressures of modern life in the city, which were the direct cause" (*Freud, Race, and Gender* 93). Sander Gilman's exhaustive analysis of beliefs regarding Jewish mental illness not only reveals the links between sexuality and modern urban life, but focuses specifically on "the world of the train." As Gilman explains, this world "was one of the public spaces, defined by class and economic power, in which the Jew could purchase status. It was part of the image of the world of 'modern life' that helped deform the psyche of the Jew. A ticket assured one of traveling among one's economic equals—but not as racial 'equals.' The association of trains and the trauma of confronting one's Jewish identity is a powerful topos at the turn of the century" (*Freud, Race, and Gender* 125).

Thus in Rothenberg's poem, the Jewish constellation of sex, madness, locomotives, and poetry is hardly accidental. The "mad" Jew on the train speaks boldly to the lady and the other passengers of "jewish alphabets," "jewish locomotives." There are, of course, "jewish alphabets" (invoking the belief in what Gilman calls "the secret language of the Jews") but this Jew also speaks Polish and confronts gentile passengers in their own tongue. The sexualized "jewish locomotive" is also a real locomotive, carrying the Jew, with his distinctively "jewish hair" and "jewish fingers" wherever he wants to go. And wherever he goes, this Jew is determined to be admired. The poem insists on Jewish endurance:

> if there are men who ride the train to lodz
> there are still jews
> just as there are still oranges
> & jars
> there is still someone to write the jewish poem
> others to write their mothers' names in light (12)

This then is Rothenberg's "jewish poem," as objective in its identity as a jar or an orange, an utterance that "madly" refuses assimilation, that asserts its minority status while freely circulating in the general society. The poet will teach us to appreciate such poems, which in their very being preserve and renew their origins and which (given the traditional Jewish notion of matrilineal descent) "write their mothers' names in light." We will become connoisseurs of Jews, however disturbing or alien or mad they may appear, for in *Poland/1931*, Jewish madness is equated with Jewish difference, which in turn is equated with Jewish survival itself.

This brings us around to some of the most fundamental questions concerning identity, tradition, and language in Rothenberg's work. I have been arguing that this work represents the strand of Jewish universalism that has its origins (like its antithesis, Jewish exclusivism) as early as the Hebrew Bible. Rothenberg's fascination with the diversity of linguistic expression in Jewish tradition, which is seen most clearly in *Exiled in the Word*, corresponds to his fascination with the diversity of linguistic expression in all cultural traditions: thus when the Native American "iggle" in "Cokboy" gives the Baal Shem (the founder of Hasidism) the "hey heya heya" song, it gets translated into the Yiddish "yuh-buh-buh-buh-buh-buh-bum" (*Poland/1931* 146). In discussing his anthologies, Rothenberg writes that he conceives of "the book as a poem, a large composition operating by assemblage or collage." What follows next is crucial:

> In *A Big Jewish Book* I've carried it (or it's carried me) the furthest: a bigger space & less "my own" than *Poland/1931*, say, in which I was likewise using procedures like assemblage. . . .
>
> The space is big enough to do it all, but in the end it isn't the idea of (so-called) "Jewishness" that most concerns me—rather a specific set of language plays, feats of word magic & language-centeredness (in its most profound sense) that come to a visible point within the illusion of the ethnically specific (the Indian in *Shaking the Pumpkin*, the Jewish here, etc.). (*Pre-Faces* 143)

Rothenberg's use of the term *illusion* in regard to the specificity of the language-events in *A Big Jewish Book* is especially provocative. Why does the author consider the cultural specificity of his various anthologies, which reflects such thorough knowledge of those cultures combined with such imaginative reach, as illusory? Why claim, in regard to his Jewish anthology, that "in the end it isn't the idea of (so-called) 'Jewishness' that most concerns me"? What is this "(so-called) 'Jewishness'" for which Rothenberg has less concern? And finally, why is this "(so-called) 'Jewishness'" too much "my own" in *Poland/1931*?

All of these questions relate to the historical representation of Jewishness in Rothenberg's poetry. In *Poland/1931*, Rothenberg obviously is interested in presenting a particular vision of Jewish history and identity, the dark underside of Jewishness as it is understood by the assimilated (or at least acculturated) Jewish community of postwar America. The ethnopoetics of the book produces history as myth, intended, as Eric Selinger notes, to "deliver the postmodern Jewish American Poet from the burden of belatedness—or, more simply, from the guilt of not belonging to generations of belief or of immigrant struggle. All Jewish Culture is contemporaneous, it says; a Sephirah is an eternal state of mind" (11). In the kabbalah, a sephirah is an emanation of the Godhead; thus, Rothenberg's goal is the contemporaneousness or synchronicity of Jewish (and all other) culture, as expressed most clearly in the language play that features prominently in *Poland/1931* and makes up so much of his Jewish anthology. *Poland/1931* follows a loose sort of chronolgy: from the Old Country of fathers and mothers, rabbis and students, through the tragicomic narratives of Esther K. and Leo Levy as they make their way to America, to the absurd Jewish conquest (sexual and otherwise) of the American West in "Cokboy." In Selinger's terms, it moves from the older generations of belief (however heterodox), through the struggle of immigration, and then on to a vision of Jewish life renewed through its engagement with the primal myths of America. But mythic history of this sort reflects "an eternal state of mind." In this respect, the narrative of Jewish history in *Poland/1931* that Rothenberg has made "his own" through phantasmagoria is as "timeless" as the language play of amulets, ancestral scenes, and ritualistic events that punctuate the book. Indeed, even the section called "A Book of Histories" is actually a set of assembled texts from other Jewish writers, as a variety of fictional expressions of Jewish life becomes a single moment.

In an interview he conducted with Rothenberg, William Spanos voiced the following reservations about ethnopoetics, history, and myths:

> I'm still a little uneasy about your account of the "greater enterprise," as you call it, especially about what I see as a tendency to minimize man's historicity. On both the cultural level and the level of literary history, what you say seems to me—I may be exaggerating—to emphasize universals, organic, to be sure, but universals nonetheless—inclusive/timeless paradigms or models (myths)—at the expense of historical differentiation. Historicity loses its priority to form, tends to get absorbed, in other words, into a timeless structural whole in which change is, in fact, extension from a fixed and stable center. (*Pre-Faces* 19)

There is much to be said for this critique, to which Rothenberg never responds. And perhaps there is little he could say when faced with the binarism of historicity versus myth, differentiation versus universality: it seems that the ethnopoetic project, including Rothenberg's Jewish writing, stresses cultural diversity in order to point to the underlying structural unity of the mythic imagination, the "CREATION" invoked in the Pre-Face to *Exiled in the Word*. But given the exuberance and beauty of Rothenberg's achievement, as well as its fidelity to a liberal vision of Jewish culture and tradition, it becomes the critic's task to historicize the mythic imagination, keeping in mind that the writing shuttles between diachronic and synchronic discourses, self-consciously and productively pulled between the poles of history and myth.

The first poem in *Poland/1931*, "The Wedding," begins as follows:

> my mind is stuffed with tablecloths
> & with rings but my mind
> is dreaming of poland stuffed with poland
> brought in the imagination

to a black wedding
a naked bridegroom hovering above
his naked bride mad poland
how terrible thy jews at weddings
thy synagogues with camphor smell & almonds
thy thermos bottles thy electric fogs
thy braided armpits
thy underwear alive with roots o poland (3)

The placement of the speaker and the nature of the utterance are relatively straightforward at the beginning of the book: the poet dreams or imagines the dark, orgiastic underside of his ancestral Polish-Jewish milieu; that is, he actively projects a phantasmagoric vision of a Jewish wedding, willing himself into this scene. Here we see the relation of Rothenberg's ethnopoetics to the Romantic dream-vision, which, like all such texts, tend to be derived from art rather than life. "The Wedding" owes a great deal to such scenes in Singer's fiction, such as the infernal wedding ceremony in "The Gentleman from Cracow." The hovering figures in the poem seem to have floated out of a Chagall canvas. Even the image of the "braided armpits" (this is, after all, a vaudeville performance) is derived from that old ethnic joke, "How do you tell the bride at a Jewish [or Polish, or Italian . . .] wedding?" As Rothenberg exclaims, "poland/we have lain awake in thy soft arms forever" (3), as this imaginary land itself becomes the poet's mystical bride.

Yet however much "thy grooms shall work ferociously upon their looming brides" (4), there remains a gap between the poet and the world he would bring into being, a space that the invocatory utterance is meant to fill. The text is less an enactment of this magical wedding than its memorialization. Like the grooms who "begin to crow" (4) at the end of the poem, the poet's cry signifies union with his bride, the Poland of his dreams. But it is only an imaginary union, and the poet is more the historian, recounting the details of the wedding, than what de Man would call "the agent of his own language," the groom himself.

These linguistic circumstances change dramatically as soon as we move to the next three poems in the volume, "The King of Jews," "The Key of Solomon," and "Satan in Goray," all of which deploy rhetorical strategies that produce a heightened sense of immediacy. The text begins its shift from a more diachronic to a more synchronic discourse, and one important measure of this movement is the status of the utterance in relation to a determinable speaker. In "The Wedding" it is the poet's mind that is "stuffed with tablecloths," and when he shifts from first-person singular to first-person plural, then we, his readers, join him in what becomes a communal vision: "let us sail through thy fierce weddings poland" (3). Later, in the section called "A Book of Testimony," each poem bears the title of an individual in the community ("The Beadle's Testimony," "The Slaughterer's Testimony," etc.): he do the shtetl in different voices. But who, we may ask, is speaking here:

THE KING OF THE JEWS

Is a stranger. Is
Sharp. Cries
For fish. Is wanting
A wristwatch.

A Poultice. One
Bathes. One intrudes
On the Nightwatch.
One steals.

Catch him. He slips
From your nets. Anoint
Him. The father of weights.
Brother of Edom. (4)

As we move from the first to the second poem in the volume, the sense of subjectivity recedes dramatically. Likewise, the diachronic sense of a historical divide gives way to a synchronic sense of simultaneity, as a mysterious voice utters enigmatic statements and commands about the equally mysterious "king of the Jews." We are drawn into what Benjamin calls *Jetztzeit,* the messianic "time of the now" (*Illuminations* 261), aware of previously hidden currents among ordinary objects and events that may yield unprecedented changes in the structure of experience. The poem, in effect, constitutes a set of verbal gestures that may be read as theurgic rituals aimed at the messianic order and as incursions against Benjamin's "homogeneous, empty time." The poem's direct syntax and its weird but simple lexicon, cast in the tight, highly enjambed quatrains, produce an uncanny sense of disruption.

This readerly sense of defamiliarization, which is often associated with avant-garde poetic techniques, is analogous to the historical sense of rupture associated with the figure of the "king of the Jews." The transgressive nature of this figure connects him to the messianic beliefs of the Sabbateans and Frankists. Sabbatai Zevi (1626–1676) was an unstable, charismatic Jew from Smyrna whose messianic claims, supported by rabbis and kabbalists, galvanized world Jewry. His career, which culminated in a shocking conversion to Islam, has had a permanent influence on the subsequent course of Jewish history. Jacob Frank (1726–1791), a Polish Sabbatean, brought the secretive doubleness of the movement to its final stage through the creation of a weird messianic sect that outwardly embraced

Christianity, as Sabbatai had outwardly embraced Islam. These seventeenth- and
eighteenth-century Jewish heresies were centered on the notion of what Gershom
Scholem calls, in the title of his famous essay, "Redemption Through Sin," the
violation of conventional Jewish law (sometimes to the point of apostasy) in the
name of messianic transformation. Rothenberg labels them "libertarian movements" and, loosely following Scholem's historical analysis, connects them to
Jewish receptivity to the forces of secularization and modernity, leading in turn to
"the critical role of Jews & ex-Jews in revolutionary politics (Marx, Trotsky, etc.) &
avant-garde poetics (Tzara, Kafka, Stein, etc.)" (*Exiled* 8–9). For Rothenberg,
there are definite historical linkages between the transgressions of messianism and
the transgressions of the avant-garde. I am aware, of course, that these are immense generalizations; I am also cognizant of the recent critique of Scholem's
historiography as represented in the work of Moshe Idel (see, e.g., Idel 264–267).
Rothenberg's concern, however, is with *poesis,* not history per se, and in all of his
work—his poetry, his translations, his anthologies, his expository prose—his goal
is "a complex redefinition of cultural and intellectual values: a new reading of the
poetic past and present": in short, a "dream of a total art" (*Symposium* xii). Given
this perspective, which is itself utopian, perhaps even messianic, it is appropriate
that Jewish mystical beliefs and theurgical practices (spells, amulets, gematria, etc.)
may be reinscribed as avant-garde textual "events." Indeed, in *Poland/1931,* the
more the work "presses for the end" (i.e., actively attempts to bring about the
messianic order), the more extravagant become the avant-garde techniques that
Rothenberg deploys.

Thus, "The Key of Solomon," following "The King of the Jews," sounds
eerily like a kabbalistic ritual rewritten as a dadaist café performance. The poem
begins with an italicized string of seemingly random nouns: "*tallow tongues of oxen
cock messias sorrel pox a glass/a root a dish an open dish a cockatrice a ring a key:*" (5).
Following the colon after *key* and looking more like conventional poetic text, is a
set of instructions and explanations:

> From the skin of a hare
> the blood of a black hen
> or a newly killed sheep
> & occasionally the meat of animals & birds
> the food is steamed with pleasant odors.
> Stand at the eastern corner.
> Bless this carpet.
> Burn a dove's feather.
> Point to westward.
> Afflict the knees
> & tyrannize over cats.
> This is the ring of travel.

This is the yellow cloth
that causes love between two people. . . . (5–6)

The apparent randomness of this text is countered by its deadpan portentousness. From where does it come, and what is its intent? The word *messias,* almost hidden in the list of nouns, indicates the messianic inclination of the utterance. Have we, the readers, become the students at some kabbalistic scene of instruction? Are we historians who have come upon some lost hermetic fragment? Solomon, the wisest man who ever lived, was naturally regarded as a master of magic. His ring was inscribed with the "Seal of Solomon" or Shield of David, the hexagram or six-pointed star that is now a universal symbol for Judaism; it was "a sign of his dominion over the demons" (*Kabbalah* 363). Are these his instructions, and if so, what mystery does this "key" unlock? There are no answers to questions such as these, and perhaps the questions are their own answers. The presence of the poem/key implies a greater absence—of wisdom, of tradition, of unity—that may or may not be retrievable. The poem appears to be a fragment, and yet is possessed of an almost magical self-sufficiency. It has a sense of (perhaps fraudulent) antiquity, but also of urgency that disrupts the normal course of time.

It is followed by "Satan in Goray," a collage-like arrangement of brief texts that play on themes from Singer's novel, set in a seventeenth-century Polish village possessed by Sabbatean fanaticism. Despite these historical coordinates, however, this poem is an even more extreme example of synchronicity and verbal immediacy, adopting the repetitions and transformations of Gertrude Stein's compositional technique to the transgressive content of Sabbateanism (see Pacernick 36). One section, parenthetically signed "G. Stein," plays on the terms "Pass over" and "Pass water": the sacred and the profane just two syllables apart. Another invokes the renegade messiah: "Sabbath./Sabbatai Zevi./Sodom Sodom./Sodom Sodom." Through the name of Sabbatai, we move from one of the most blessed Jewish notions to one of the most accursed biblical locales. Yet another, consisting entirely of the words "Holy Muhammed," reminds us of Sabbatai's apostasy. We are also presented with the single phrase "Something is Presence"—and whether that "Something" is holy or demonic is beside the point. Beyond even those messianic sectarians who sought "redemption through sin," Rothenberg insists that in Jewish tradition—as in all others—the holy and the transgressive carry the same cultural charge insofar as they are both expressions of human creativity. *Poesis,* linguistic making, is an impure act, and Rothenberg's own poetry not only inhabits but celebrates the fallen world. This is the world of the *kelipot,* the husks or shells, sparks of the *sefirot* or divine emanations that broke and fell because they could not contain the pure light of the godhead for which they were intended. The kabbalist seeks to "raise the sparks" through acts of holiness, and thus restore the cosmic order. Rothenberg, however he may appropriate kabbalah for his "symposium of the whole," is in this respect diametrically opposed to the kabbalistic project.

Yet the term "Presence" implies that there are powers that determine belief and shape experience, and that language is the medium of their expression among us. Indeed, given kabbalistic belief, language itself is such a power. As Scholem observes, "The secret world of the godhead is a world of language, a world of divine names that unfold in accordance with a law of their own. The elements of the divine language appear as the letters of the Holy Scriptures. Letters and names are not only conventional means of communication. They are far more. Each one of them represents a concentration of energy and expresses a wealth of meaning which cannot be translated, or not fully at least, into human language" (*On the Kabbalah* 36). So "Something is Presence" and can be known through human language, but only (pace Objectivism) obliquely and never fully or immediately. In his extraordinary meditation on divine and human language, Walter Benjamin suggests that with the Fall, "[t]he word must communicate *something* (other than itself). That is really the Fall of language-mind. The word as something externally communicating, as it were a parody by the expressly mediate word of the expressly immediate, the creative word of God, and the decay of the blissful, Adamite language-mind that stand between them" (*Reflections* 327).

Parody, of course, is very much a part of Rothenberg's stock-in-trade, and I would argue that there is just this sort of "deep parody," as it were, going on in the language play of *Poland/1931*. The messianic aspect of Rothenberg's project is directly related to "the decay of the blissful, Adamite language-mind," for language, like all else that is human, will be redeemed on the arrival of the messiah. But to what extent do Rothenberg's texts seriously enact the "parody by the expressly mediate word of the expressly immediate," and to what extent are they simply learned but still profane jokes? Selinger, meditating on the shadowy photograph of Rothenberg having *tefillin* (phylacteries) layed on him by a solemn female figure (*Poland/1931* 28) detects a genuine sense of "deliverance." As he explains it, "It's clearly a staged, performative gesture: not a performing of the mitzvah, done l'shem yichud, in the name of the Holy One & his Shekhinah, but a poet's decidedly heterodox and aesthetic invocation of that act. Yet there is nothing stagy or kitchy or forced about it" (11). These outwardly devout yet fundamentally agnostic gestures, these performances of spiritual, not merely formal indeterminacy, constitute the postmodern Judaism of Rothenberg's work. The more we consider the balance between the serious and comic in these poems, the more uncanny they become:

Word Event

He sits in a house whose walls are decorated with fresh vegetables, praying & singing psalms, & reading from *The Book of the Law*.

Then he begins to move the letters that he sees, until they make new words & sounds.

Quickly he jumps from word to word, letting the words form thoughts in any order.

Finally he drops the words out of his mind: word by word until he thinks of nothing.

Freed from thought, the consonants dance around him in quick motion. Forming a mirror in which he sees his face. (73)

On one level, the unnamed subject of this "event" is Abraham Abulafia, the thirteenth-century kabbalist and would-be messiah whose mystical writing practices Rothenberg links to such modern experimentalists as Apollinaire, Tzara, and MacLow. The "house whose walls are decorated with fresh vegetables" is presumably a *succah,* to which Abulafia has retired to worship, study, and engage in what he called *Hokhmath ha-Tseruf,* the combinations and permutations of Hebrew letters that lead to knowledge of the Divine Name and ecstatic union with God. As Scholem explains, "all things exist only by virtue of their degree of participation in the great Name of God, which manifests itself throughout the whole Creation. There is a language which expresses the pure thought of God and the letters of this spiritual language are the elements both of the most fundamental spiritual reality and of the profoundest understanding and knowledge. Abulafia's mysticism is a course in this divine language" (*Major Trends* 133). Abulafia's "Path of the Name" includes a textual practice called *dillug* or "jumping," which "unites . . . elements of free or guided association and is said to assure quite extraordinary results as far as the 'widening of the consciousness' of the initiate is concerned" (*Major Trends* 136). For Abulafia and his followers, these word events (to use Rothenberg's term) are ultimately intended to produce a state of prophetic ecstasy, a union of man and Torah. Scholem quotes a kabbalist of Abulafia's school: "one day I sat and wrote down a Kabbalistic secret; suddenly I saw the shape of myself standing before me and myself disengaged from me and I was forced to stop writing!" (*Major Trends* 142). Thus "Freed from thought, the consonants dance around him in quick motion. Forming a mirror in which he sees his face."

But to what extent does this scholarly gloss "explain" Rothenberg's text? Read in the broader context of the "yiddish surrealist vaudeville" that is *Poland/1931,* the poem produces an effect of comic defamiliarization: a house decorated with vegetables, a writer jumping from word to word, dancing consonants, and so on. The title of the poem, the lack of historical referents, and the use of present tense all heighten the synchronicity for which Rothenberg strives when he reworks traditional material. The figure of the medieval mystic merges with that of the modern avant-gardist; in both instances, language play leads to an emptying of conventional meaning that is the only way one may truly see oneself. But whereas the mystic seeks the union of that self with divinity, the avant-garde poet/ethnographer/performance artist finds meaning in the immediacy of the event itself, however much it resonates with similar events in the past.

Noting Abulafia's messianic pretensions, including his attempted visit to the Pope in 1280, Rothenberg names him "A model, therefore, of the poet/rebel in language & in life, common to Jewish & other marginalities within the monolithic nation-state" (*Pre-Faces* 161). The constellation of messianism, poetry, and rebellion, however volatile, is a longstanding one. Scholem calls messianism an "anarchic breeze" that blows through halakhic Judaism's "well-ordered house," and observes that "in every historical hour in which the Messianic idea entered the mind as a power of direct influence, the tension which exists between these two forms of religious authority immediately became noticeable" ("Messianic Idea" 21–22). For Scholem, Judaism pays a heavy price for the spiritual renewal that each outbreak of messianic fervor brings with it: messianic authority, never as clearly defined as halakhic or rabbinic authority, depends more on the charismatic power of the "poet/rebel" whose inspired, visionary outbursts may produce unexpected and even disastrous results.

In *Poland/1931*, Rothenberg's messianic pretender is Leo Levy, "[a] lion by birth a liar later, hah!" (91). His arrival from China, where the Jewish community is said "to go perhaps back to the lost tribe of Asher, one of the famous ten lost tribes of Israel" (87) is announced to Esther K., mistress of "the Governor," by whom she has had "[a] white-haired child which smelleth of old laundry" (86). Although "for the Jewess who has tasted of the Gentile's honey there is no reunion in her father's tent" (86), she is still the Shekhinah gone into exile with the Jewish people; her fate and that of Leo Levy are bound together to form Israel's messianic destiny (see Pacernick 43–44). Yet as is indicated by the absurd erotic comedy of "Galician Nights" and "Esther K. Comes to America," the two sections of *Poland/1931* in which these characters appear, there is more than a touch of melodrama and chicanery in this mystical union. In the fake newspaper ad that announces this "Novel in Progress," "Mrs. L. L. nee E. K." is presented as "Mme. Shekinah," "Jewish Soul Healer & Adviser" (82). Leo Levy "went to sleep in Jewishtown woke up early the next morning feeling how forlorn it was to be lost & foundering from three directions" (90); he is angry at himself, at his reduced circumstances filled with "dirt & corruption" (91), and most of all, at Esther K., against whom he chants a long, repetitive "*Angry Song*" similar to the Native American "Horse-Songs" that Rothenberg has translated. In some respects, Leo Levy's fate is to become an anti-Semitic stereotype, suffering "Contagion./This comes from being a jew" (91). Sander Gilman, citing Heine's poem on the Jewish hospital in Hamburg, observes that the poet "used tropes for his Jewishness taken from the vocabulary of anti-Semitic discourse, and shaped them to his own ends" (*Difference and Pathology* 150). Rothenberg, as we have seen in "The Connoisseur of Jews," does much the same. "Why had he brought his powers to this place" asks Leo Levy in Jewishtown, looking at the "[b]rown of piss in pot" (91). The answer lies in the dynamics of his messianic mission. Followers of Sabbatai Zevi explained his conversion by arguing that he could only perform the act of redemption by spirtually descending into the fallen world. By assuming his enemies' degraded image of himself, Levy, like Sabbatai before him, can, in effect, "descend into the realm of the *kelipot* [husks or shells]" in order "to rescue the divine sparks still imprisoned there" ("Messianic Idea" 95). When last seen, Levy and Esther K. sit together in "The Wilderness," a Manhattan cafeteria filled with "stale odors: Leo Levy/going every morning to the chicken market/pursues his dream of power/ Esther K. wonders: how was I ever trapped/inside this body?" (108). The primal Jewish couple continues to wander in the wilderness; the union of the messiah and the people of Israel remains indefinitely deferred: "thus history repeated itself with marked rapidity/leading her to first meet/& then lose/Leo Levy . . . the poor under your window & the poor/around your table/will always be there" (109). For Scholem, "[t]he magnitude of the Messianic idea corresponds to the endless powerlessness in Jewish history during all the centuries of exile, when it was unprepared to come forward onto the plane of world history. . . . It diminishes the singular worth of the individual, and he can never fulfill himself, because the incompleteness of his endeavors eliminates precisely what constitutes its highest value. Thus in Judaism the Messianic idea has compelled a *life lived in deferment,* in which nothing can be done definitely, nothing can be irrevocably accomplished" (*Messianic Idea* 35). *Poland/1931* is an excellent example of a messianic work caught in the endless regress of exilic history, which becomes a perpetual "crisis":

> the good life of the timid
> beckons: it is a value
> to be learned: a source of fortune
> only too distant without refinement
> both will grow sick & die
> much later: separate beds
> wait for them
> chimeras dressed as chorus girls
> to direct & love: his name
> changed to Ben Messiah
> hers to his: an aged couple
> smelling of wet sheets (109–110)

Messianic hopes diminish individual experience while strengthening the endurance of the people; "the Wilderness/has shrunk them" says Rothenberg of this "aged couple," though as he declares at the end of "Portrait of a Jew Old Country Style," "I count the failures of these jews/as proof of their election" (119).

"The Wilderness," of course, is not only the Manhattan cafeteria of Esther K. and Leo Levy but the American west of "Cokboy" as well; thus it defines both the bitterwsweet end of the Eastern European Jewish experience and the phantasmagoric "coming-forth" of the American Jewish experience, "a little Moses" born of the Baal Shem and a Native American Shekhinah, "daughter of a chief."

But the poem that concludes *Poland/1931,* for all its phallic extravagance and mad parturient imagery, actually shuts down the volume's messianic project. The Jew and the Indian may be mystically united in an ethnopoetic vision, but the "American disaster" proves overwhelming. Rothenberg's protagonist wanders "past mining camps Polacks were panning gold in/& other pure products of America" (151): the ironic reference to the violence of Williams's "To Elsie" indicating that for the Jews, the Diasporic experience in the New World may not be so different from that of the Old. Cokboy (or is it the poet?) is "kept from/true entry to the west true paradise/like Moses in the Rockies who stares at California spooky in the jewish light" (151). Looking out from that vantage point, he falls silent. Will America bring forth a new Jewish vision? Rothenberg's frequent references in his essays and interviews to the "monoculture" that modern American produces indicates that it might not, however flourishing the largely assimilated world of American Jewry may appear. Be that as it may, the messianic impulse in *Poland/1931* opens the door to a traditional past that also leads to the future. Thus it becomes "a neglected dream of beards" (*Poland/1931* 18), a visionary promise that remains to be fulfilled.

Rothenberg's most recent Jewish work is *Khurbn,* part elegy, part nightmare, and wholly concerned with the near extermination of European Jewry. Begun in 1987 on his first visit to Poland, the poem is in one important respect the complement to *Poland/1931,* which was written over ten years before. In his introduction, the poet looks back on his earlier work, noting that "at a great distance from the place [Poland], I decided deliberately that that was not to be a poem about the 'holocaust'" (*Khurbn* 3). As I have observed, the earlier book follows a loose chronological pattern, starting with an ethnographic re-creation of Jewish Poland and then moving on through the immigrant experience to America. Though shadowed by the Holocaust, it is still a poem about the transformations of modern Jewish life, not its destruction. *Khurbn,* on the other hand, arises out of the loss of the poet's own relatives and their fellow Jews in the town of Ostrow-Mazowiecka, "only fifteen miles from Treblinka." Rothenberg tells us that "The poems I first began to hear at Treblinka are the clearest message I have ever gotten about why I write poetry. They are an anwer also to the proposition—by Adorno & others—that poetry cannot or should not be written after Auschwitz" (4).

Rothenberg's treatment of the Shoah plots a middle course in comparison to Reznikoff's *Holocaust* and Grossman's poems in *A Harlot's Hire.* On the one hand, *Khurbn* conveys a far greater sense of the poet's subjectivity than *Holocaust,* in which only the barest hints remain of a persona standing in or behind the text. On the other hand, Rothenberg is far more concerned with the function of the poem as testimony than Grossman, who believes that the transformative power of poetic discourse can cleanse and redeem the horrors of history and restore the moral dimension of human life. Rothenberg does not assume this degree of transformative agency, and given his relation to Objectivism, he would probably find in

Grossman's stance the arrogation of a power that the poet may not rightfully claim. Yet he does not follow Reznikoff to the endpoint of Objectivism's testimonial trajectory that *Holocaust* represents. Instead, like the shaman in a tribal culture, he opens himself to the dead and lets them speak through him. In becoming such a vessel, he maintains a sense of poetic agency, but at the same tries to allow the victims to speak, as it were, for themselves. Rothenberg finds that the emptiness of Treblinka is "in sharp contrast to the crowds of tourists at Auschwitz (Oswiecim) & to the fullness of the other Poland I had once imagined [in *Poland/1931*]. The absence of the living seemed to create a vacuum in which the dead—the dibbiks who had died before their time—were free to speak. It wasn't the first time that I thought of poetry as the language of the dead, but never so powerfully as now" (*Khurbn* 3).

Were it not for the poet, the dead would remain speechless; they would remain consumed, as in the first section of the poem, "IN THE DARK WORD, KHURBN" (5). Instead, Rothenberg "would take it from your voice/& cradle it// that ancient & dark word." To do so, he must experience "Dos Oysleydikn" ("The Emptying"), a psychic experience that parallels the emptying of the Polish towns, still inhabited by Poles but betraying an uncanny absence:

> empty bakery & empty road to warsaw
> yellow wooden houses & houses plastered up with stucco
> the shadows of an empty name still on their doors
> shadai & shadow shattering the mother tongue
> the mother's tongue but empty
> the way the streets are empty where we walk
> pushing past crowds of children
> old women airing themselves outside the city hall
> old farmers riding empty carts down empty roads
> who don't dispel but make an emptiness (6)

As Dan Featherston observes in his essay on *Holocaust* and *Khurbn*, "The emptying is both the emptying out of lives destroyed in the Holocaust, and an emptying into language those absences, those silences that inhabit both the streets and the poem, filled, as it were, with emptiness" (135). The lost Yiddish of the Polish Jews, their "mother tongue" (*mamaloshen*) that has been emptied into silence, is heard again in Rothenberg's American speech. The poem is marked throughout by such uncanny verbal phenomena, to be experienced simultaneously as absent and present. In the glossary section presented at the end of the book, Rothenberg tells us that "In the case of untranslated Yiddish words in particular, I would strongly urge the reader to catch them in their initial incomprehensibility before checking these notes towards their apparent 'clarification.'" Furthermore, "The spelling of Polish place names, etc., have sometimes been modified toward something like their sounds in Yiddish" (111). The language of the silenced Jews, both heard and

unheard, is analogous to "the shadows of an empty name still on their doors"—
the marks left on the doorposts after the Jews' *mezuzoth* have been removed,
indicating how during and immediately after the Shoah, Poles moved into houses
previously owned by Jews. *Mezuzoth* are often marked with the Hebrew letter *shin*
for "shadai" (Almighty), which in the Shoah has become "an empty name." Not
only has the trace of the physical object been left behind, but the Name, that once
seemed omnipotent to the faithful Jews, has likewise been emptied of all its might.

The play of absence and presence, particularly in relation to language, is
sustained throughout the poem. It is related in turn to the idea of the dibbik, the
possessing spirit of one who has died prematurely, as in "The Dybbuk," S. Ansky's
mystical Yiddish drama. "Once a dibbik," observes Rothenberg, "was a singular
occurrence. It is now repeated many million times as the result of so much early
death. Into whom do the dead souls enter? Each one contains a dibbik, or some of
them contain a world of dibbiks" (27). In *Khurbn,* the poet is possessed by both a
single dibbik—that of his uncle, who joined the partisans but committed suicide
upon hearing of his family's death in Treblinka—and by a world of dibbiks. In
"Dos Geshray (The Scream)," the poet instructs himself (or the dibbik instructs
the poet) to " 'practice your scream' " and the poet declares that "because it was his
scream & wasn't my own/it hovered between us" (11). It is this scream "that allows
the poem to come" (12): only the primal utterance of extreme anguish can bring
language back out of silence, so that the voices of remembrance (the remembered
voices) can be heard. An instant later, we begin the section called "Dibbukim
(Dibbiks)," as Rothenberg moves from a single spirit within him into the world of
the dead:

> spirits of the dead lights
> flickering (he said) their ruakh
> will never leave the earth
> instead they crowd the forests the fields
> around the privies the hapless spirits
> wait millions of souls
> turned into ghosts at once
> the air is full of them
> they are standing each one beside a tree
> under its shadows or the moon's
> but they cast no shadow of their own (13)

In some respects, this vision of a world of dibbiks emerging out of the
Khurbn is a significant departure from the traditional Jewish understanding of the
dibbik in kabbalah, folklore, and earlier literature. The Yiddish word "dibbik" is
derived from the Hebrew *davok,* "cleave." Although the idea of demonic possession dates back to Jewish antiquity, the term appears, according to Scholem,
"neither in talmudic literature nor in the Kabbalah." Rather, it "was introduced

into literature only in the seventeenth century from the spoken language of German and Polish Jews. It is an abbreviation of *dibbuk me-ru'ah ra'ah* ('a cleavage of an evil spirit'), or *dibbik min ha-hizonim* ('*dibbik* from the demonic side'), which is found in man." The dibbik was originally a devil; eventually, the notion developed "that some of the *dibbukim* are the spirits of dead persons who were not laid to rest and thus became demons. . . . They were generally considered to be souls which, on account of the enormity of their sins, were not even allowed to transmigrate and as 'denuded spirits' they sought refuge in the bodies of living persons. The entry of a *dibbuk* into a person was a sign of his having committed a secret sin which opened a door for the *dibbuk*" (*Kabbalah* 349).

Ansky's play "The Dybbuk" (1912–1917), one of the most famous works of Yiddish literature, modifies these beliefs by adding a great element of pathos to the act of spiritual possession. When the soul of the student Khonon possesses Leah, the daughter of the wealthy hassid Sender, it is an act not of evil of but divine justice, for Sender and Khonon's father Nissen originally agree that their children should marry before either child is born. Nissen moves to a distant town and dies shortly after his son's birth; Khonon, who, like his father, studies kabbalah, wanders about searching for his mystically intended bride. Khonon meets and falls in love with Leah, but he dies on hearing the news that Sender has betrothed her to another. Khonon's ghostly possession of Leah leads to the revelation of the truth that Sender has suppressed, but even then, Khonon's spirit refuses to leave Leah until he is threatened with excommunication. Forced to abandon his spiritual haven, Khonon departs; whereupon Leah immediately expires and their souls are finally united in the beyond. Leah's possession by the dibbik may thus be seen as part of a divinely ordained process of purification, for Khonon's mystical obsessions, which have led him to the point of heresy, are focused on the idea that extreme devotion can cleanse even the worst of sins.

But unlike the dibbik in Ansky's play, the ghosts of the Khurbn that possess Rothenberg are the victims of genocide, the most heinous of crimes, for which there can be no rituals of purification. These dibbiks are furious; "they lap up fire water slime/entangle the hair of brides"; one hears their voices "carrying across the fields/to rot your kasha your barley" (14). Their anger continues to build as the poem goes on and the crimes against them are recounted, eventually culminating in a long litany called "Di Toyte Kloles" ("The Maledictions"). This section ends with the declaration "Let ghosts & dibbiks overwhelm the living/Let the invisible overwhelm the visible until nothing more is seen or heard" (*Khurbn* 35): because the living humanity of Eastern European Jewish life has been wiped out, it seems that the poem can only inscribe negation, leading back to the Nothingness that is the God of the Khurbn.

And yet this is not, finally, the case. If what I have observed about the dialectic of absence and presence in *Khurbn* is true, then Rothenberg's poem summons presence through absence at every point in the text. In the last section of the poem, "Peroration for a Lost Town," the horror recedes somewhat before images of Ostrow-Mazowiecka as it was before the Shoah. Even the church bells seem to sing a Yiddish tune ("bimbom"),

> that call forth death o death o pale photographer
> o photos of the sweet town rubbed with blood
> o of its streets the photographs its vanished folk
> o wanderers who wandered o bodies of the distant dead who stayed
> o faces o dimming images lost smiles o girls embracing girls
> in deathless photographs o life receding
> into images of life you beautiful & pure sweet town
> I summon & I summon thee to answer (37)

In the end, the poet/shaman, still possessed, takes on the equally poetic and magical role of the summoner of spirits, providing images of all that has been lost. But he remains the ethnographer as well, as he and his dibbik speak to the Poles who remain: "Then he asked—or was it I who asked or asked *for* him?—were there once Jews here? Yes, they told us, yes they were sure there were, though there was no one here who could remember." The questions and answers that follow indicate how clouded legend and reality become in such a short span of time, among what remains an almost instinctively anti-Semitic populace: "They had six fingers on each hand. Their old men had the touch of women when we rubbed against them. One day they dug a hole and went back into the earth. They live there to this day" (38–39). And so they do, until Rothenberg, with his Jewish magic, calls them forth.

Jewish magic? In the Pre-Face to *Exiled in the Word*, Rothenberg reads Exodus 22:17 as "thou shalt not suffer a shaman to live," though the noun *michashaiphah* is usually rendered "witch" or "sorceress." In Exodus, and again in Deuteronomy (18:9–22), the Israelites are forbidden to adopt the magical practices of the older Canaanite tribes, which constitute, according to Rothenberg, a "language-of-vision in a culture that was communalistic, anarchic, & egalitarian, that the newer city-states tried to destroy" (5). Yet as we have seen, Rothenberg would restore some of the most archaic functions of the shaman and apply them to a modern poetic sensibility, thus revealing (or creating) a bridge between the two forms of culture. *Exiled in the Word* traces a broadly Jewish "tradition of *poesis* that goes from the interdicted shamans (= witches, sorcerers, etc., in the English Bible) to the prophets & apocalyptists (later "seers" who denied their sources in their shaman predecessors) & from there to the merkaba & kabbala mystics, on the right hand, & the gnostic heretics & nihilist messiahs, on the left" (5). Ethnopoetics represents the rediscovery of this tradition under the aegis of anthropology, and its application to new acts of *poesis*, which, in this respect, are not "new" at all. In Rothenberg's project, the idea (or perhaps we should say, the myth) of tradition as continuity, enduring despite the vicissitudes of history—the spasms and ruptures of thousands of years of conquest, exile, persecution, and genocide—is a given. Yet as I observed in relation to *Poland/1931,* much of Rothenberg's poetry is a sort of "deep parody," and his reinterpretations of the old ways gesture to both the continuities and the ruptures of tradition. A plangent note of irony resonates throughout this work, and irony always implies a distance that language cannot bridge, a loss that *poesis* cannot restore. And it is at this point that we turn to Rothenberg's colleague, Armand Schwerner, whose work is even more deeply parodic, more firmly marked by a consciousness of discontinuity. Culminating in his serial poem, *The Tablets,* Schwerner's poetry is altogether true to the univeraliz-ing spirit of ethnopoetics, yet increasingly ironic in its expression of that spirit.

Schwerner's concerns with native cultures and languages, the play of varied discourses in common speech, the fundamental ground of the human body, and the synchronicity of the archaic and the modern, parallel Rothenberg's in many respects. At the heart of Schwerner's multifaceted project is the desire to articulate a radical, indeed an ecstatic alternative to the homogeneity and artificiality of our culture, to preserve and reinvigorate the act of *poesis* through "the immediacy of the oral, which is the immediacy of the tribal, the archaic, the so-called primitive, which was gone for a long time. . . . The question of poems as oral transmission from one generation to another for hundreds, even thousands of years, is a question of a buried tradition, a 'whispered tradition,' the Tibetans sometimes say, the stuff of one being connected to another being" ("A Conversation" 81, 82). Schwerner's poetry, from his early work in *The Lightfall* (1963), *(if personal)* (1968), and *Seaweed* (1969), and on through the various editions of *The Tablets,* presents a great range of forms and procedures. But what is to be found consis-tently, both on the page and in Schwerner's extraordinary readings, is the underly-ing assumption that language, particularly spoken language, embodies a kind of primacy which, when discovered anew (a discovery that is to be made endlessly), can restore a fundamental sense of wonder to human existence.

Part of this wonder is derived from the nature of the poetic process. As Schwerner explains, "The made thing, poem, artifact, product, will appear to the maker as Other and yet give the pleasure of recognition, to breed other discoveries. The voices of the made thing, poem, object, need no ascription by the maker. He does not know the necessary identity of a voice or many voices. They speak him in a way he later discovers. The locus appears later" (*Tablets* 131). This statement pulls together a number of the most important aspects of ethnopoetics as an original artistic tendency—original in Pound's sense of "make it new" and original in the sense of a return to origins. When Schwerner describes the artifact's con-fronting the maker as an Other, he reflects a typically postmodern skepticism regarding the unitary self and its expression in the poem. The current notion that language speaks us, rather than vice versa, is likewise found in the image of unknown voices speaking the poet. But the sense of otherness that obtains be-tween subject and utterance is also very ancient, going back to the shaman's trance, the possession of the tribal poet by a god, ancestral spirit, or totemic power. But whether one regards the phenomenon from an archaic or postmodern perspective, it is clear that what the maker fashions is not self-expressive or experiential in any conventional sense. And as Schwerner further asserts, "there is no nuclear self" (*Tablets* 130).

Because poetic form is experienced as both recognition and otherness, it is magical or uncanny. In Schwerner's work, this linguistic quality is most apparent in those texts that rehearse the spoken word, such as the early "Poem at the Bathroom Door by Adam":

> push-car woman do you love me
> watch woman do you love me
> iron woman do you love me
> bye woman do you love me
> happy woman do you love me
> store woman do you love me
> bird with a heart in his mouth and a kiss in his mouth
> present woman do you love me
> ask woman do you love me
> that's all I can think of (*Seaweed* 23)

In this poem, the speech act of Schwerner's young son takes on, as the boy's name appropriately implies, the adamic quality of primal naming. The chantlike quality of the verse, the use of repetition and variation, and the play of parts of speech, are not only qualities of the child's language, but are reminiscent of the poetry of "primitive" cultures as well. Rather than sentimentalize either the childlike or the primitive, however, the poem *enacts* the oral immediacy which the poet finds so valuable.

This same sense of immediate connectedness—of sincerity, that quality so valued by Objectivists such as Zukofsky and Oppen, whom Schwerner knew personally—is also to be felt when the poet uses the first-person pronoun. "Bar-mitzvah poem for my son Adam" ends with these lines:

> bar mitzvah, son of a good deed
> I was told, life-bearer, man of red earth,
> *pri haadamah* fruit of yourself, we can only know
> present moments calm decisions to cut off the snapper's head
> when the hook is irretrievable, gullet
> beyond repair son of your finite seconds
> you touch the living world gently
> as a man in a fullness learns. you are earning
> your face, you are this man.
>   love, father
>   (*sounds of the river Naranjana* 5)

The play on the Aramaic *bar mitzvah* (son of a good deed) and the Hebrew *adam* (red) and *pri haadamah* (fruit of the earth) links the ritual moment to any moment when the young man may know the world in its fullness and in effect give birth to himself. For Schwerner, as for the other poets of his generation who are even more directly influenced by Objectivism, poetry's linguistic immediacy provides an understanding of life as "fatal," in the sense of fate as a succession of unknowable moments of surprise. As the poet observes in "the boat,"

> . . . It's not dramatic,
> just fatal, a vivid life like the life
> of the poem is the life
> of the senseless calm surprise, the profound greeting
> in the kitchen and the streets and the field
> to the not-known unpredictable in the beings
> and to the call within the burnished and rusty things
> of this world. (*sounds of the river Naranjana* 36)

The invocation of "the not-known" or what Schwerner earlier in the poem calls "no-mindfulness" indicates the way in which the epistemological and phenomenological concerns of Objectivism coincide with the poet's extensive studies of Buddhism. It is a coincidence out of which comes some of his most lyrical work, as in this brief passage from the serial poem "sounds of the river Naranjana":

> for a week watch the river Naranjana flowing
> for a week, walk, and for a week watch
> the bark of the balsam fir. now
> the red-wing lights on it. now
> the river eddies, now when you walk you walk.
> (*sounds of the river Naranjana* 24)

The voice speaking here is that of a sage instructing us on the path of enlightenment, which is an experience of the totality in and of every present moment. In many respects, it is similar to Schwerner's translation of the Yiddish poem by Peretz Markish, which appears in *Exiled in the Word*:

> *Now*
> is my name. I spread my arms, my hands
> pierce the extremes
> of what is. I'm letting my eyes roam around
> and do their drinking from the fountains
> of the world

eyes wild, shirt ballooning,
my hands separated by the world, I don't know
if I have a home
or have a homelessness
or am a beginning or an end. (151–152)

With this passage in mind, we are led to ask in what ways Schwerner, given
the extraordinary range of his work's multicultural references as well as the sense of
groundlessness or homelessness that permeates the writing, is a specifically Jewish
poet. And in a certain respect, we have just answered our own question: since so
much secular Jewish literature of the last century has dealt with the groundlessness
of Jews in diaspora, the notion of the Jew as *luftmensch,* it could be argued that the
ethnopoetics of Schwerner and his colleagues is, in effect, the clearest expression of
this groundlessness as well as a counterforce posed against it. The experience of
feeling rooted or at home in even the most remote cultural practices need not be
limited to Jewish writers. But the Jewish tendency to incorporate a sense of
cultural otherness into what is already a diasporic, wandering identity, warrants
some consideration. In his attempt to explain this phenomenon, Jonathan Boyarin, meditating on the "nomadic" work of Edmond Jabès, recalls the story of
Abraham:

> Estrangement from the self, or at any rate a double consciousness, is con-
> stitutive of Jewishness not because we persist only through being repeatedly
> rejected by others but because there was a time before the Jew was a Jew.
> Abraham becomes the first Jew when he leaves his father's ways and his
> father's house to follow an invisible God. Coming to be Jewish is coming to
> be Other. What is relevant here regarding the possibility of a distinctively
> Jewish ethnography is that Judaism contains the Other in its own genealogy,
> that is to say, its own imaginary. This does not mean, of course, that Jews are
> inherently any more (or any less) tolerant or empathetic than any other
> given group of people, nor that the potential I am pointing to is exclusive to
> Jews. Yet it is extraordinary as a model of an elaborately inscribed identity
> constructed in the awareness of difference. (*Storm from Paradise* 66)

Like Jewish ethnography in Boyarin's definition, Schwerner's masterpiece,
The Tablets, contains the Other in its own genealogy or imaginary, and the
identities it inscribes as it zigzags across the millennia are elaborately constructed
in the awareness of difference. Genealogically, *The Tablets* goes back further than
almost any other exercise in ethnopoetics. The deepest of deep parodies, it is a sort
of Joycean hoax: a sequence of texts that purports to be translations of Sumerian/
Akkadian clay tablets more than 4,000 years old. Riddled with signs indicating
untranslatable or missing passages, filled with notes and speculations in a variety of
real and fictive, living and dead languages, *The Tablets* is presented as the work of

the "Scholar/Translator," an eccentric, perhaps even mad figure in constant dialogue with the voices of the archaic past, as well as with the equally strange tradition of research from which he comes. Much of the weird humor of the work arises from the manic discrepancies between the Scholar/Translator's observations and the material he has managed to decipher with varying degrees of certainty. This fundamental lack of temporal and discursive stability distinguishes *The Tablets* from other literary works of an "archaeological" nature: as Brian McHale notes in his essay comparing Schwerner's poem to Geoffrey Hill's *Mercian Hymns* and Seamus Heaney's bog poems, we are never presented with the "archaeological primal scene." McHale explains: "Nowhere in *The Tablets* are we *shown* the translator actually confronting the artifacts (the clay tablets or cylinder seals, or a photo of them); at most we hear him discoursing *about* them. Rather, it is *we readers* who enact the primal scene every time we look into *The Tablets*, every time we turn its pages, for the translated tablets are themselves the artifacts, or as close as anyone will ever come to them. No need to represent the encounter with an artifact when the text itself *is* that artifact" (247). It is this quality that leads Rachel Blau DuPlessis to observe that as the work develops, *The Tablets* reflects the evolving concerns of the ethnopoetics movement, from "the search for origins or primary emotional and cultural ground" to "the nature, functions, ideologies, and interests at stake in the transmission and the transmitter" (212).

In the "Journals/Divagations" appended to *The Tablets*, Schwerner himself discusses the form of his major work, explaining its attraction for him, and by implication, its importance for ethnopoetics in general:

> The modern, accidental form of Sumero-Akkadian tablets provides me with a usable poetic structure. . . . The uses of the past, by means of these found archaic objects, are thus more than ironic and other than nostalgic. The context of sober translation creates a mode suitable for seductions by the disordered large which is the contemporary, and the narrative, which is out of honor in the most relevant modern poetry. The context also makes me feel comfortable in recreating the animistic, for which I have great sympathy, and which, subject to my sense of the present, I have been unable to approach as a poet without such contextual personae and forms as I have found in these archaic leftovers. (*Tablets* 134)

Schwerner's opposition to nostalgia, as well as his inability to re-create the animistic except through such a pseudo-archaic invention as *The Tablets*, are both connected to his relation (or nonrelation) to what is ordinarily conceived to be "Jewish American literature." In a letter to the author (10 September 1993), Schwerner complains of "a profound lack of risk-taking" in the work of certain other Jewish American poets, "so that the learning and the praiseworthy connections to the complexities of tradition tend to inertness. My profound disinterest in almost all manifestations of 'Jewish' Americana is one of the factors that led me 5,000 years back to find, represent and embody my relatives the Akkadians." Schwerner thus avoids the pitfalls inherent in directly addressing what Bloom would call "the Sorrows of American-Jewish Poetry" (and American-Jewish culture in general), which include sentimentality, nostalgia, and the paralyzing weight of the Jewish textual tradition. Instead, Schwerner goes back to a time before the Jews were Jews, before that moment, as Boyarin would have it, when the Jewish worldview presented itself as an Other. He produces his own Dead Sea Scrolls (or pre-Mosaic tablets), what Kathryn Van Spanckeren describes as "a self-reflexive or deconstructive exploration of Western consciousness. The Tablets revel in the condition of brokenness, illegibility, and loss" (18). But rather than offer up this archaeological reconstruction in a quasi-sacred fashion (as is the case, perhaps, of the "Talmudic" books of Edmond Jabès), Schwerner delights in presenting the Rabelaisian profanity of his ancient "relatives." From Tablet V:

is the man bigger than a fly's wing?	what pleasure!
is he much bigger than a fly's wing?	what pleasure!
is his hard penis ten times a fly's wing?	what pleasure!
is his red penis fifteen times a fly's wing?	what [pleasure]!
is his mighty penis fifty times a fly's wing?	what pleasure!
does his penis vibrate like a fly's wing?	what terrific pleasure! (23)

Through the temporal warpings of *The Tablets,* the literal shards of a civilization that existed thousands of years in the past, Schwerner constantly reminds us of the founding cultural dialectic of the sacred and the profane. Body and spirit veer about and collide in the text in ways that continually expose the inadequacy of modern religious thought regarding our somatic being. For Schwerner, this is "not poetry as obeisance to the sacred, but as a creation of it in all its activity; not as an appeal for its survival in spite of a corrosive sense that the sacred is lost, but as a movement which itself might add its own small measure to reality" (*Tablets* 130). How does the sacred arise out of the profane, how does the profane enhance our sense of the sacred? How does this dialectic contribute to our sense of reality? Consider the opening lines of Tablet VIII:

go into all the places you're frightened of
and forget why you came, like the dead

what should I look for?
what should I do? where?
aside from you, great Foosh,
who is my friend? a little stone,
a lot of dirt, a terrible headache
and more than enough worry about my grave. Hogs
will swill and shit on me, men
will abuse me (29)

Part prayer and part *kvetch,* this passage resonates with an existential melancholy worthy of Bellow or Malamud, but supposedly precedes even Job or Eccle-
siastes by many centuries. At the beginning of Tablet VI, we are informed that
"Foosh" is the last in a long list of ridiculous names (including "Sore-Ass-Mole-
Face-Snivel-Kra," "Anxious-Liar-Fart-Flyaway," and "The Porous Poppycock"),
though "we have no information about the identity of the addressee; anger and
ridicule are directed toward some immanent power which keeps changing its
attributes" (25). No wonder then that the speaker in Tablet VIII is so distraught!
From the tone of the address, Foosh is, in all likelihood, some sort of deity, and
there is a note of intimacy in the passage that is reminiscent of a patriarch's or
prophet's speech with God in the Hebrew Scriptures. But if this god's attributes
keep changing, then a sense of uncertainty enters into the life of the speaker,
leaving him with nothing but headaches, worry, and abuse.

It is at such points that one feels the modernity of *The Tablets,* and not
merely in the anxieties of its ancient speakers. "[T]he right words wait in the
stone/they'll discover themselves as you chip away" declares the voice in Tablet
VIII: *writing* becomes the means through which the speaker deals with his worries,
and finding himself "getting stiff" in a "cold place," he composes a poetic curse
("this curse/better work" he cries) to free himself:

> *If you step on me*
> *may your leg become green and gangrenous*
> *and may its heavy flow of filth*
> *stop up your eyes forever, may your face*
> *go to crystal, may your meat be glass*
> *in your throat and your fucking*
> *fail. If you lift your arms in grief*
> *may they never come down and you be known*
> *as Idiot Tree and may you never die* (29–30)

And so it goes for another three stanzas: surely one of the funniest send-ups of "the
primitive" in the entire body of ethnopoetics. Yet just as Rothenberg's treatment of
Jewish folk material conveys a sense of immediate presence and conviction that
goes beyond any historical reconstruction of the material, so too Schwerner's
Sumerian/Akkadian curse (along with the hymns, love songs, plaints, meditations,
and other speech-acts found throughout *The Tablets*) is charged with the urgency
of the fully lived moment, however remote in time. It is a moment when rhetoric
counts, when poetry comes as close as possible to magic in the power it is believed
to hold over reality.

Schwerner does not relegate this sense of the magical to the primitive or the
archaic alone, however, and this is one of *The Tablets'* greatest strengths. In his note
following Tablet VIII, the Scholar/Translator reflects on the course of his work:

> Looking back myself to that first terrific meeting with these ancient poems,
> I can still sense the desire to keep them to myself all the while I was straining
> to produce these translations—desperately pushing to make available what
> I so wanted to keep secret and inviolable. . . . There is a growing ambiguity
> in this work of mine, but I'm not sure where it lies. Some days I do not
> doubt that the ambiguity is inherent in the language of the Tablets them-
> selves; at other times I worry myself sick over the possibility that *I* am the
> variable giving rise to ambiguities. Do I take advantage of the present unsure
> state of scholarly expertise? On occasion it almost seems to me as if I am
> inventing this sequence, and such fantasy sucks me into an abyss of almost
> irretrievable depression, from which only forced and unpleasurable exercises
> in linguistic analysis rescue me. (31–32)

The Scholar/Translator's fantasy is true, of course: not only is the sequence an
invention, but he himself, forced into unpleasurable linguistic exercises, is an
invention as well. Schwerner's metafictional fun with his character is one indica-
tion that the magical power of writing holds even in the realm of "objective"
modern scholarship. Like the scribes and librarians of Kafka and Borges who are
his closest kin, the Scholar/Translator is fanatically devoted to a text that is his
world; the book is the scholar's author, rather than the scholar authoring the book.
The ambiguity that the Scholar/Translator experiences is derived from this intri-
cately folded condition of fiction and reality, creator and creation, past and present, magic and science, original and translation.

   It is this last dichotomy, fundamental to the Scholar/Translator's identity,
that puts such a strain on this figure. The Scholar/Translator regards it as his
responsibility to translate, and thereby "make available" to a general readership, or
at least to other experts in the field, a set of texts that he regards as "secret and
inviolable." By the time we reach Tablet XXVI (subtitled "From the Laboratory
Teachings Memoirs of the Scholar/Translator"), it has dawned on the Scholar/
Translator that "I am involved in process of formation of the canon of this sacred
material" (95). To what extent is he the rational scientist engaged in the objective
study of these artifacts, and to what extent is he an initiate into the sacred truths
that they may contain? At what point does the modern student of the sacred
participate in the practice of the sacred? And given what we have seen of the
Tablets and the world from which they come, where does ritual end and poetry
begin? "I would also call attention," notes the Scholar/Translator, "to the power of
the unsullied literary imagination evident in the texts which are the objects of my
studies, a power generously evident in the work of the so-called scribes, who were
of course redactors, a vector we usually ignore. Thus often the line between
redactor and author is hard to draw" (71). From author to redactor to Scholar/
Translator to Schwerner, the poet himself pulling all the strings: the lines become
increasingly hard to draw, but "the power of the unsullied literary imagination"—
what Rothenberg calls *poesis*—deconstructs the binarisms that structure Sch-

werner's masterpiece. Or as Schwerner observes, "Prose is eloquence, wants to instruct, to convince; wants to produce in the soul of the reader a state of knowledge. Poetry is the producer of joy, its reader participates in the creative act. Thus Commentary and Text in *The Tablets?* (Is that distinction stupid?)" (132).

Despite Schwerner's joking tone, these are not altogether rhetorical questions, for they lead us back to one of the more important—and importantly Jewish—aspects of *The Tablets.* According to Scholem, for the rabbis and scribes, "Revelation needs commentary in order to be rightly understood and applied— this is the far from self-evident religious doctrine out of which grew both the phenomenon of biblical exegesis and the Jewish tradition which it created" (*Messianic Idea* 287). For Scholem, the efforts of "the exploring scholar" or "seeker after truth consists not in having new ideas but rather in subordinating himself to the continuity of the tradition of the divine word and in laying open what he receives from it in the context of his own time. In other words: Not system but *commentary* is the legitimate form through which truth is approached" (*Messianic Idea* 289).

In *The Tablets,* this lofty ideal is both upheld and ironically undercut every time we witness the Scholar/Translator uncover and attempt to interpret the ancient artefacts before him. The uncanny symbiosis of prose and poetry, commentary and text, present and past, that intensifies as the sequence proceeds, indicates that in *The Tablets,* these distinctions exist so as to be subsumed by the maker's art. Yet that art of *poesis,* both original inscription and inventive commentary, seems always to be in crisis. In Tablet XXVI, a figure called "the blind artificer" emerges out of a welter of (computer-generated) pictographs, and we hear one of the most poignant laments to emerge from Schwerner's ancient world:

> When I was young they would praise
> just about all I'd say, as if I breathed
> with them; my times are bad, the past is a joke,
> former admirers hound me, alone and treed
>
> what's left of my ties with them who
> praised anything out of my mouth—my voice
> now that life floors me and they cut
> my best song, seeing what, lies?
>
> what we had together is lost; they praised me once
> for any language at all; I'm now to fall,
> now in my troubles; my merit is my seeing,
> their hate infects my days (90)

"[T]he oracle/turns dunce" (90) says this poet-prophet of himself, but even as he mourns the loss of his visionary power, his lyricism reaches across the millennia, edging *The Tablets* away from satire to an increasingly elegiac register. The powers he represents, the powers his civilization have posited as truths, are perceived to be failing; faced with his apparent death, the process of cultural meaning falls away and a mournful voice declares that "The abyss is a hope/Yawning between mouth and star" (91).

Schwerner understands that the same is true for his contemporaries as well. As he says of his poor Scholar/Translator in a conversation with Willard Gingerich, "The S/T has an inclination towards meaning, but he's got a problem which he avows covertly and indirectly and with pain. He has a suspicion that his inclination towards meaning must find other paths from those he has been given by his own modes of scholarship and research, his own culture, his own theological antecedents. And that's the main problem; that's also the problem of Western civilization . . ." (32). What is remarkable about Schwerner is that he may have found one means of addressing this problem; what is remarkable about ethnopoetics is that it may represent an alternative path.

5

Objectivist Continuities:
Harvey Shapiro, Michael Heller,
Hugh Seidman

One appropriate text with which to begin a discussion of the second generation of Jewish New Yorkers writing in the Objectivist mode is surely Michael Heller's groundbreaking book on the first Objectivist generation, *Conviction's Net of Branches* (1985). As might be expected of an inaugural study of a relatively neglected set of writers, Heller's work does not focus on the specifically Jewish aspects of Objectivism; rather, he places Zukofsky, Reznikoff, Oppen, Carl Rakosi, and Lorine Niedecker in the broader historical and philosophical contexts of modern poetry, thereby arguing for their literary significance. Thus in his chapter on Reznikoff, Heller writes of emphasizing "Reznikoff's importance as a poet rather than as a social documentor of city life, of Jewish life, and so forth" (62), despite the fact that the essential sense of "wonder" in Reznikoff's Objectivist stance "was to embrace the urban experience, in particular its relation to the life of newly immigrant Jews" (59). Reznikoff's poetic is inextricable from his urban and largely Jewish milieu, but even if we momentarily bracket off that milieu and consider some of Heller's general remarks about Objectivism, we shall see the relevance of his analysis to our consideration of this mode as an expression of a specifically Jewish American sensibility.

Some of Heller's most provocative observations involve Objectivism's relation to time, history, and tradition. Throughout this book I have argued that Objectivism reflects the modern Jewish preoccupation with the historicity of experience, a preoccupation which in turn indicates a deep awareness of historical rupture and of a crisis of cultural transmission. Heller writes of Objectivist poetry's "time-bound adeptness. The poet's precise function is in arriving at—not in dictating—some language (the poem) which embodies a skillfulness in apprehending the present" (105). In contrast to modernists like Ezra Pound, who attempt to draw historical lessons based on the assumption that "all ages are contemporaneous," the Objectivists experience history "less like a lesson than a pressure" (104) that shapes their response to the immediacies of their present circumstances, the moment of poetic composition. Furthermore, "what distinguishes Objectivist work is its sensitivity to the spirit of the tradition as a whole, not to any particular instancing of it. . . . The informing elements of a new tradition, its particular 'recencies' [the term comes from Zukofsky], knowledge, a sense of history and the prior traditions of which one is part, are gathered as a unique occasion of work and thought" (101, 102). This is why, as Heller asserts elsewhere in his book, "the impulse behind Objectivist poetics" lies "in creating an art which aspires to complete transmissibility" (30).

What does it mean for an artist to aspire to complete transmissibility, and what, as it were, would the Objectivists transmit? "You are not required to complete the work" says Rabbi Tarfon in the *Aboth,* "but neither are you free to desist from it." Yet the modern poet is no Talmudic sage, and we often think of the poet in the same terms that Walter Benjamin uses to describe the novelist in comparison to the storyteller: cut off from any sense of community or wisdom tradition, the novelist "is the solitary individual, who is no longer able to express himself by giving examples of his most important concerns, is himself uncounseled, and cannot counsel others" (*Illuminations* 87). In Chapter 1, I cited Benjamin's belief that "[t]here is a kind of transmission that is a catastrophe," noting how Reznikoff's serialized, fragmented work is an attempt to "rescue" phenomena from a reified conception of "heritage." However, there is Benjamin's observation that Kafka "sacrificed truth for the sake of clinging to its transmissibility, its haggadic element" (*Illuminations* 144). Transmission involves risk, but it is a risk that must be taken if the work is to continue.

For Heller, whose work is shot through with references to Benjamin and, as we shall see, is deeply haggadic in its own right, it would appear that "complete transmissibility," related to "the spirit of the tradition as a whole," means a particularly temporal awareness. The poet, confronted, more often than not, with the breakdown of tradition, becomes particularly attuned to haggadic possibility, the "unique occasion of work and thought" that presents itself in a moment of clarity. The poem does not present wisdom or truth content in any conventional sense; we are speaking, after all, neither of halakhic law nor even folk custom. Rather, it can only gesture to a certain set of contingent circumstances from which wisdom may possibly be extrapolated.

These circumstances usually consist of what Heller in his poem "Knowledge" calls

This something simpler than metaphor

The world
Which spoke back
In facts, to him(*Wordflow* 24)

The unyielding facticity of the world (one inevitably thinks of Manhattan's glass, concrete, and steel) has always been a crucial reason for the Objectivists' emphasis on immediacy and material detail, their scrupulous avoidance not only of abstraction, but of sweeping, Poundian visions of history as well. What Hugh Seidman names, in a poem set on the E Train, "the hard terrains and facades" (*Collected Poems* 144), are not only simpler than metaphor, but *resist* metaphor. The modern urban world presents itself as something that merely is. The Jewish Objectivists (both first and second generations) emerge into this world from a cultural matrix that has endured the attentuation of tradition, the decay of wisdom, the shocks of immigration and assimilation. If they aspire to a poetry of complete transmissibility, it is the transmissibility of meaning won from what Oppen calls, in *Of Being Numerous,* "the existence of things/An unmanageable pantheon" (148). Oppen's masterpiece, which is our most complex poetic investigation of this "pantheon," raises—and by no means completely answers—the most severe doubts regarding cultural transmissibility:

> Clarity
> In the sense of *transparence*
> I don't mean that much can be explained.
> Clarity in the sense of silence. (162)

The ironic possibility that clarity equals silence, that in the present very little bears explanation, that what we once knew can no longer be communicated or passed down—it is in the face of this possibility that the Objectivist project goes on. And as with the original Objectivists, we find that Jewish attitudes, culture, and textual traditions often help a second generation of poets to uncover, as Oppen would say, "The roots of words/Dim in the subways" (159).

Consider the career of Harvey Shapiro. Born in Chicago in 1924, educated at Yale and Columbia, an Air Force gunner during World War II (his early sequence "Battle Report, revised through a number of his books, is one of the few classic American poems to come from that conflict), Shapiro settled in New York and worked as a journalist, serving for eight years as the editor of the *New York Times Book Review* and eventually becoming a senior editor of the *New York Times Magazine.* A poem such as "Borough Hall," from *The Light Holds* (1984) presents an understated summation of both an aesthetic and a life:

> In Brooklyn I knew Louis Zukofsky
> and George Oppen. I saw the Bridge
> and the Statue of Liberty.
> I had a wife, two sons, a house.
> All this is recounted in my poems.
>
> No horseman will
> pass by my stone.

If I am remembered
let it be
by a young woman on the IRT
getting off at Borough Hall. (34)

This playful jab at "Under Ben Bulben" and its elegiac Romanticism comes relatively late in the game, and is in some respects just as elegiac as the Yeats original. A friend not only of Zukofsky and Oppen but of Reznikoff as well (Shapiro and David Ignatow were the two poets chosen by Marie Syrkin, Reznikoff's widow, to read at Reznikoff's funeral), Shapiro gradually assumes an Objectivist stance, bringing a wry, urbane tone and a practiced eye for detail to numerous poems set in Brooklyn and Manhattan.

As we noted in chapter 1, Shapiro's rhetoric, by 1972, is close enough to that of Reznikoff, Zukofsky, and Oppen to provoke a pointed critique of his work by Harold Bloom in "The Sorrows of American-Jewish Poetry." According to Bloom, Shapiro's poetry "lacks only a language adequate to its genuine and accurate apprehensions of Jewish dilemmas," since "the spareness of this style is rarely adequate to Harvey Shapiro's own intensities" (255). As in the case of Reznikoff, the poet's Jewish sensibility, his understanding of his place in Jewish and American cultural traditions, and his emotional proclivities are all held back, supposedly, by his style. Bloom cites a poem called "The Way" (from *This World* [1971]) as an example of Shapiro's misguided attempt to follow the Objectivist model in dealing with Jewish material; he appreciates its "fine economy," finding it "[s]pare and moving," but nevertheless "laments the attachment of Shapiro to so minimal a modernist tradition" (256).

I have already analyzed Bloom's opposition to Objectivism, and will only add here that ironically, Shapiro's rhetoric, particularly in relation to his Jewish poems, undergoes a number of changes over the years, and cannot at any point be labeled "Objectivist" in any simple sense of the term. His earliest collection, *The Eye* (1953), appears very much the product of the New Criticism. Many of the poems are studied set-pieces; they adopt a reserved tone, make neat use of rhyme and meter, and deal with subjects drawn from high culture, such as Dante's dark wood, a Cellini saltcellar, Nijinsky's dancing. A poem for William Langland, purported author of *Piers Plowman*, addresses him as "the shadow sitting by the tree of sorrow,/Who speaks with Christ's leech upon his chest" (33); another, called "Landscape and Figure-Piece," describes a woman resembling those of Dante, Yeats, and Eliot, who "moves into the garden, and her smile/adorns the perfect habit of the rose" (18). Yet in addition to the first version of the harrowing "Battle Report," we find in *The Eye* another poem which stands apart from the derivative early pieces, a poem which, significantly, Shapiro republishes in a number of his subsequent volumes, including his most recent *Selected Poems* (1997). It is called "Death of a Grandmother," and the woman we meet in it is quite different from any we may encounter in Eliot's rose garden:

My grandmother drank tea, and wailed
As if the Wailing Wall kissed her head
Beside the kitchen window;
While the flaking, green-boxed radio
Retailed in Yiddish song
And heartache all day long. (*Selected* 17)

Among the careful and genteel poems of Shapiro's first volume, this wailing grandmother and her equally wailing Yiddish radio shows come as something of a shock. "To what sweet kingdom do the old Jews go?" exclaims her grandson, suddenly moved to wail as well. The line is as penetrant as "the cry of the gunner" (*Selected* 25) shot from the sky in "Battle Report," for despite his obvious scholarship, it is war and *Yiddishkeit* that the author of *The Eye* knows best.

The "sweet kingdom" to which the old Jews go becomes, in effect, the subject of Shapiro's third collection, *Mountain, Fire, Thornbush* (1961), a book that achieves precisely the "highly colored, biblicizing idiom" that Bloom claims to miss in Shapiro's writing overall. Apropos to the work in this volume is Shapiro's first encounter with Reznikoff's poetry. After coming upon Reznikoff's *Inscriptions: 1944–1956* in the Gotham Bookmart and purchasing it, Shapiro noted that "In the care and precision of those lines, people and objects maintained their own lives, were not just material for rhetoric. . . . Curiously, it was not his poems on Jewish themes that attracted me then. That's because in my own poetry I was trying to use those themes but with a high rhetoric, returning the images to their mythic beginnings. I could not understand Charles' casual way of treating them" ("Remembering Charles Reznikoff" 86). As we shall see, the further Shapiro goes, the more "casual" his treatment of Jewish themes becomes; thus the Jewish poetry with a high rhetoric and mythic imagery to which Shapiro refers is no doubt the poetry of *Mountain, Fire, Thornbush*.

Indeed, the rhetoric of Shapiro's most completely Jewish collection is remarkably similar to that of another largely Jewish volume of poems published in 1961, Grossman's *A Harlot's Hire*, and quite different from that of a third, Ginsberg's *Kaddish*. Nevertheless, as we observed in chapter 3, Shapiro reviewed *Kaddish* with great enthusiam in *Midstream*, and it is worth noting that David Ignatow's review of *Kaddish* in *The New Leader* also considered *Mountain, Fire, Thornbush*. For Ignatow, the difference between the two books is obvious, but he wisely decides that "It is idle to choose between them. The point is that from widely divergent sections of our society two very different poets converge upon the fear, mystery and worship of their one God" (25). Ignatow describes Shapiro's tone as "ruminant, putting one in mind of his acknowledged rabbinical masters. The language is precise yet flowing, the images drawn from history. The vision is penetrant. A studied, controlled calm pervades the whole" (24–25).

What Ignatow intuits about *Mountain, Fire, Thornbush*, especially in comparison to the teeming contemporary world detailed in Ginsberg's *Kaddish*, is that

Shapiro, in turning his imagery back to what he himself calls its "mythic beginnings," is attempting to write a poetry that participates in Jewish thought and
history without being limited to a particular vision of Jewish ethnicity. This is why
I would link Shapiro, at this stage of his career, less with the Objectivists than with
a poet like Grossman. We have seen that Grossman regards *Kaddish* as a work in
which "the poetic identity must supersede the ethnic identity if the poet is to
survive"—a remark I consider more relevant to Grossman in *A Harlot's Hire* than
to Ginsberg. Like Grossman, Shapiro is also "in the process of transcending
parochial limits": unlike the ethnicity of "Death of a Grandmother," we find the
poems of *Mountain, Fire, Thornbush* to be what Grossman would later call "theophoric" or "God-bearing," often returning to biblical and rabbinic origins in
order to understand the power of the Law and the overriding demands of the Holy.

   Two midrashic treatments of the Exodus from Egypt demonstrate these
concerns with particular urgency. The first is simply called "Exodus":

> When they escaped
> They carried a pack of bones
> In a mummy-coffin like an ark.
> Of course they had the pillar
> Of clouds by day and fire by night,
> But those were like dreams
> Or something painted in the sky.
> God was in the bones
> Because Joseph had said,
> God will remember you
> If you take me hence.
> This was before the miracle
> By the sea or the thundering mountain,
> Before the time of thrones
> And cherubim. They were
> Only now being drawn forth
> To eat the history feast
> And begin the journey.
> Why then should they carry history
> Like an ark, and the remembering
> Already begun? (*Selected* 20)

The text reads like a proleptic gloss on the first chapter of *Zakhor,* in which
Yerushalmi writes that in the Hebrew Bible, "the crucial encounter between man
and the divine shifted away from the realm of nature and the cosmos to the plane
of history, conceived now in terms of divine challenge and human response" (8).
Shapiro calls the natural symbols of God's presence "something painted in the
sky," for the true force of divinity is to be found not in nature but history. Thus,

what counts for the Israelites in Shapiro's poem is "a pack of bones/In a mummy coffin like an ark." The bones are those of Joseph, and God is in them because of Joseph's words prior to his death in Egypt: "Yosef had the Sons of Israel swear, saying:/When God takes account, yes, account of you,/bring my bones up from here!" (Genesis 50:25). The key word, repeated twice in the poem, is "remember": God has indeed remembered them, just as they have remembered Him. The coffin, like Noah's Ark in the past, and the Ark of the Tabernacle in the near future ("This was before the miracle/By the sea or the thundering mountain") is a token of that mutual remembrance, God's covenant with humanity, and with the Jews in particular. They must bear this ark though "They were/Only now being drawn forth/To eat the history feast/And begin the journey," the "feast" presumably the unleavened bread that will become the symbol of their liberation. Shapiro casts the last lines in the form of a question, but it is a rhetorical question: the Israelites *must* carry the ark, for despite their many doubts, they intuit that the covenant, the contract of mutual remembrance, will not be broken.

This is why, in the poem "Mountain, Fire, Thornbush," Shapiro declares that "there must be/Narrative." The poem brilliantly condenses the exodus story with its commentary:

> How everything gets tamed.
> The pronominal outcry, as if uttered in ecstasy,
> Is turned to syntax. We are
> Only a step from discursive prose
> When the voice speaks from the thornbush.
> Mountain, fire, and thornbush.
> Supplied only with these, even that aniconic Jew
> Could spell mystery. But there must be
> Narrative. The people must get to the mountain.
> Doors must open and close.
> How to savor the savagery of the Egyptians,
> Who betrayed the names of their gods
> To demons, and tore the hair
> From their godheads
> As lotus blossoms are pulled out of the pool. (*Selected* 19)

Even Moses, "the aniconic Jew" (who by his very nature resists or will not recognize icons or idols), apparently can comprehend the situation in which he finds himself through the visible icons with which he is confronted; thus he can "spell mystery." When he asks the Voice in the burning bush for a name, he hears "The pronominal outcry": *Eyeh Asher Eyeh,* traditionally rendered as "I Am That I Am" or in Everett Fox's recent translation, "I will be-there howsoever I will be-there" (273). Contemplating the difficulty of this "name" (which is actually not a name at all), Fox observes that "the poetics of the phrase indicate both importance and vagueness or mystery." If "knowing the true name of a person or god meant that one could coerce him, or at the very least understand his true essence," then God is "magicless, he is nameless, at least in the conventional sense of religion" (Fox 270). Nevertheless, as Shapiro knows, for the human mind, and for human belief, God's ecstatic utterance of Himself, the infinite force of divine language that is God's Name, must become "syntax," that is, must be put in some kind of limiting order, or "tamed." Likewise, that which is eternal must be bound in time: from divine revelation to religious history is a shift toward "discursive prose" and "narrative." Human discursivity involves cause and effect, the purposeful movement of events in time, as possibilities, like doors, open and close. Yet this movement is informed by divine purpose: "The people must get to the mountain" and the savage Egyptians, with their betrayals and false gods, are left behind.

"Mountain, Fire, Thornbush" is the clearest instance in Shapiro's work of this period of the way in which religious history coincides with linguistic self-consciousness, as if the return to the "mythic beginnings" of Jewish belief is congruent with the equally mythic beginnings of language, both oral and written. "The Talker," drawn "from a midrash," connects Adam's God-given dominion over Creation to his ability to speak, to intuitively name all the creatures that have just come into being. As Shapiro tells the story, God first

> Bade angels say the simple names
> That mark in place each bird and beast.
>
> But they were dumb, as He foretold—
> When man stepped from his shuddering dust
> And lightly tossed the syllables,
> And said his own name, quick as dirt.
> Then angels crept into their spheres,
> And dirt, and bird, and beast were his. (*Selected* 18)

Adam, of course, is made of "dirt," and it is with deep irony that the poet observes how he "tossed the syllables,/And said his own name, quick as dirt," thus taking possession of "dirt, and bird, and beast." "Quick" means both rapid and alive, while dirt and dust are terms associated with mortality. Human language is implicated in the fundamental human condition, the limits of life and death. Adam may name the creatures, but unlike divine language, his speech does not literally bring things into being. As Walter Benjamin says in his meditation on divine and human language, "The infinity of all human language always remains limited and analytical in nature in comparison to the absolutely unlimited and creative infinity of the divine word" (*Reflections* 323). Furthermore, just as the Fall brought death into the world, so too, according to Benjamin, "the Fall marks the birth of the *human word,* in which name no longer lives intact, and which has stepped out of name language, the language of knowledge, from what we may call its own immanent magic, in order to become expressly, as were externally, magic. The word must communicate *something* (other than itself). That is really the Fall of language-mind" (327). Perhaps this is why, at the beginning of the poem, "all the choiring angels cried:/Creation's crown is set awry!" Although they cannot name Creation, in their silence they remain perfect, unlike precocious Adam, who for all his clever speech will be responsible for setting Creation's crown awry. Or as Shapiro puts it in "A Short History," "From the fiery limits of His crown/The brawling letters broke,/In the beginning" (*Selected* 22).

Humanity fares somewhat better in "Aleph," a consideration of written language. The original pictograph is an "Oxhead, working in/The intelligence. First sign,/Alphabet's wedge" (*Selected* 21). Although the letter moves to "Hebrew-Phoenician abstract/And so to Greek," the goal is

> . . . to return to first
> Signs when the world's
> Complex—
> The head of an ox
> Blunt, blundering,
> Withal intelligencer
> Pushing forward, horns raised,
> Stirring the matter
> To make a beginning
> For Amos, Homer,
> And all who came first
> In that sign. (21)

Amos is not the most important of the Hebrew prophets, but he was a herdsman and knew the ox, the thing itself from which the letter came. Inspired by divinity, the primacy of his vivid language is linked, presumably, to that of Homer, first poet of the West. Though the original words of Amos and Homer were spoken, they have since been written down, and written language, clumsy though it may be, is still our "intelligencer/Pushing forward, horns raised." In the *Grammatology*, Derrida elaborates the distinction between the spoken and the written word: "In every case, the voice is closest to the signified, whether it is determined strictly as sense (thought or lived) or more loosely as thing. All signifiers, and first and foremost the written signifier, are derivative with regard to what would wed the voice indissolubly to the mind or to the thought of the signified sense, indeed to the thing itself . . . The written signifier is always technical and representative. It has no constitutive meaning" (11). Nevertheless, in "Aleph," the inscribed signifier assumes lasting power, always "Stirring the matter," always able to take us back to "all who came first/In that sign." As Derrida would have it, "the intelligible face of the sign remains turned toward the word and the face of God. . . . The sign and divinity have the same place and time of birth. The age of the sign is essentially theological" (13–14).

The theological nature of the written sign in Jewish life is the concern of two of the most ambitious poems in *Mountain, Fire, Thornbush,* elaborately rhetorical but urgent works that bring together the themes of history, language, and identity. Both "The Book" and "Feast of the Ram's Horn," stress the human response to the original power of divine language, the way in which Torah, regarded as the word of God, also becomes a binding force of communal identity for the Jewish people over the course of time. This move from the eternal to the historical is evident in the first stanza of "The Book":

> Violent in its blood, the dark book
> Hangs like a tree of night upon the sky.
> It batters history, that genesis,
> Word that whelped a world up,
> While priest and king and all
> Raged at the syntax they were swaddled by. (*Mountain* 13)

The imagery of the first two lines will return at the end of the poem to underscore the human dimension of the divine Word, which comes into being as the book "batters history." Indeed, the book creates history, "that genesis"; it is the ordering "syntax" (the same word used in "Mountain, Fire, Thornbush") that swaddles priest and king and against which they rage. On one level the book is simply metonymic of the parental God who shapes Jewish history through the demands of the law, to which the Jews, more or less obedient, respond. Nevertheless, if the book is associated with divinity, it also passes rapidly into human truth. With the loss of Kingdom and Temple, we move from biblical rage against the Word to rabbinic acceptance, subordination, and interpretation:

> And this is law, or so is said
> Within the darkening synagogue
> By old men, honored in their beards
> By the unsealed, heroic sounds.
> Celebration without end, the dark book
> Whispers to the wind,
> Wind cradles the destructive globe.

As is often observed of Jewish history, law and synagogue replace Kingdom and Temple, as the centralizing tradition of rabbinic interpretation transforms the Jews into the People of the Book. The "old men, honored in their beards" reading the "unsealed, heroic sounds" determine the course of Jewish life in a "Celebration without end." The book "whispers to the wind" which in turn "cradles the destructive globe": no longer battering the Jewish people, the breath of language protects them against the destructive conditions they must endure. Inextricably bound to the book, it becomes, in effect, their life: "What hangs upon the tree is man./With his blood the book is written." These last lines, with their defiant reversal of Christian imagery, confirm the Jews' devotion to the book. Man, not God (or God-Man), hangs from the tree, and given the human sacrifice for the sake of the book, it has come to be inscribed in human blood.

The communal devotion of the Jewish people to the Book is at the heart of one of the grandest of Shapiro's early poems, "Feast of the Ram's Horn," which draws on Genesis 22, the Akedah, or Binding of Isaac (the Torah portion read on the second day of Rosh Ha-Shanah), and on Nehemiah 8, the reading of the Law to the people at the Water Gate by Ezra the Scribe on Rosh Ha-Shanah, after the return from the Babylonian exile. The poem emphasizes devotion and memory rather than judgment; the Jews "Hear the ram-rod summons beat their heels" and gather in the synagogue so the shofar may "Speak for all the living and the dead,/ And tell creation it is memorized" (*Selected* 22). Underlying the text, as we have observed in other poems of this period, is the theme of reciprocal memory—the Jews' memory of God's acts and God's memory of the Jews' response. The acceptance of the Torah at Sinai and the renewal after exile of the people's devotion to the Book at the Water Gate in Jerusalem are commemorated in two stanzas that capture both the historical and the eternal:

> For they are come again to this good turning:
> That from the mountain where their leader goes,
> In ten days' time they greet the Law descending.
> And these are ancient stories from a book
> That circulates, and for them has no ending.
>
> All stand as witness to the great event.
> Ezra, their scribe, before the water gate
> Takes up the book, and the people rise.
> And those who weep upon the word are bid
> To hold their peace because the day is holy. (22)

The book "[t]hat circulates, and for them has no ending" refers to the circularity of the Torah portions read weekly, year after year in the same order, though the "ancient stories" of that book also circulate among the people, passed down through generations. Time is both cyclical and progressive, a sense that is experienced at the moment of the year that is Rosh Ha-Shanah, just as the Jews are a historical people gathered together as one figure, Isaac, whom God remembered and redeemed:

Let Isaac be remembered in the ram
That when the great horn sounds, and all are come,
These who now are gathered as one man
Shall be gathered again. . . . (23)

At no point after this will Shapiro write with such high formality and
unquestioning faith in Jewish tradition. Indeed, in terms of its relation to tradition, *Mountain, Fire, Thornbush* is one of the least agonistic books of Jewish
American poetry, and one of the few that would meet Cynthia Ozick's extravagant
but still relevant definition of "liturgical" Jewish writing: "Liturgy is in command
of the reciprocal moral imagination rather than of the isolated lyrical imagination
. . . Liturgy is also a poem, but it is meant not to have only a private voice. Liturgy
has a choral voice, a communal voice: the echo of the voice of the Lord of History"
(169).

In a recent autobiographical essay, Shapiro makes an observation of particular relevance to the changes in his poetry after *Mountain, Fire, Thornbush*. Considering his bitterness toward "Western culture" in the years following the
Holocaust, he tells us that

There was a period after World War II when I wrote only on Jewish themes
and published only in Jewish magazines and conceived of my audience as
being different from that of other poets. I was making a little ghetto for
myself in the spirit of Jacob Glatstein's poem, "Good Night World." Had
there been in those days a real community for me to join I might well have
stayed in the ghetto. But my ghetto was not real and my audience, such as it
was, and mostly wasn't, was not Jewish. And so I had to enter the dangerous
world.

("Uncreated Identity" 22)

The period to which Shapiro refers is no doubt the period during which he
writes *Mountain, Fire, Thornbush*. Why, one wonders, was there no "real community" for Shapiro to join, despite the deeply Jewish qualities of his work? A
number of possible answers present themselves. Shapiro, unlike Glatshteyn, writes
in English rather than Yiddish: he does not have an audience that is, however
small, Jewish by definition. Furthermore, at that time he is writing a formal and
rather lofty language with obvious connections to the British as well as to the
American poetic traditions; the work is Jewish in theme, but quite English in tone
and structure. In terms of readership, the Jewish American poet may want "a little
ghetto" for himself, but if he is as talented as Shapiro and publishes his work (and
not only, as the acknowledgment pages of his early books indicate, in Jewish
magazines), his audience is bound to include non-Jews as well as Jews. Even the
Jews who would read his poetry could not in any real way constitute a "ghetto,"
since it is mainly assimilated, secular Jews who read poetry of any kind in the first

place. Glatshteyn himself must have intuited this when he wrote his scathing "Good Night, World" in 1938, looking back at the worsening situation in Europe from his vantage point in America:

> Good night, wide world,
> great, stinking world.
> Not you, but I slam the gate.
> With the long gabardine,
> with the yellow patch—burning—
> with proud stride
> I decide—:
> I am going back to the ghetto.
>
> . . .
>
> Back to my kerosene, tallowed shadows,
> eternal October, minute stars,
> to my warped streets and hunchbacked lanterns,
> my worn-out pages of the Prophets,
> my Gemaras, to arduous
> Talmudic debates, to lucent, exegetic Yiddish,
> to Rabbinical Law, to deep-deep meaning, to duty, to what is right.
> World, I walk with joy to the quiet ghetto light. (Glatshteyn 101)

The urgent, even desperate nostalgia of Glatshteyn's poem, his vituperation of the "Prussian pig and hate-filled Pole," the dramatic declaration that "I disown/ my liberation" would certainly appeal to Shapiro, but for both poets, going back to the ghetto, or even a fully observant lifestyle of "Talmudic debates" and "Rabbinical Law," is out of the question. For Glatshteyn, the émigré modernist, the only alternative was to become the American standard-bearer of secular Yiddish culture in a time when that culture was being destroyed in the Old World and disappearing in the New. For Shapiro, a Jewish poet born in America and writing American English, the only alternative is "to enter the dangerous world" of American letters, burdened with the knowledge, as he says in "ABC of Culture," that

> . . . the angel of death whistles Mozart
> (As we knew he would)
> Bicycling amid the smoke of Auschwitz,
> The Jews of Auschwitz,
> In the great museum of Western Art. (*Selected* 28)

Whistling Mozart, Dr. Mengele, the "angel of death" responsible for the *selektions* at Auschwitz, is connected to modern American poetry through the reference to the fascist Pound's *ABC of Reading,* a book that "tutored" Shapiro ("Uncreated Identity" 21), as it did so many other poets of his generation. Both European and American traditions are tainted; as an ideal site of culture, "the great museum of Western Art" is no more acceptable than in the "warped streets and hunchbacked lanterns" of Glatshteyn's beloved ghetto.

The poems such as "ABC of Culture" that appear in *Battle Report* (1966), the book following *Mountain, Fire, Thornbush,* testify to a growing sense of dissatisfaction, of existential doubt and formal disjuncture. The poems grow shorter, more epigrammatic. In their terseness and greater use of free verse (and as Shapiro becomes friends with Oppen, Reznikoff, and Zukofsky), they become more identifiably "Objectivist" in style. Lacking the orderliness and definite closure of the earlier work, they are less confident of their stake in Jewish tradition or history, and much less apt to assume a biblical stance. As Shapiro says in "Purities," "What was ceremonially impure, he knew,/Was his life. The laws were not followed./The god was unhonored./Anxiety sat on every road" (*Selected* 28). But how can the laws be followed? In a fallen world, the poet is fallen, and whether it is intended for a secular or a religious purpose, language itself is in a fallen state too. Thus "The Six Hundred Thousand Letters":

> The day like blank paper
> Being pulled from my typewriter.
> With the six
> Hundred thousand letters of the Law
> Surrounding me,
> Not one of them in place. (*Selected* 30)

The poem refers to the many kabbalistic notions surrounding the mystical textuality of the Torah. In "The Meaning of the Torah in Jewish Mysticism," Scholem recounts the belief held by some kabbalists that the original Torah given to Moses consisted of six hundred thousand letters, corresponding to the six hundred thousand souls of Israel gathered at Sinai to receive the Law. When Moses broke the first set of tablets on seeing the Golden Calf, he had to return for a second Torah, the Torah we have today, with some three hundred forty thousand characters. This "shortened" Torah indicates the fallen condition of Israel and the Law—but like the mystical Torah in Paradise, the Torah of the messianic age will be a fully restored, purely spiritual entity, with each letter again corresponding to one of Israel's holy souls.

Meanwhile, as Shapiro clearly indicates, the writer facing the blank page, facing another day of life, is sure to go wrong. Even so, the poem must be written, however imperfect. "Dumb Adam," from the same period, draws on another kabbalistic belief in an ur-Torah that preexisted Creation, from which God read in letters of black fire on white fire. As in "The Six Hundred Thousand Letters," the poet cannot quite get it right:

I forget. Was it to be
Letters of black fire on white fire
Or letters of white fire on black fire?
But here are the words.
The vines of heart-shaped leaves
Bind the trees
Yet the topmost branches remain free
To receive signals. (*Battle Report* 38)

In its relation to tradition, in its relation to meaning itself, poetry is a binding and an unbinding. The Jewish poet in particular is bound to the Word as "The vines of heart-shaped leaves/Bind the trees"; and as deeply Jewish a poem as this one reminds us of Grossman's crucial formulation: "The Jew's word, strictly speaking, is One (holy, sacred, *Kadosh*), and is unlike all other words in that it does not signify by difference but rather serves the Master who is difference—which is to say, existence itself" (*Long Schoolroom* 162). Yet in that relation, the poet must find the freedom to receive signals, must be unbound at least to the extent that signals from the Outside (as Jack Spicer, that most gnostic of poets, would say) come in and make the poem its own utterance. In "Dumb Adam," Shapiro calls this "The freedom to glide, to coast." In one respect, this freedom is the freedom to forget, a partial forgetting in which tradition is not abandoned, but opened and reworked with productive ambiguity: "Was it to be/Letters of black fire on white fire/Or letters of white fire on black fire?" In addressing "dumb Adam," the poet addresses himself:

Dumb Adam, slow-footed,
You are like the farmers
I pass in their fields;
Your world has vanished.
It is all the wind and water
Of before creation.

Along the night routes
In the brightness of cities,
I read letters of black fire
On white fire.

Adam, as we saw in "The Talker," names Creation, but Creation comes into being before him, and is there waiting to be named. To imagine a vanished and uncreated world, with only *tohu va-vohu* remaining, as at the beginning, is an impossible dream. Adam himself would be dumb, a thing of earth like the farmer in his field; he would hardly exist at all. In the end, the poet must reconcile himself with the Word, which always already precedes him, deriving his creativity from

that great original. At night, the city, the created world Shapiro knows best,
spreads itself before him to be read, a Torah of black fire on white fire, as the poem
is called forth in emulation of the first act of reading and making.

    Shapiro's interest in Jewish mysticism, though not as fundamental to his
poetic as it is to that of Jerome Rothenberg, continues to work its way into the
poems of his next volume, *This World* (1971). If Scholem serves as one of Rothenberg's most important guides, then for Shapiro, as he freely notes, "Martin Buber
has been an influence throughout" (*Contemporary Poets* 771). Shapiro is particularly fond of quoting a hassidic saying found in Buber's Preface to his *Tales of the
Hasidim:* "A story must be told in such a way that it constitutes help in itself" (v).
The forthright practicality of this attitude has undoubtedly shaped Shapiro's
poetic, and coincides with the Objectivist virtues of sincerity of expression and
direct presentation of experience. But there is also a certain magical dimension to
this notion: in the anecdote connected to the saying that Buber recounts in his
Preface, a rabbi whose lame grandfather was a disciple of the Baal Shem Tov tells
that "he related how the holy Baal Shem used to hop and dance while he prayed.
My grandfather rose as he spoke, and as he was so swept away by his story that he
himself began to hop and dance to show how the master had done. From that hour
on he was cured of his lameness. That's the way to tell a story!" (vi). From the Baal
Shem, to the grandfather, to the rabbi, to Buber, to Shapiro: if we ask what is
kabbalah, the answer, as in Shapiro's "A Message from Rabbi Nachman," turns out
to be surprisingly direct:

> Kabbalah—
> A transmission
> From mouth to ear.
> The words of my friend
> Steady my world
> Even as I say them. (*Selected* 40)

The word "kabbalah" is usually translated as "tradition" or "reception"; in this
respect, it is indeed a transmission, a passing down of words that have efficacy, that
bind soul to soul and steady the world. The poem concludes:

> *There are stones—*
> How else will the house
> Be built—
> *Like souls*
> *That are flung down*
> *In the streets.*

    The certainty of tradition or kabbalah is represented in the image of a
spiritual edifice built not of rarefied souls but of common souls, like stones flung

down in the street. If hasidism, as many historians and theologians have argued, results in part from the popularization of the Jewish mystical tradition, then the influence of hasidism on Shapiro is certainly in evidence here. The potential for mystical union with the divine is present throughout mundane existence; it hovers over Shapiro's poetry despite his modern skepticism and the resolutely secular, sometimes even profane attitude of many individual pieces. The popular mysticism of hasidism serves as a kind of spiritual ground bass in the work; one senses it even when the conditions of belief, as is often the case, grow cloudy and obscure. "Kabbalah," a strange poem that begins with what Rothenberg would describe as an alphabet or word event, literally presents the cloudiness of tradition and the struggle to achieve what Shapiro often calls "the Way":

> **K**een **a**s **b**reath
>
> **B**lack **a**s **l**aw
>
> **A**nd **h**eaven
>
> Moving through darkness, clouds,
> And thick darkness.
> Returning through darkness, clouds,
> And thick darkness.
> Some lift up their heels
> And some jump. (*This World* 56)

The word "kabbalah," transformed (in English) into an acronym, opens into ambiguity. Here, the law itself is a kind of darkness; the Way is obscure; and those who persist in the midst of such conditions must "lift up their heels." The image is that of a weirdly comic leap of faith, or perhaps of a hasid dancing ecstatically but still lost in the clouds. That particular sense of religious loss is definitive in Shapiro's poetry. As Walter Benjamin says of Kafka, "His assistants are sextons who have lost their house of prayer, his students are pupils who have lost the Holy Writ" (*Illuminations* 139). Tradition or the Way, however lost or hidden, remains palpable, presents itself as a possibility, despite the poet's skepticism or common sense. Or as Shapiro puts it in "The Argument":

> All right, there are thrones upon thrones.
> There is suffering and redemption.
> There is exile and return.
> But to myself, gripping this pavement?
> Thrones upon thrones.
> You keep placing them there,
> Pyramiding them there

In a golden game.
Art and imagination.
But on this pavement,
In this life, with these eyes? (*This World* 74)

"A middle-aged man," writes Shapiro, "wanders about the city looking for the Way. He seems harassed by the life he leads, but he takes joy in much of what he sees—until he remembers that there is no real joy for the man who cannot figure things out. He could be a Jew" ("Uncreated Identity" 23). In both his poem and this prose statement, Shapiro conducts an argument, tries to "figure things out." With whom does he argue? Himself? Another Jew more sure of his faith? God? It doesn't really matter, for the terms are the same: the limited, limiting certainties of mundane urban life, the typical milieu for millions of American Jews, posed against the enormity of redemptive history, the grandeur of mystical beliefs. In "The Argument," fundamental religious concepts seem to exist in a dimension entirely apart from the ordinary life of the modern (Jewish) man on the street, a figure who is not quite a schlemiehl but is still "gripping the pavement," just hanging on. He is reflective enough to recognize what strikes him as the utter incongruity between the life he leads and his Jewish heritage, which nevertheless imposes itself on him with an uncanny force and immediacy to which he must concede. That concession is heard in the first two words of the poem, that weary sigh of an "All right," against which is raised the "But" of those two lines that invoke the pavement, the obdurate reality to which the Objectivists so often refer. Whoever is arguing with the poet keeps "pyramiding" the items of faith "In a golden game," imposing an Egyptian oppression on the already burdened Jew. Curiously, the phrase "Art and imagination" stands free, a separate line, a separate sentence. Its status, of course, is ambiguous. What role do art and imagination play in this argument? Are they behind the golden game? Is Jewish redemptive history ultimately a humanly authored fiction? Do we read too many miracles into Jewish destiny?

Shapiro's skeptical art, the Objectivist's art of seeing the life of the pavement with one's own eyes, would seem to be opposed to such exalted narratives. His understanding of imagination is closer to William Carlos Williams's definition in that inaugural Objectivist work, *Spring and All* (1923): "To refine, to clarify, to intensify, that eternal moment in which we alone live there is but a single force— the imagination" (89). "[T]hat the particulars/of my life," Shapiro insists, "become manifest/to me walking these dark streets" (*Selected* 75). Yet Shapiro's art, like that of the earlier Objectivists, would not be as compelling without the transcendental horizon from which they cannot turn away for long. Indeed, this Objectivist credo is from a sequence called "A Jerusalem Notebook," and in this instance, the dark streets are not those of New York, capital of the diaspora, but Jerusalem, always the spiritual, if not the political or social center of Jewish being.

The tension between the life of the streets and the life of the spirit is a permanent feature in Shapiro's later work; it continually marks his language, which in turn marks the Way. In Jerusalem, Shapiro tells us,

> . . . it is all
> swept clean, except for
> a faint pink in the sky and on the old
> stones of the city, and language in my head
> that I brought with me, that I carry,
> that I use to mark my way. (*Selected* 74)

The language that the poet has brought with him—a language, not incidentally, of a great diaspora community—marks the poet's way in the world, even in Jerusalem. And it also marks the Way, which Bloom, even in his critique of Shapiro, notes "is *halakhah* or right conduct, based on the Mishnaic word meaning 'to walk.' . . . Shapiro laments the universality of the departure from halakhah, as far away in Israel as in America" ("Sorrows" 255–56). But what is truly remarkable about Shapiro's work, as in Reznikoff's and the work of the first generation of Jewish Objectivists in general, is not only that the Way is lost, but that it is found again under what would appear to be the least likely circumstances. Yet even discovering the Way, or rediscovering it, at most leads, as we saw in Reznikoff's case, to a messianic waiting, a kind of patience that is definitive of the Jewish condition but seems at times to be too much to bear. Consider "47th Street":

> In the delicatessen
> The countermen
> Were bantering about the messiah,
> Lifting the mounds of corned beef
> And tongue. He wouldn't come,
> They said, you couldn't
> Count on it. Meaning:
> They would die in harness. (*Selected* 54)

If Shapiro turns such fundamental religious categories into Jewish jokes, it is not because he takes them any less seriously in his later, more casual poems than he did in his earlier, more rhetorically elaborate ones. Aggadic legends recount that in the days of the messiah, the righteous will feast on the flesh of Leviathan and Behemoth, but for the time being, these countermen, unlikely participants in traditional messianic speculation, must labor to provide the corned beef and tongue for the sandwiches of their fellow New Yorkers. You can count on these countermen to make your lunch, but they themselves cannot count on the coming of the messiah. The colloquial speech and ironic attitude of such figures recur constantly in Shapiro's poems, even when they shift from a secular to a religious locale, as in "In the Synagogue":

> The new year. Five thousand what?
> God's deliberate flatness
> In his scrolls, with touches of
> Megalomania and song. (*Lauds & Nightsounds* 63)

It takes a good deal of chutzpah to characterize God's (or J's) style in the Torah as one of "deliberate flatness" "with touches of/Megalomania and song," but it's a fairly accurate description too. In the year "Five thousand what?" the Jews ought to know that style well enough, as well as the quirky personality of their God as depicted in his scrolls. For nearly five thousand eight hundred years, they have taken his megalomania seriously and honored his commandments, knowing full well the consequences of disobedience.

  "Jews, departure from the law/Is equivalent to death," cries Shapiro in his darkly ironic Yom Kippur poem "Riding Westward." The title plays off against John Donne's "Goodfriday, 1613. Riding Westward," in which the poet contemplates the Easter paradoxes of east and west, of sunrise and sunset, and of Christ's life and death:

> Hence is't, that I am carried towards the West
> This day, when my Soules forme bends toward the East.
> There I should see a Sunne, by rising set,
> And by that setting endlesse day beget;
> But that Christ on this Crosse, did rise and fall,
> Sinne had eternally benighted all. (Donne 307)

By contrast, "Riding Westward" depicts Shapiro, among other "crazy Jews," "on the road,/Finished with fasting and high on prayer." With services over, he is on the Long Island Expressway, heading for the cemetary on "Utopia Parkway/Where my father lies at the end of his road." However irreverent his tone, Shapiro cannot escape his awareness of a brooding, divine judge and His grim, angelic servant overhead:

> . . . Cemetaries
> Break against the City like seas,
> A white froth of tombstones
> Or like schools of herring, still desperate
> To escape the angel of death.
> Entering the City, you have to say
> Memorial prayers as he slides overhead

> Looking something like my father approaching
> The Ark as the gates close on the Day of Atonement
> Here in the car and in Queens and in Brooklyn. (*Lauds & Nightsounds* 6)

For the Jewish Shapiro as opposed to the Christian Donne, death is no illusion or paradox; it bears a kind of finality that religious faith must help him accept. Thus the image of the Angel of Death is folded into that of the dead father, which is folded in turn into the image of the Ark closing at the end of the final Yom Kippur service, and of the heavenly gates closing as the Day of Atonement ends, allowing no more prayers to ascend to the Throne. In short, what Shapiro is addressing in this poem is the notion of *closure* both in human and divine terms. On Rosh HaShanah the fate of every individual is decided and on Yom Kippur it is sealed. The father is literally "at the end of his road" (even if that road is named Utopia Parkway!); his fate has been determined, as will be that of his son, and thus in the figural and psychic economy of the text, he becomes the trope of death and judgment, "sliding overhead."

The verb itself is revealing, for figures and frames of reference slide in this poem, as if the concern for our ethical choices under the pressure of mortality causes both verbal compression and verbal instability. We see this again in a one-line poem called "Poets & Comics": "To make a little noise before death" (*Lauds & Nightsounds* 85). Poets and comics are metonymically condensed here because they both take it upon themselves to speak, to make a little noise and affirm their being against death's inevitability. Theirs is an ethical choice; they choose life, as Jews are instructed to do in Deuteronomy 30:19, a verse that is never far from Shapiro's thoughts. And in the recent poem "Prague," images slide again in the face of the most horrific moment of death in all of Jewish history:

> The Gothic half-light
> in which moulder
> the stones of the Jewish cemetary,
> a tumbling mass of stones
> crowded on each other
> like the cadavers in the camps,
> so that you keep sliding out
> of one picture into the other.
>
> 'The world is a narrow bridge,'
> said Rabbi Nachman,
> 'the important thing
> is not to be afraid.' (*Selected* 97)

If the world through which we must make our way is a narrow bridge, then what we find on all sides of us is the abyss, as the images in the first stanza of the poem make all too clear. From Nachman's eighteenth to Hitler's twentieth century, that bridge, for the Jews, became increasingly narrow. "They have been driven insane by history,/my tribe" declares Shapiro in "Loyalty," "They are totally crazy." Shapiro refers to the contemporary situation of the Jews in Israel and the United States, but at the same time reminds himself that

> God can forsake them, whenever.
> Hasn't He?
> He has the option.
> I don't. (*Selected* 91)

The flat language of assertion in this poem indicates just how far Shapiro has moved from the rhetoric of his earlier work, and the degree to which he has absorbed the lessons of the earlier Objectivists. Casual, forthright, and decidedly American, Shapiro has found an enduring poetic means of dealing with Jewish history. And yet his understanding of language is also profoundly Jewish, as we see in "Ancient Days":

> Great things had happened.
> They felt called upon
> To bear witness.
> The words, in themselves,
> Became events. (*Lauds & Nightsongs* 80)

Shapiro knows that the biblical Hebrew *davhar* is both word and thing. Words, in themselves, do become events; God speaks and acts; the Jewish prophets bear witness and their testimony likewise take on the power of the deed. And so, by implication, the poet's words become events, when great (and even small) things occur.

The frequent haggadic occasions that we find throughout Shapiro's work prove that what Michael Heller calls the Objectivist concern for "complete trans-missibility" remains a vital force in recent Jewish American poetry. And as with Shapiro, Heller himself exemplifies this uncanny vitality in the face of cultural discontinuity. Drawing on the historical dialectics of Walter Benjamin, who calls for the historian "to brush history against the grain" (*Illuminations* 257), Heller searches for what he calls "countercontinuities": "that is, a notion of poetry in which one sought to bring a meaning to a poem that could directly war with other existing meanings, not procedures that out-foxed meanings or went somewhere else or even invented their meaning, but rather one that was always in relationship to a kind of prior order of experience" (Foster, "Interview" 50). Heller originally develops this notion as part of his powerful critique of the contemporary avant-garde formation known as language poetry, which attempts to radically decenter the subject and challenge conventional practices of representation through various methods of verbal discontinuity. What happens, asks Heller, "when the literary work attempts to free itself from historical time and historical beings who make utterances in speaking and writing?" ("Avant-Garde Propellants" 23). The answer: "The artist no longer works on the edge of being but at the margins of form where novelizing the object and specialization of skills take precedence over feeling or thought or sentiment" ("Avant-Garde Propellants" 8).

The concern expressed here for maintaining the historicity of literary discourse, an agonistic but feeling relationship to "a prior order of experience," indicates how, in a figure like Michael Heller, the thought and attitudes of the Objectivists and of Walter Benjamin coincide. "Oppen and Benjamin," Heller observes, "have similar resonances in my mind in the sense of the project of the poet and the difficulty of that project, as well as, of course, Benjamin's tremendous ambivalence about his Jewishness and his ambivalent, though professed, faith in Marxism. All of these were very pregnant issues as I was trying to think my way into poetry" (Gardner, "Interview" 308). Benjamin, the scion of a highly cultured German Jewish family, was deeply committed to an apocalyptic messianism that was both Jewish and Marxist in nature, and engaged in avant-garde writing practices meant to challenge normative habits of reading and thought. Like Benjamin, George Oppen, the poet who probably has had the greatest influence on Heller, also came from an assimilated, well-to-do family; he began as an avant-garde poet influenced by Ezra Pound, gave up literature to work as a Communist Party operative, and returned to poetry after a long hiatus, producing dialetically honed work that was both a critique and an endorsement of populist politics and experimental writing. (Zukofsky and Reznikoff, as we have noted, were more working class and originally less assimilated; they were variously engaged with leftist politics, but did not commit themselves to anywhere near the same degree as Oppen.) As Heller declares in his poem "For Uncle Nat":

> . . . Not to make
> Too much of it, but I know history
> Stamps and restamps the Jew; our ways
> Are rife with only momentary deliverance. (*Wordflow* 89)

Heller is not merely addressing his personal antecedents here, for history has also stamped and restamped those writers closest to the heart of his project. Traditional observance, bourgeois assimilation, leftist activism, avant-garde poetics: through the vicissitudes of history, all provide only momentary deliverance, though the desire for such deliverance never ceases. According to Heller, in the Objectivist poem (and, I think he would add, the work of writers like Benjamin), "one enters a temporality which bears history's burdens." Such writing is "communicative, intersubjective, in that it wishes to entangle its reader in its momentary convictions (*Conviction's Net* 6). Momentary deliverance, momentary convictions: such moments seem to suffice.

The value that Heller places on writing of this sort makes a great deal of sense, considering his background and early work. Indeed, there is something almost paradigmatic to the course of Heller's career; it is another tale of Jewish transformations, historical stamping and restamping. Heller was born in Brooklyn in 1937. His paternal great-grandfather, David, was a revered rabbi in the Polish city of Bialystock; David's son Zalman, also a rabbi, emigrated to the United States in 1911 and settled with his family in the Williamsburg section of Brooklyn. Heller's father Philip (later Peter) was a businessman; his mother Martha, née Rosenthal, was a schoolteacher until a heart condition led to her early retirement. It was for this reason also that the family moved to Miami Beach in 1943, where Heller spent most of his childhood and teenage years. Originally trained as an engineer (he received a B.S. from Rensselaer in 1959), Heller first worked as a technical writer and gradually turned to literature in his twenties, living for a year and half in a Spanish village during the mid-1960s and returning to New York to begin a second career as a poet, critic, and teacher at New York University's American Language Institute.

Heller's first volume of poetry, *Accidental Center* (1972) is a work in dialogue not with the Jewish past, but with the scientific present and the rationalistic discourses in which he was originally trained—what he calls, in a statement on the book's cover, "these later gods." The objectivity of science and technology, as appealing as it might be in its epistemological power, is regarded as insufficient: although it reveals us to be, as he says in the poem "Madness," "isolate particles/ suspended in our fates and faiths" (73), Heller still tries, according to his statement, "to pose something *as language* which gives more force to a human argument of the world." These concerns already align Heller with an Objectivist aesthetic, especially that of Oppen, as can be seen in the first poem of *Accidental Center,* called "In the Difficulties":

    in the difficulties of the rough seas
    of the passage—for that
    is what it was—a thing to be endured,
    but for the beauty of the powerful lunges
    of the dolphins seen
    from the deck, a wildness
    in the seas, as wild as seas &
    natural, as we knew
    ourselves not
    in the blindered shuttered salon (*Wordflow* 1)

The modern poet must master two techniques in order to make thought count: the measure of the line (look at Heller's enjambments) and the placement of the image (note the appearance of the dolphins, and then the "blindered shuttered salon"). The repetition of "seas" and the strategic punctuation make sure the center of the poem works as tightly as its margins. Here is the remainder of the text:

> as the heart jumped
> when the rose
> & its fluted vase
> fell to the table
> after an untoward roll
>   —untoward as the steel meaning
> unbending of the ship's prow
> or the rock's entrapment
> against which, a wild sea
> & wild dolphins . . .
>   kinship
> & miscalculation

To an even greater extent than the first generation of modernists, the Objectivists learned that in presenting a given experience, the whole need not be equal to the sum of its parts. Find the right tonal key, and abbreviation could take you as far as you might want to go. In a seemingly modest reflexive poem about the difficulties of a passage, phrases such as "untoward roll" and "steel meaning" gather surprising emotional intensities to themselves. The ellipsis, followed by the last lines, enjambed and spaced just so, implicate the reader in a rhetoric made of risk and trust in equal measure.

But it is in his next book, *Knowledge* (1979), that the "human argument" that Hellers works to preserve in *Accidental Center,* takes a Jewish turn. In this volume, the power of language as a means of transmissibility is fully recognized; as Heller observes in "Objurgations," "whether the word is found/Or finds us, it is inserted in history" (*Wordflow* 52). And in an extraordinary sequence of poems called "Bialystock Stanzas," it is Heller's Jewish word that is inserted into Jewish history. Occasioned by Heller's visit to New York's Bialystoker Center, where the poet went in search of information about his grandparents, "Bialystock Stanzas" embodies the delicacy and horror, the precarious comfort and certain doom of European Jewry. At the Center, Heller was shown a book of photographs from the town; hence the subtitle "*from a book of old pictures.*" As he reports, "I'd look in this book and write poems about each of these things. It was a way of holding my heritage somewhat at arm's length and yet dealing with some of the most difficult things about Jewish history—the Holocaust, for instance" (Gardner, "Interview"

304). Thus, in "Bialystock Stanzas," we view these pictures through two lenses, that of the photographer and that of the next generation, the American generation, the fortunate children of those who got away. Impossibly, perhaps thankfully remote, the poet still tries to get as close as he can:

> Light—
> The scene filled with photographer's light
>
> The sparsely furnished room
> In the corner of which
> A china-closet Ark
>
> The old men
> Under green shaded bulbs
> Reading *Torah*
>
> The prayers are simple,
> To what they think larger
> Than themselves
> —the place almost bare,
> Utterly plain
>
> The flat white light
> Adds no increment
> But attention (*Wordflow* 26)

"A photograph," writes Susan Sontag, "is both a pseudo-presence and a token of absence. Like a wood fire in a room, photographs—especially those of people, of distant landscapes and faraway cities, of the vanished past—are incitements to reverie" (16). In this respect, the pathos of the Objectivist poem is close to the pathos of the photograph. But in "Bialystock Stanzas," reverie (and nostalgia, its close attendant) is implicitly understood as the inevitable violation of a historical space, a psychic zone that can maintain its dignity only in the medium of mute memory. The photograph having been taken, reverie follows its course, which leads, sooner or later, to poetry. And poetry, in order to maintain *its* dignity, must restrain itself as much as possible, so that like the photographer's "flat white light," it "adds no increment/But attention."

Nevertheless, that attention to detail illuminates a lost world: thus the poet acknowledges his responsibility to the circumstances from which his poems arise. In confronting the photograph, Heller is reminded that his experience is an extension of his people's experience, and yet is incommensurate with what has gone before. The scrupulous language maintains the transmissibility of culture and faith, but the ruptures of emigration, assimilation, and genocide that largely constitute modern Jewish history are felt as a kind of palpable absence in the text, transforming it into a vessel filled only with the light of attention. Like the old men reading Torah, or, as in the following poem, at prayer, Heller devoutly attends to the past, however distant he may be:

> The old bind with phylacteries
> between the leather turns
> The pinched flesh bulges, the old
> Skin, the hairs burn
>
> As if to do this is also
> For the pain
> —to explain
> To Him of what it is
> They are made
>
> Thus, why they fail (29)

Heller speaks to the Jewish past as the Jew in his phylacteries speaks to God. The admission of failure in both cases is inevitable, but the *mitzvah*, the command-ment that is also a good deed, has been performed. Humility achieves authority despite itself; inadequacy proves greater than any accomplishment. Recall the name of the volume from which "Bialystock Stanzas" comes: *Knowledge,* from which may be derived, the poet ironically observes in the title poem, "something simpler than metaphor." For Heller, knowledge is the experience of the negative, of lack, of emptiness, of "Toys and an ache" (*Wordflow* 24). In this respect, he follows Benjamin's interpretation of Kafka: "To do justice to the figure of Kafka in its purity and its peculiar beauty one must never lose sight of one thing: it is the purity and beauty of a failure" (*Illuminations* 144–45).

The recognition of this "failure" (and it is a "failure" that is to be found throughout modern Jewish literature) may be said to abolish the conventional distinction between the practice of justice and the practice of art, between ethics and aesthetics. According to Heller, "the incarnated sounding of the thought (poetry) abolishes the dichotomies imposed by the separation of the individual from the knowledge of which he is the instrument. Here we can see that Zukofsky's definition of poetry as a 'rested totality' is an act of reaching, a 'desire for an inclusive object,' as he says in 'An Objective,' which signals and even at times abolishes the disposition of rhetorical forces between humans and their institutions. In this lies poetry's ethical dimension" (*Conviction's Net* 31). The abolition of dichotomies in the rested totality of the poem, the way in which the achievement of form synthesizes the "I" as knower and the "I" that is known, explains Heller's (and the other Objectivists') ceaseless attempts to both follow and go beyond the limits of perception, in a practice that participates, in effect, in both the aesthetic and the ethical.

Yet there are moments that prove nearly too much for such a poetic practice,
and for the Jewish poet, as we have seen before, those moments are found at the
brink of annihilation. The section of "Bialystock Stanzas" called "Terrible Pictures" is divided into smaller units simply labeled by the page number of the book
of photographs. Thus "*Page 153*":

Grimly
They lie closely packed
Upon each other
In the mass grave

Looking now
Like figures of saints
Carved across cathedral doors

—but beyond image or irony,
The empty wrongness.
Here, all death
Was made untimely (*Wordflow* 33)

To a poet dedicated to the practice of attention, what lies on the far side of image
and irony? An "empty wrongness," or perhaps a horrified religious silence. Heller
does not go quite so far; rather, looking at the next few photographs he simply
repeats their captions, such as "died in the ghetto" or "fell in battle . . . 1944" or
"killed . . ." (34). As he explains, "I realized I couldn't even describe the pictures: I
just put the captions in. It would be trading on someone's terrible misery to start
describing those pictures. I wanted to respect that distance" (Gardner, "Interview"
304). Finding his own voice again when facing the last photo of a burnt synagogue, and contemplating the mass executions in Bialystock, Heller concludes
"Words can add nothing/That flame itself was without a light" (35).

Against the dark flame of destruction is posed the light of attention; the
former swallowing speech, the latter illuminating it, sometimes with an almost
equally frightening power. The penultimate poem in the Bialystock sequence,
"From the Zohar," captures the apocalyptic intensity of Jewish mysticism in a
moment when "The lights, in unity, are merged/Illumined world/in which above
and below/Are blessed" (36). Yet that moment is endlessly deferred. Instead, the
last section of "Bialystocker Stanzas" is given over to Heller's grandfather under the
title "Senile Jew":

One God. One boiled egg.
Thirty *dy-yanus,* and the Paradise
Not yet given a number.

Eight nights, eight lights.
Which break the dark
Like a cat's wink.

I think the boot is not gone—
Whose boot? I ask
Do you wear the boot?
Or does he who wears the boot
Wear you?

Coat of my pain, cloth
Of pain, winding sheet of
My horror. Just a rag,
Just a *shmata*. You
Are not my pain, not you.
My pain is me: I am the Jew. (37)

Dy-yanu ("it would suffice us") is the refrain sung at the Passover seder
during the recitation of the miracles God performed for the Jews during the
Exodus, while the eight nights and eight lights refer to the candles lit during
Hannukah to commemorate the miracle of the oil in the Menorah of the Temple
after the Maccabees' victory. But for all the marvelous events of Jewish history
woven into the fabric of the present through repeated religious celebration, it is
still the Nazi boot and the "cloth/Of pain" that prove the most memorable. Age
and suffering turn Heller's "senile Jew" into a prophet for whom "One boiled egg"
is as significant as the "One God." As Yerushalmi points out, Jewish belief holds
that God's miracles create a history that is a continuous, lived present. In the
Passover Haggadah, we read that "In every generation, one must look upon
himself as if he personally had come out of Egypt, as the Bible says: 'And thou shalt
tell thy son on that day, saying, it is because of that which the Eternal did for me
that I went forth from Egypt.'" But perhaps the horror lives on as well: "Do you
wear the boot?/Or does he who wears the boot/Wear you?"

These questions, followed by the resigned yet strangely proud last line ("My
pain is me: I am the Jew") indicate why Objectivist procedures such as Heller's,
despite their nearly obsessive sense of tact, their implacable decorum, still prove so
serviceable when the Jewish American poet must confront the worst in modern
history. Heller admits that before he wrote the poem, his grandfather "was often a
problem to me. I didn't want to be around him." A poem of this sort provides "a
way you learn to relate to people, learn to take uncertainty as a given rather than
wanting to change it or force it to be other than what it is. That in itself allows that
relationship to exist" (Gardner, "Interview" 303). This lesson, which Heller
teaches himself through the attention he pays to his literary models and to the
experiences out of which his own poems arise, continues in a set of poems in his

next volume, *In the Builded Place* (1989). This set deals mainly with what Heller calls, in his wry prose poem "Some Anthropology," "my lost tribe of Jews, American Jews." Heller compares his tribe to the Tasaday, members of a native culture whose "false primitiveness and naïveté" may actually have been a hoax by Ferdinand Marcos of the Philippines to fool visiting anthropologists. American Jews are likewise, "part hoax and part invention, whose preserve is sheltered under brick where limousines hum and one hears the faint, familiar babble of the homeless." "Strange, then," comments Heller, "the anthropology of the poet, who must build his poems out of the myths he intends to falsify" (*Wordflow* 86).

"*No Myths* might be the Objectivist motto" (*A Homemade World* 187), says Hugh Kenner in one of the first considerations of the Objectivists. But rejecting myths (so fundamental to precursors like Eliot and Pound) is quite a different matter from intending to falsify myths. In this respect, Heller's Jewish poems take us back to our discussion in chapter 1 on the relation of Objectivism to Judaism in Reznikoff's work. A Jewish poet who chooses to address Jewish history inevitably must deal with the enduring, mythologizing force of remembrance, a force that often creates religious narratives that are at odds with history in the more modern, objective sense of the term. Furthermore, Objectivism, however one may define the term, is committed to what is, not the mythic but the real: no myths, Kenner goes on to explain, because "Myths stand between facts and words" (187). The contradictory or dialectical tension between the two perspectives that we identified in Reznikoff's poetry appears to be operating in Heller's statement as well. Heller's Jewish "anthropology" depends on a mythic view of history, yet as an Objectivist, his treatment of that mythic history is bound to "falsify" or demystify it. In his secular modernity, he cannot fully participate in the mythic narrative of remembrance—but he cannot reject it completely, for it is too basic a part of his identity.

This dialectical tension may be seen in a pair of poems about Heller's grandfather Zalman, "The American Jewish Clock" and "In a Dark Time." The first poem opens with the grandson's bemused questions:

> When did Solomon (for Zalman) Heller, my grand-
> father, come here, his time folded into America
> like honey layered in middle-European pastry?
>
> When did he arrive? After his pogroms and wars,
> And before my father's. Was he naive? To arrive
> like an autocrat, to enter like a king, in the train
>
> of minor victories. Zalman, here called Solomon!
> With a new syllable to lengthen his name. In the vast
> benumbed space of us, a little more sound to place him. (*Wordflow* 87)

Zalman becomes Solomon; the *pintele Yid* taking on added dimensions, even a kind of borrowed grandeur, as he enters the new world. The myth of immigration, of America as the *goldener medina,* cannot be denied, despite the poet's skepticism. "He had been brought into redeeming time," declares grandson of grandfather, "each stroke the echo of his unappearing God." The stroke of what Heller half-jokingly calls the American Jewish clock, measures the time that, from his perspective at least, is both mythic and historical—from the struggles of "those Twenties and Thirties, when profit/turned to loss, and loss to profit," on to the postwar years "when the synagogues swelled/with increase and were tethered like calves/on suburban lawns." The mock-biblical description cannot altogether hide Heller's admiration for Jewish accomplishment in America, his desire to accept the myth of America's virtually redemptive promise to his people. Perhaps that "unappearing God" has manifested Himself after all. Yet Heller is also among those of the following American generation, who came of age in the rebellious Sixties: "the young walked out, walked back/to the cities, prodigals of emptied memory." And here too we sense Heller's ambivalence: those prodigals might be seeking new identities by leaving their secure suburbs for the cities their parents left, but with emptied memory, they have abandoned the founding commandment of their ancestors: *zakhor.*

The poem comes to no definite resolution, though the issue of memory certainly takes on a more grim tone in the companion piece, "In a Dark Time, On His Grandfather." Here, in the light of disastrous events, remembrance appears to bring only bitterness, while religious faith and devotion to tradition seem beside the point:

> There's little sense of your life
> Left now. In Cracow and Bialystock, no carcass
> To rise, to become a golem. In the ground
>
> The matted hair of the dead is a mockery
> Of the living root. Everyone who faces
> Jerusalem is turned back, turned back.
>
> It was not a question of happiness
> Nor that the Laws failed, only
> That the holy or sad remains within. (*Wordflow* 88)

"Only that historian," writes Benjamin, as it becomes clear to him that he would not escape the Gestapo, "will have the gift of fanning the spark of hope in the past who is firmly convinced that *even the dead* will not be safe from the enemy if he wins" (*Illuminations* 255). In Heller's poem, it is as if this terrible prophecy has somehow come true despite the Nazis' defeat. Those Jews who left Europe before the Holocaust; who, like Zalman, reached a safe haven, maintained their faith; and who even managed to prosper after all they had endured—those Jews represent, to their children and grandchildren, the irrevocable end of a more genuine way of life. The devout Zalman was the purported author of a lost religious work called *The Just Man and the Righteous Way.* Heller alludes to this work in the last lines of the poem, implying that with the passing of his grandfather's generation, Jewish cultural and religious traditions will find "no issue" in the new world:

> . . . My father
> Never spoke of your death,
>
> The seed of his death, as his death
> To come became the seed, etc. . . . Grandfather,
> What to say to you who cannot hear?
>
> The just man and the righteous way
> Wither in the ground. No issue,
> No issue answers back this earth.

This proves, however, to be only part of the story. For most Jews of Heller's generation, the old ways may be gone, but they are neither forgotten nor is their creative potential truly lost. Heller's "For Uncle Nat," which, as we have observed, is one of the poet's clearest articulations of modern American Jewry's relation to its past, develops this theme in terms of religious practice, ethnicity, genetics, and language. The first two stanzas recount how Heller, "walking down 20th Street with a friend," is approached by a member of Congregation Zichron Moshe: "May I,"/He says to my companion, "borrow this/Jewish gentleman for a moment?" (*Wordflow* 89). The secular Jew has been "borrowed" by a small group of his more observant coreligionists to make up a *minyan,* to "stand as one among the necessary ten"—not an uncommon event in some neighborhoods of New York. Through this act, Heller is called on to obey the commandment *zakhor*—remember—as part of a congregation named *Zichron Moshe,* the memory or remembrance of Moses, who brought the Law to the Jews. Having agreed to participate in the service, Heller watches as the Ark is opened, "an unfolded/ Promissory note," for the Torah remains God's gift and promise:

> The braided cloth, the silver mounted
> On the scrolls, even the green of the palm
> Fronds placed about the room, such hope
> Which breaks against my unbeliever's life.

Yet this is not quite a moment of *teshuvah,* return or repentance, in the traditional sense. The anecdote proves to be prelude to Heller's revision of his

Jewish heritage; the service, with its *minyan* and ark, a paradigm drawn from the tradition which the poet will rewrite. If, as in "In a Dark Time," there appears to be "no issue" from the ground of European Jewry, then the American experience still produces an unexpected turn in the course of Jewish history. Appropriately, it is Uncle Nat himself that requests the poem: "My uncle was turning eighty or eight-five, and he said, 'Michael, you're a poet and you've never written a poem about me. How about writing a poem for my birthday?' We would always meet. . . . And yet there was some kind of powerful thing going on there between us that had very little to do with this broken record of a conversation: a kind of sacred space for ritual that the synagogue fills at the beginning of the poem" (Gardner, "Interview" 306).

And so, still the unbeliever, Heller addresses his uncle in the last stanza. Family resemblances, the habits of ethnicity, and above all, history's power to both preserve and transform Jewish linguistic expression all combine to produce some of Heller's most resonant lines:

> So I ask, Nat, may I borrow you, for a moment,
> To make a necessary two? Last time we lunched,
> Enclaved in a deli, in the dim light, I saw
> A bit of my father's face in yours. Not to make
> Too much of it, but I know history
> Stamps and restamps the Jew; our ways
> Are rife with only momentary deliverance.
> May I borrow you for a moment, Nat. We'll celebrate
> By twos, the world's an Ark. We'll talk in slant,
> American accent to code the hidden language of the Word. (*Wordflow* 89)

For Heller, "The operative word is 'code' . . . The hidden language, of course, is the Adamic language we'd all like to write. . . . Perhaps it would take two Jews with an accent to arrive at this code" (Gardner, "Interview" 305–306). Thus, the deli replaces the synagogue, spoken American English is heard instead of chanted Hebrew, a minyan need only be a Jewish I and Thou, the entire world becomes an ark to house the Word—and poetry, reaching toward the kabbalistic *Ursprache,* bears the promise of deliverance.

Heller's concern for that *Ursprache* means that, however strongly American linguistic circumstances may bear on his work, he will always turn back toward Europe, and the linguistic circumstances of European Jewry, for an equal measure of poetic inspiration. "Europe was your father/who cast you on the path,/hungry, into constellated cities" (*Knowledge* 68), writes Heller in "Constellations of Waking," his poem on the suicide of Walter Benjamin. It is in Benjamin's essay "On Language as Such and On the Language of Man," as well as in the kabbalistic research of Gershom Scholem, that Heller finds the notion of an Adamic language. He learns, as we have seen in regard to Shapiro's poetry too, that after the

Fall, "The word must communicate *something* (other than itself). That is really the Fall of language-mind" (*Reflections* 327). Benjamin wished to write a book consisting wholly of quotations, a book that was, so to speak, authorless, free of the mark of human subjectivity, and perhaps in this respect closer to the Adamic language. Heller alludes to this in his poem:

> So to consider
> as ultimate work
>
> that sea bed of
> all citation—
> you'd allow nothing of your own—
>
> thus the perfected volume.
> No author?
> And then no death?
>
> The sea inscribed
> with *The Prayer*
> *for the Dead.* . . . (69)

Death, of course, inscribes both the life and the text; citation is always a partial act, an ineluctably human gesture of an I toward a Thou, and thus the text is always written under the sign of the fallen language-mind. A more recent poem about Paul Celan, another great figure who emerges from the linguistic matrix of European Jewry, invokes what Heller calls

> Omnivore language,
> syntax of the real, riddling over matter,
>
> more difficult to ken
> than the talmudic *angelus*. . . . (*Wordflow* 107)

It is an apt description of Celan's poetry (and for that matter, Benjamin's prose), a vision of language contoured to the twists and turns of history but always conscious of its own gaps and silences, lacunae that measure the distance between itself and the impossible idea of verbal immanence. The impacted lyricism of Celan's post-Holocaust German bears the mark of numerous languages, including French, Russian, English, Romanian, Yiddish, and Hebrew. "What sets one free/ within the sign and blesses the wordflow//without barrier?" asks Heller. Celan, in the next lines, provides an answer: "*Not literature, which is only for those//at home in the world/*while air is trapped in the sealed vessel." In "The Meridian," the speech Celan gave when he received the Büchner Prize in 1960, the poet urges "'a radical calling into question of art . . . to which all present-day literature must return.' The reason for this questioning 'lies in the air—in the air that we have to breathe'" (Feldstiner 165). The extremity of the artist's situation in the twentieth century impels this radical interrogation, this reconsideration of the value of "art" in the face of the most urgent social conditions. In this respect, Celan is remarkably similar to Heller's mentor George Oppen, who writes throughout his career (and especially in *Of Being Numerous*) of how dubious the category of art may be under the volatile conditions of modernity.

The Jewish writer in particular is aware of this instability, which expresses itself as both a desperate need for utterance, however impeded it may be, and the equally strong need to avoid lapsing into the easy solaces of the merely aesthetic. In another recent poem, "In Paris," "the bomb at Boulevard/St. Michel" and "the slaughtered diners at Goldenberg's in the Marais" (*Wordflow* 119) remind Heller that to be a Jew today in one of the capitals of modernity remains fraught with danger. Paris, for Heller, is "the City of Light/where hope was stifled once between *le mot juste* and *le mot juif.*" Flaubert's *mot juste* stands as one of the earliest ancestors of the Objectivist attitude toward language. But far older is *le mot juif.* Heller knows that he cannot reconcile these competing verbal and existential modes, but in its austere refusals and sudden revelations, his work never fails to take them both into account.

Le mot juste, le mot juif. The antimony that Heller posits between the two terms could apply equally well to the poetry of his friend Hugh Seidman, who at first glance would appear to be an unlikely candidate for election as a major Jewish American poet. To be sure, Seidman writes with the edginess often associated with an urban Jewish milieu, and over the years, his poems have become increasingly concerned with the family romance, that most famously guilt-ridden Jewish subject. But despite occasional references, he rarely addresses matters of Jewish identity, culture, or history head on. The author of five books, including, most recently, his *Selected Poems* (1995), Seidman published his first volume, *Collecting Evidence* (1970) in the Yale Younger Poets series, and went on to garner praise from figures as diverse as Adrienne Rich, Robert Creeley, W. S. Merwin, and Stanley Kunitz. But despite these solid credentials, Seidman is probably underread: a poet's poet, his poise, timing, and condensed diction are bound to appeal more to his colleagues than to today's poetry audience, which usually reaches for easier classifications of identity and style, including, I suppose, that of Jewish American poet.

But then, the same could also be said of his mentor, Louis Zukofsky, with whom Seidman studied at Brooklyn Polytech. Apropos of *let mot juste,* from Zukofsky, Seidman learned that "[t]he economy of presentation in writing is a reassertion of faith that the combined letters—the words—are absolute symbols for objects, states, interrelations, thoughts about them. If not, why use words— new or old?" (*Prepositions* 14). This passage, from the inaugural essay of Objectivism, Zukofsky's "An Objective" (1931), hovers over a crucial statement about poetry that appears on the back cover of Seidman's fourth book, *People Live, They Have Lives* (1992):

> Do these poems struggle? driven to the language that cannot change a life— until it does. Or as might be said: poetry doesn't care about us.
>   At the same time, the syntactical object interests endlessly. At first an almost believable order. Then, one sees (hears) that it fails. The transparent now opaque—like the centipede who cannot walk for thinking on its legs.

This statement (which goes on to equally remarkable insights) reflects an invaluable Zukofskian teaching about language: poets must have faith that "the syntactical object" actually has something to do with their lives—though they also know that it doesn't. The fascinating struggle for verbal economy likewise may become an object of faith—until the "almost believable order" one achieves fails. Why use words indeed? Seidman's response to his teacher: "Silence will not do, though not the worst solution and an obvious temptation."

As one would suspect, Seidman writes tough, even fierce poems that are perfectly willing to accept the inevitable failures of art and life. "Your son bows his head in reverence for failure" (*SP* 182), he declares in a sequence about his senile mother. The work has a "let's face it" tone and hides none of the compassion and bitterness of a New Yorker who has spent a lifetime observing the gradual disintegration of urban culture, that same culture that the first-generation Objectivists presented in such precise detail. An early poem, "Affair," sounds like Reznikoff or Oppen in a particularly bleak mood:

> The black pigeon straggles under the parked car
> I feel the pain of the cracked wings
> I reach to it but it hides near the wheel
>
> Later I see the bloody and headless
> Half-body of a pigeon lying in the street
>
> The ease of such comparison persists
> We struggle to survive these sentiments (*SP* 29)

The last lines indicate that even as an apprentice, Seidman recognizes one of the necessary limits of the Objectivist project: through a process of comparison, these snapshots of the world, poems as objects made out of other objects, ennoble (to use Oppen's term) what would otherwise be mere, hardly permissible sentiments. Given the inherent austerity of any variety of modernism, the patent inadequacy of individual feelings to the high demands of art means that the "affair" of the poem must involve something else, some other object. In Zukofsky's formulation, sincerity is admirable, but objectification is the greater goal of the poem. But the patent inadequacy of that other object—red wheelbarrow, saw horse, dead pigeon, you name it—is just as acutely understood. Caught between a reduced subject and an equally reduced object, "We struggle to survive these sentiments."

What makes the struggle particularly difficult for Seidman, and what makes him, however problematically, into a centrally Jewish poet, is the remote, brooding presence of that which is neither self nor world, neither subject nor object, the figure of judgment who calls him into utterance, named in the title of Seidman's second book: *Blood Lord.* Although Seidman is not a religious poet in any conventional sense, he is always aware, as he says in another early piece, of "How the Lord of Death came to lay his moist finger at my throat." Here is the rest of this prophetic fragment, which is called, appropriately, only "Poem":

> I went to the fork of the streets
> But the distances were different and had lengthened
> I heard the voices behind me as I ran
> And awoke to the leaves which were the wind
> Insane with tiredness and distant from myself
> And how I awakened beside you years ago
> To fend away your touch turning in half sleep
> For the loss of love does not cease in this world (*SP* 33)

Like a modern Jonah, Seidman tells us that "I heard the voices behind me as I ran." And as Harold Bloom would surely observe, the leaves in the wind, a trope for poetic prophecy that comes from Shelley via Wallace Stevens, is a sure sign of Seidman's uncanny election. When the Lord of Death fingers the poet, neither the material world nor the world of human relations are any longer adequate. The poem breaks off on a note of desolate resignation: "For the loss of love does not cease in this world."

The entrance of this "Lord of Death" results in poems that are a dying into utterance, premised on the ongoing experience of loss, and the demand—indeed, the commandment—to speak out of that loss. Over the course of his career, Seidman moves between unflinching realism and nightmarish phantasmagoria, though never with a loss of Objectivist precision. His condensed strength of architecture, syntax, and diction mark him as a master of lyric form. Together, the poems become an accumulative litany of minor tragedies and horrors, however mundane each item in that litany may sound. "[T]hese things are indelible" (*SP* 62) Seidman declares in a poem from *Blood Lord* that bears the phrase "Death, Which Is" as both title and refrain. "Lord/I begged you to break me of bitterness" he cries in "The Artists," another poem in that volume, in which images of a slaughterhouse, an artist's studio, and perhaps a concentration camp are conflated to express the terror of his calling:

I see how the blade slides
the punctured skin
I know the pleasure
of the dipped brush
the certainty that one is clear
that all must pay
but I swear
death there was not yours
and the stones were being
hammered to believe (*SP* 75)

But it is not until Seidman's third volume, *Throne/Falcon/Eye* (1982) that the poet is sufficiently hammered into belief so that he is truly broken of his bitterness. It is in this collection that Seidman comes upon a mythos of sufficient power and resonance to provide him with the means to broaden his struggle beyond the self to include family and community. References to myths from various cultures appear with some frequency in this book, but of greatest importance is the story of the Hebrews in Egypt and all that it symbolizes: exile, captivity, liberation, redemption. In a handful of extraordinary poems, we may infer a complex dance of analogies: the Hebrews are held captive in Egypt as people's lives are held captive by the degrading powers of modernity and as the family is held captive by emotional stress, economic instability, disease, and mortality. The texts are dominated by Egyptian deities and religious practices, while the actual story of the exodus remains in the background. Seidman is obsessed with exile and enslavement, while freedom and redemption are but remote possibilities. The respect, duty and love of the individual for the community and of the son for the parents are constantly challenged: like Israel in Egypt, both beaten and seduced by an alien people and foreign gods, the poet can barely keep his faith. No Moses, he usually represents himself as a Jew who has forgotten the Lord of his people, alternately brutalized and seduced into the worship of corrupt but deified rulers and a pantheon of gods and goddesses, half-human, half-animal. Here are the opening stanzas of "Concubine," from the sequence called "Cult of Isis":

How much is enough to pay or too much
or not enough, sphinx:
fur in the alley at Thebes, forget
the ascetic Aton sun

The eye is etched black at the brow
of gold below the jeweled scorpion
or the aquiline nostril
is offered in profile

As under the gallery's fluorescents
her edge of face talc
glints like a scar

Sleek deco cat guardian:
the immaculate oiled under tindery silk
she who has set the snake on Pharaoh's head
and bloomed the sand's
revenge and dismemberment
from the ennui of mud (*SP* 97)

As we noted in chapter 2, in regard to Zukofsky's comments on Reznikoff, Aton (or Aten), god of the sun, is the deity that the pharaoh Akhenaton imposed on the Egyptians, leading to what some scholars believe was one the first versions of monotheism. Freud appropriates this notion in his uncanny "historical novel," *Moses and Monotheism,* in which he transforms Moses into an Egyptian trying to bring a belief in one God to the recalcitrant and ultimately murderous Hebrews. The ambivalent speaker in Seidman's poem turns from the ascetic, severe father-god to the sensuality of Isis, the "Great Mother" (*SP* 97), the primal force of savage nature that brought forth the Egyptian kingdom out of the flooded Nile, "the ennui of mud." But despite the sexual lure of the concubine-goddess, the poet is still appalled by the idolatrous worship of her followers "in their lust and rage/ before that insensible stone" (*SP* 98).

Like so many other Jewish American writers, Seidman is capable of exploiting his religious and cultural ambivalence, compounded with filial responsibility and guilt, to great effect. "For I was the circumcised as if drugged before the heat of the mouth of/the Gentile combing her gold hair at the floors and floors of the city" he declares in "Hymn," a poem in which fragments of Egyptian myth are swirled wildly among images of the family romance, "because Israel had always wandered and warred as the idolaters/of the cow head in the desert on the pillar" (*SP* 131). Here, the poet tells us,

I saw in the dark the hawk head at the head of my
         father the engineer
who had courted with the gilt-edged Victorian sonnets
         in leather
like the equations of a war that was never to be won between
         a man and a woman (*SP* 130)

The erotic drive that founds the family takes on mythic proportions, as the courting father is revealed to be the hawked-headed solar deity Horus, child of the primal couple, Isis and Osiris. In turn, the poem ends with an early sexual experience of the son, the poet himself, with "the fourteen year old with oiled pubic hair/in Brooklyn in a yellow sweater/luminous as the blue double of Pharaoh the *ka* in the dark when I touched her" (*SP* 134). In Egyptian belief, the *ka* is the double or detached self of an individual that guides one's destiny and with whom one is united after death. To reach toward the desired other is to reach toward deified kingship, but to reach into the realm of death as well.

Seidman's transformation of the living Jewish family in Brooklyn into a pantheon of dead Egyptian gods is one of the most uncanny rhetorical gestures in recent Jewish American literature. The son in the throes of the oedipal complex often fantasizes "the replacement of both parents or of the father alone by grander people." According to Freud,

> these new and aristocratic parents are equipped with attributes that are derived entirely from real recollections of the actual and humble ones . . . Indeed the whole effort of replacing the real father by a superior one is only an expression of the child's longing for the happy, vanished days when his father seemed to him the noblest and strongest of men and his mother the dearest and loveliest of women. He is turning away from the father he knows to-day to the father in whom he believed in the earlier years of childhood; and his phantasy is no more than the expression of a regret that those happy days are gone. (300)

Seidman gives the Freudian model an additional twist. Jewish parents take on the characteristics of the gods and rulers of a people regarded as one of the first great oppressors of Israel. Mother and father become as remote from themselves as possible while still maintaining their "actual and humble" characteristics.

Thus, in "The Front," a poem about early childhood during World War II, we learn that "a son/must be healthy/wealthier than a Jew skeleton," so his mother feeds him "raw milk, vitamins/and his wheat bread, every day/and the broiled meat" (*SP* 117). Weirdly conflating the voice of child and man, Seidman continues:

> She knows he will eat
> or it is quick, quick to bed
> to make no noise that might wake
> a father and mother
> while they lie dead (*SP* 118)

Like the figures of Isis, Osiris, and Horus on the Egyptian stele, a photograph of which appears on the original paperback edition of *Throne/Falcon/Eye*, father, mother and son are posed hieratically in their beds. The son innocently aspires to solar godhood: "But listen, O listen/he beamed only to be their sun/their bright one." Like Horus, he will be "mother's hero/in the old bad world," for it is the hawk-headed god who revenges his parents after Osiris is dismembered by his brother Set. But the child's oedipal anxieties inevitably arise as he lies in his tomblike bed:

> And how old is he
> as old as the dead?
> or the fur chubby teddy
> he cuddles to sleep
> or the yellow-soft rabbit who creeps
> O bunny
> will they broil *you?*

The macabre image of the broiled stuffed toy chimes with the lean meat that the mother serves, the threat of the father lying "dead" with the mother, and the "Jew skeleton" of the Holocaust that the son must not become. In effect, the ritual entombment of the son and the threat against his "yellow-soft rabbit" is the price he pays for misbehavior "in the bad old world." This misbehavior is at least partly sexual: put to bed, the boy has "naughty hands taught/where they are not to be." The poem moves resignedly toward loss and exile: we hear the "father coo/don't cry don't cry/we hear you through the stone/our sonny who plays alone/so sad he can't come home" (*SP* 119).

For Israel in Egypt, there is no home, of course; that home has yet to come into being. Seidman takes on this issue in "Out of Egypt," and the result in this extraordinary poem is both deeply moving and deeply ambiguous. The piece is divided into three brief sections: "Promised Land," "Exodus," and "Pharaoh," which in effect reverses the order of the biblical narrative, and ironically undercuts the poem's title. Here is Seidman's "Promised Land":

> So had not the *Testament* said
> that my people ate no bread in the desert
> and were given the Commandments
>
> And at the Fifty-ninth Street station of the Express
> the old Jew pretzel man blames each man
> and smokes at the DO NOT SMOKE sign
>
> And surely the poor are not free
> yet had I not thought obsessed
> that he too thinks he shall profit—nonetheless (*SP* 126)

Like Zukofsky and Reznikoff before him, Seidman uses oddly placed rhyme to lyrically tease the past from the New York Jewish present. But the reined-in bitterness here is pure Seidman. New York is no promised land, even to what remains of the old immigrant generation. The Jews in the desert ate no bread and received the Commandments, but in Manhattan the old Jew sells pretzels, disregards the law, and thinks of profit. Is this a free man or a slave? I just suggested that the order of the poem's sections reverses the biblical narrative, but perhaps New York is actually Egypt, where the Jews still labor underground, among immensities of stone.

If this is the case, how then are we to judge the poet as Moses, given this "Exodus":

> Skull-capped boys talking ball scores
> black beards in black overcoats and fedoras
> among Italians, Ukrainians, Chinese
>
> Where the B train bolts Brooklyn
> where a dark-eyed fidgety girl blurts though no car comes:
> *Mister, Mister, cross me, Mister*
>
> Amazed, I am she decades back, but daughter
> what first-born stranger to Israel
> still leads you before the Gentile (*SP* 126–127)

In an ethnically mixed Brooklyn neighborhood, the Hasidim are indifferent to the girl's plight. We cannot tell if she is Jewish or not; in either case, of course, these ultra-Orthodox Jews could not take her hand, and it is left to the secular poet, who is, presumably, that "first-born stranger to Israel," to take her across the street. Her plaintive cry evokes a powerful childhood memory for Seidman, but what role does he now play? Is he Moses, as reluctant as in the past, leading a remnant of his people across a Brooklyn version of the Red Sea? Or does this "stranger to Israel" lead her "before the Gentile" as a captive still? In either case, the poem is suffused with aching guilt, which propels Seidman into "Pharaoh," the last section of the poem:

> In Flatbush at the tarred-over trolley tracks
> I went back to the doors of many dreams
> though I could decipher no bell
>
> Nor remember no night nor dream
> where in a photo I sleep with my bear
> where my parents sleep and breathe
>
> But I had pitched pennies
> traded baseball cards, played stickball, hoarded marbles
> where Turner Place was vast dirt and weeds

Just as under Ocean Parkway in the sealed tunnel
my teddy, my bed, my broom-handle bat
wait to bear me through the underworld (*SP* 127)

As in "The Front," we have returned to the primal scene of the family in bed, as
the parents "sleep and breathe," and the child, after playing in the vacant lot that
has since been developed, is once again transformed into an entombed god-king.
The trolley bell tolls like a death-knell as the poet is led "back to the doors of many
dreams," finding himself with his teddy, bed, and broom-handle bat, the objects
that will accompany him into the underworld, "under Ocean Parkway in the
sealed tunnel." Fleeing a life fraught with oedipal and cultural anxieties, the poet is
ironically apotheosized. In short, what this weirdly comic dream-vision tells us is
that the only way a modern, secular Jew can be brought "out of Egypt" is to
become Egyptian. And yet, confronted with the pathos of the pretzel man and the
girl crossing the street, it is only this "pharaoh"— like Moses, the "Egyptian"
prince—who feels compassion for his downtrodden people.

Thus, Seidman's appropriations of biblical narrative and Egyptian myth are
uncanny psychic defenses against the disintegration of a people, a family, a self.
But the poems in *Throne/Falcon/Eye* and subsequent volumes that carry less myth-
ological armor are also blasted memorials to the Jewish soul's struggle from slavery
to freedom. Due to the very cultural, religious, and psychological ambivalence that
makes Seidman's work so troubled and compelling in the first place, they are
remarkably free of sentimentality, yet still reveal the depths of Seidman's
compassion.

"Kaddish" (which Seidman curiously chose not to republish in his *Selected
Poems*) is one of the poet's most direct and painful explorations of the boundaries
of secular Jewish identity. According to Allen Grossman, "the *kaddish* functions to
effect the restoration of the created world after its diminishing by death by
reestablishing and also overcoming the difference between God and man as in the
creation. But the *kaddish* also aggregates death to the severe rationality of the
sanctification of the name ('sanctified be his great name') that is at once holiness—
the right order of the world—and martyrdom, the gathering of all being into the
one sign, the name, which is the shadow of his wings" (*Long Schoolroom* 185–86).
Seidman's kaddish poses one of the most important questions to be found in
modern Jewish poetry: in the absence of normative belief and observance, how can
being be gathered and sanctified? How can one effect restoration (*tikkun*) of the
created world, especially after the experience of loss, when the source of creation,
the name, is likewise held in doubt or understood as an absence? And in more
personal terms, how can one cope with a lingering sense of Jewish responsibility
when one cannot avow Jewishness with any confidence? "Kaddish" is less an
answer to these questions than an existential cry, an expression of heartfelt grief
and indignation over the fact that such questions must be posed at the moment
when loss is most acute:

O TORAH TORAH TORAH
downtown but uptown
and in gold on black bronze and lead:
This Obelisk Shall Outlast

O Dream Dream Dream
yet I fasted not nor atoned
I made no tabernacle
on Tish'a Be'ab with Solomon

O Mitzvah Mitzvah Mitzvah
I faked the Hebrew
I the circumcised
stubborn as the metal

O Life Life Life
I yelled to the *mohel*'s knife
I bewailed myself
like any for the dead (*Throne* 56)

For whom is this kaddish recited? In a few years, Seidman will write
movingly of the illness and death of his parents, but I would speculate that this text
is to be chanted in memoriam to Seidman's Jewish self. The structure and terms of
the piece indicate that the poet has endured a disastrous falling away from Jewish
practices and beliefs: he cannot mourn the loss of Solomon's Temple on Tish'a
Be'ab; he "faked the Hebrew" at his Bar Mitzvah; he is as "stubborn as the metal"
of the *mohel*'s knife that circumcises him; and though he cries "O Life Life Life"
like an eight-day-old boy at the thought of that initiating event, he simultaneously
bewails himself "like any for the dead." Each quatrain begins with a fundamental
term, ritualistically repeated three times, while the subsequent three lines undercut
its primal force.

Yet however these terms are ironized or negated, they still possess the poet's
psyche, defining an identity that is not merely historical, but tribal in the most
archaic sense:

O Jew Jew Jew
of God's pagan blood
I was a man in a blue suit
suede shoes and gold ring

O Israel Israel Israel
though I had no tribe
and my parents lay
under the bronze and lead

O TORAH TORAH TORAH
uptown but downtown
but O father, O mother
who would mourn Zion if you were dead (*Throne* 56–57)

Though he may claim to have no tribe, Seidman still clings to the figures of his parents not merely as his immediate forebears, but as representatives of the people Israel, bound to God through the Torah and the "pagan" covenant of blood. The reference to blood leads back to both nationhood and circumcision, vexed Jewish notions in the modern world. In their essay on circumcision and headcovering, "Self-Exposure as Theory: The Double Mark of the Male Jew," Jonathan and Daniel Boyarin observe "that an acceptance of the mark of circumcision and all of the involuntary connections that it implies place a Jewish male into a 'dreamtime' or . . . 'totemic time' and outside the progressive time of modern self-making." For the Boyarins, "it is worthwhile focusing at least briefly on Jewish circumcision as a 'tribal rite'—a scary one, more consequent and disturbing than ethnic foods, for instance—persisting within the heart of the enlightened, civilized world" (39). This notion is presented even more vividly by Philip Roth at the end of *The Counterlife*, when Nathan Zuckerman tells his pregnant wife, Maria, that the disturbingly "tribal" aspect of circumcision is "what the Jews had in mind and what makes the act seem quintessentially Jewish and the mark of their reality. Circumcision makes it clear as can be that you are here and not there, that you are out and not in—also that you're mine and not theirs. There is no way around it: you enter history through my history and me" (323). Seidman's Jew, the modern "man in a blue suit/suede shoes and gold ring" who yet bears the mark of the covenant on his flesh, who denies and affirms his tribal identity, and who mourns and celebrates Zion, is likewise a figure in a "dream time." The rites that are performed on him and that he performs deny the existentially irresponsible freedom of modern self-making and insist on the conditional, historicized nature of the individual. In the Jew, for all his modern ambivalence, tribal dream and historical reality coincide.

The power of this reality manifests itself with remarkably little ambiguity in "On TV." In this deeply moving poem, which demonstrates how carefully Seidman has studied Zukofsky's dialectic of sincerity and objectification, the poet responds to a TV report on a Holocaust survivor, a woman who "had been nude before the SS/so devout she fasted on Tish'a Be'ab/and refused bread on Pesach" (*SP* 124). For Seidman, the documentary is an occasion to continue the Jews' ancient argument with God:

I mean: I think God had guilt
when she worked to cremate
the suicides, the starved, the ill

I mean: she survived thus
for three years for love of God
who commands: endure

She who *would not forget*
though she live as long as God
one like any who outlives him

She who now prays to Solomon's God
twenty-five centuries old in Jerusalem
and who now plants the olive (*SP* 124–125)

In effect, this Holocaust survivor visiting Israel is more faithful to the
covenant that God made with the Jews than God Himself. She *"would not
forget"*—which is to say she *remembers,* in a way that, during the Shoah, God failed
to do. Once again we are reminded of Yerushalmi, who explains in *Zakhor* that the
collective memory of the Jewish people, which this woman shares, comes into
being through God's intervention in Jewish history. In biblical Judaism, "the
crucial encounter between man and the divine shifted away from the realm of
nature and the cosmos to the plane of history, conceived now in terms of divine
challenge and human response" (8). This fundamental notion, involving faith,
nationhood, and above all, the responsibility of memory, remains at the heart of
Jewish identity to this day. Like nearly all the other Jewish writers under discussion
in this book, Seidman is yet another of those "fallen Jews" for whom "history, not
a sacred text, becomes the arbiter of Judaism" (86). The testimony he offers in the
face of the woman who kept the *mitzvah* of memory after the most devastating
event in Jewish history, a woman "who now prays to Solomon's God/twenty-five
centuries old in Jerusalem/and who now plants the olive" indicates that in the
wake of historical rupture, he respects but cannot enter into the kind of Jewish
experience that is governed by traditional faith. Yet the sense of an ongoing Jewish
history remains crucial for Seidman; like poetry itself, it is a source of wonder and
doubt, resulting in an art that chastises as much as it nourishes. "I don't know why
we believe," he declares; "[a]nd I don't know why so many suffer/in this world,
though I know that this poem/has no right to name them" (*SP* 140–141). The
poem offers no redemption, for Seidman is too skeptical, if not of language itself
than of the ways we use language, of what he calls in the title of this poem, "The
Great Ego of the Words." Seidman is determined to avoid that ego; thus, what
goes unnamed in his poems manifests itself through substitution, ellipsis, implication, and absence.

But despite the hermeneutical play or circulation of tropes that these terms
imply, Seidman, as I have implied, is on one important level an *iconic* poet, who,
in the light of the Second Commandment, risks transgression at every turn. The
cat figures and hawk-headed deities in his Egyptian poems, the stuffed animals

and stickball bats ritually transformed into tomb objects, are graven images set into the text to propitiate or ward off psychic demons. And if, as Geoffrey Hartman notes in his essay on the Jewish imagination, the Second Commandment was "formulated in the context of religions with animal and astral gods" (452), what are we to make of "Mr. Bear":

> Mr. Bear stares wistfully at the lovers
> Lover's brown, stuffed toy animal.
>
> His close-set eyes seem wistful to the lovers,
> Who think of the woods of Mr. and Mrs. Bear.
>
> And Mr. Bear yields his silence to the lovers,
> Like a secret to each at the ear.
>
> Yes, the lovers are clarified after love
> By Mr. Bear in his beneficence.
>
> And they hold Mr. Bear in their arms,
> And the electricity sparks off his coat.
>
> And Mr. Bear outpours the ions of bear,
> Charged with the volts of the lovers.
>
> And Mr. Bear is the ancient philosophical bear
> Before the Great and the Little Bear.
>
> Though the bloody paw and muzzle
> Lurk always at the force of the lovers.
>
> But now Mr. Bear triumphs in beneficence:
> Greatest dipper shining over the lovers. (*SP* 137–138)

Love as cloying sentiment, as animal violence, as philosophical instigation, as astral motion: Mr. Bear carries us into the world of the lovers, and in doing so, grows increasingly in psychic stature. As an icon, his worship is the lovers' worship, as Mr. Bear gathers to himself all of the qualities of the lovers' career. The poem, with the stuffed toy at its center, *idolizes* the lovers. Indeed, in opposition to the Second Commandment, the poem itself is an idol; we go the poem to celebrate the glory of human love and its cosmic implications.

Hartman speculates that in Jewish tradition, the prohibition against graven images may "have channeled imaginative energies into writing, into graphic rather than graven forms" (453). Recalling Erich Auerbach's distinction between biblical and Homeric narrative, he notes that the former creates "a hermeneutic rather than iconic—pictorially clarified—space" (465). The distinction between the hermeneutic and the iconic certainly holds for lyric utterance as well as narrative, and in Seidman's case (and, I would argue, for many other modern Jewish writers), the tension between the two modes can be a risky but powerful incitement. In her critique of Harold Bloom's theory of poetic influence, Cynthia Ozick cleverly argues that Bloom transforms poetry into a decidedly un-Jewish mode of idolatry, a closed aesthetic system that is ahistorical and ultimately "indifferent to the world and to humanity" (*Art & Ardor* 189). But as Ozick herself recognizes, "if there *can* be such a chimera as a 'Jewish writer,' it must be the kind of sphinx or gryphon (part one thing, part another) Bloom himself is, sometimes purifying like Abraham, more often conjuring like Terach, and always knowing that the two are icily, elegiacally at war" (198).

In the most compelling Jewish literature, this struggle between icon-maker and iconoclast results in a dialectical play that remains, as we have seen, strongly conscious of history. In Seidman's uncanny poem "14 First Sentences," we confront what appears to be a series, perhaps even a random series, of iconic moments:

> He had never kept a journal.
> Sometimes he wanted to write prose about first love.
> Once he heard Auden lecture: Don't falsify history.
> He used to feel better if people in novels were rich.
> Williams wrote: Old woman, all this was for you.
> He was going to type: The form of a life changes little.
> Reich said the Eskimos say: Don't thwart a child.
> Zukofsky taught: The poet makes one long poem.
> Mathematicians say: Notation is notion.
> The dream voice said: Imagination fails the dream.
> He read in the paper: the poor, mired in poverty.
> Sometimes he remembered the books forgotten in libraries.
> Do we sleep only because night falls?
> How shall one speak how another suffers? (*SP* 143)

In their isolation from each other, the individual names, circumstances, and observations in these lines could indicate a condition of existential fragmentation. The self-referentiality of such momentary experiences thwarts any attempt to understand the psychic wholeness of the subject and its place in the meaningful process of history. The realization of each instant is never to be carried forward; it stands in a "pictorially clarified," self-sufficient space, constituting the first line of a poem that cannot be written.

Or can it be? To be sure, each of these lines could be the beginning of an extraordinary poem. Arguably, each in turn proposes an interpretive challenge to the reader, who must hermeneutically "complete" the text, much as the midrashist will expand on a biblical verse in order to explain apparent discrepancies or discontinuities of Scripture. Seidman's "Scripture" here is not Torah, but rather an ideal notion of Poetry toward which he and all other poets strive, symbolized by the number fourteen, the number of lines in the sonnet, that most tightly unified of forms, which the present poem cannot become. The lesson of Zukofsky, that "The poet makes one long poem" likewise points toward this ideal, but we also hear a "dream voice" saying that "Imagination fails the dream." Ours is a history of failure, of poverty, suffering, forgetfulness, and falsification. Be that as it may, the poet's responsibility remains that of the rememberer, who must suggest, even if he cannot elaborate, the form of a life in history.

This brings us finally to "Icon," one of Seidman's most moving poems of familial and cultural memory. The poem quietly takes on the greatest icon in western culture, that of the cross, against which Seidman poses a highly charged object of his own, introduced in the first quatrains:

> My father's photo in his dark-stained frame:
> eight-pointed, etched star
> at each notched vertex.
> Boys High wood shop, circa 1920.
>
> Teenage, old-master matrix
> inferred from Poland's
> martyrs above the candles
> before he sailed here at six. (*SP* 174)

Note the rhymes and off-rhymes on the *x* sound in "etched," "vertex," "matrix," and "six." These sounds, which will return at the end of the poem, emphasize the contested notion of the iconic cross. In both of the books in which the poem appears, a small sketch of the crossed picture frame appears above the title, indicating the importance of the high school shop project to the memory-work of the text. This "Object of meticulousness," which the poet's father made "for his meticulous, seamstress mother," comes to the poet as a "gift from Aunt Florence the day/Uncle Nat's granite is unveiled" (*SP* 174–175), tying generations together on an occasion specifically intended for acts of memory. The crafted object is, in this case, not in the least self-sufficient, and though it houses a human image, it is by no means "pictorially clarified." Rather, this icon is an instigation to the hermeneutic process of memory, a process in which psyche and language become increasingly intertwined:

> The Rabbi raised the cloth.
> *Stone not stone but love of unknowable God.*
> I nodded; I heard.
> I wept but raged at a photo.

No son could do less.
Fists pressed to the eyes.
Puzzle of meticulous light closed to nothingness.
Forgive my father for he knows not.

Forgive my father for he knows not
that he tries
to halt Death in the wood shop.
He worked; took night school;

helped his hard, jobless father.
And his mother love told untold times.
Thus, he was my hard mother
when Mother was depressed. (*SP* 175)

The son's anger at the father's failures is balanced by his love and forgiveness.
Jesus' words on the cross ("Father, forgive them; for they know not what they do")
are Jewishly ironized, as the all too human father is forgiven by the son, who finally
recognizes his self-sacrifice. Returning after "the Zion noon" from the cemetery
"through eternal Brooklyn," the family's car is "consecrated" by a child at an open
fire hydrant:

And I touched the waters
forgiving of the guilt unforgiven by what self
for anger at the father?
Father. Dearest friend.

Amen. Amen.
Perhaps this is God's axiom:
each day does not stop the errors
between this one and this one.

And there is no rebuttal.
Only birth, story.
Only barter: one thing for the next.
Only the four starred crosses of the matrix. (*SP* 176)

The compassion for human limitation comes from learning "God's axiom": there
is no point in arguing that life is error and misunderstanding, a story of continuous emotional "barter" or exchange. In the end, we frame memories that are
both iconic and hermeneutic, like the (Jewish?) stars superimposed on the crosses
of the matrix: seemingly static, they engage us, as does Seidman's poetry, in an
interminable dialogue with the past.

There is a poem by George Oppen that has always had a talismanic power for me. It is called "From Disaster" and comes from *The Materials* (1962), the first volume Oppen published after his return to poetry:

Ultimately the air
Is bare sunlight where must be found
The lyric valuables. From disaster

Shipwreck, whole families crawled
To the tenements, and there

Survived by what morality
Of hope

Which for the sons
Ends its metaphysic
In small lawns of home. (29)

There is nothing specifically Jewish about this poem, though the experience to which it attests is that of American Jews among any number of other ethnic groups in the twentieth century. The attitude is typically Objectivist: just as the "lyric valuables" must be found in the limits of "bare sunlight," that is, the material world and nothing more, so too the "morality/Of hope" must be found in the terribly constrained circumstances of historical "disaster" or "shipwreck," the latter a term that Oppen will develop with wrenching power some years later in "Of Being Numerous." In "From Disaster," the shipwreck is that of western, or specifically, European culture, and the concomitant social transformations visited on European societies by the violent forces of modernity. The families of immigrants that fled the disaster of modern Europe to find the opportunities and insecurities of America live first in the tenements and then, with hard work and good fortune, make their way by the second generation to the outer boroughs and suburbs, with their "small lawns of home." "Metaphysic," another highly charged term that Oppen uses at certain critical points in his work, indicates that he is adumbrating a process that is not merely socioeconomic in nature. As he says of the poets in "Of Being Numerous":

They have lost the metaphysical sense
Of the future, they feel themselves
The end of a chain

Of lives, single lives
And we know that lives
Are single

And cannot defend
The metaphysic
On which rest

The boundaries
Of our distances. (165)

In both poems, Oppen is concerned with an existential boundary condition, the boundaries of futurity confronted by ordinary people in their daily struggle to get by, a struggle that many poets tend to forget. The boundary may be defined by a suburban lawn, the fulfillment of a dream for one generation but a limit that must be transcended in the struggle of the generation that follows. Indeed, we have seen Heller responding to Oppen in "The American Jewish Clock" when he observes that "the young walked out, walked back/to the cities, prodigals of emptied memory (*Wordflow* 87). Now it is clear that some poets do not forget, and that in their acts of remembrance the metaphysical sense of the future is preserved.

Afterword

Saying Kaddish:
Holiness, Death, and the
Jewish Difference in Poetry

> I call-as-witness against you today the heavens and the earth:
> life and death I place before you, blessing and curse;
> now choose life, in order that you may stay-alive, you and
> your seed . . .
>
> —Deut. 30:19

As I bring this book to an end, I wish to return to the issue of Jewish distinctive-
ness or difference in poetry. My focus has been on Jewish American poetry, but we
have seen in the statements of figures such as Bloom, Hollander, Grossman, and
Rothenberg that when it comes to "the Jewish question," American poetry glides
into the larger category of poetry in English, or the even larger one of poetry in the
west. One wishes to avoid sweeping generalizations about the poetry of a given
people, especially a people that has mingled and sometimes nearly become one
with other peoples in a long succession of variously organized societies and diverse
cultures. Furthermore, literary theory's attack on (and dread of) "essentialism,"
and the multiplicity of "subject positions" recognized as operative within a single
text, make any discussion of such a difference even more risky. Consider this coda,
then, to be a speculative midrash on the part of a passionate, if rather eccentric
reader, as well as a reflection on his own work by an American poet who has also
written out of relation to his Jewish heritage.

"Now choose life, in order that you may stay-alive." In Everett Fox's new
translation of the Five Books of Moses, the phrase takes on an archaic tone that is
simultaneously fresh, old and new, uncanny in its originality. There seems to be a
special urgency in "stay-alive" as opposed to the usual "live." In choosing life, in
doing all they can to "stay-alive," the Jews turn from death and all that may be
associated with it. Yet in the western tradition, poetry is, in one fundamental
respect, a speaking to death. In English poetry, Shakespeare's sonnets are the locus
classicus, an extended argument with oblivion in which the power of the poet's
verse will guarantee his love's—and his own—immortality. "Not marble nor the

gilded monuments/Of princes shall outlive this pow'rful rime," begins Sonnet 55, perhaps the boldest of these declarations, set "'Gainst death and all oblivious enmity." In Donne's Holy Sonnet X, religious faith replaces the power of art, but rhetorically the effect is similar: "One short sleepe past, wee wake eternally/And death shall be no more; death thou shalt die."

But death is a strangely seductive power, as the authors of the Torah must have understood. Speak to death long enough, and this power begins to grow. Milton, great Hebraicist and classicist both, narrowly triumphs over death in *Lycidas,* and, typical of the elegist, assumes his poetic life through the death of another poet. "Sunk low,/but mounted high," Lycidas "hears the unexpressive nuptial Song/In the blest Kingdoms meek of joy and love." Entertained by "all the Saints above," Lycidas becomes audience, not poet; that role is taken over, in effect, by Milton himself in the figure of the "uncouth Swain" who "With eager thought warbling his *Doric* lay" heads "Tomorrow to fresh Woods, and Pastures new."

Milton, at the expense of Lycidas, chooses life; but Keats, his follower, listening to the Nightingale, falls entirely under death's voluptuous spell:

> Darkling I listen; and, for many a time
>   I have been half in love with easeful Death,
> Called him soft names in many a musèd rhyme,
>   To take into the air my quiet breath;
> Now more than ever seems it rich to die,
>   To cease upon the midnight with no pain,
>   While thou art pouring forth thy soul abroad
>   In such an ecstasy!
> Still wouldst thou sing, and I have ears in vain—
>   To thy high requiem become a sod.

Here, death takes on all the appeal of luxurious, eroticized vitality, in contrast to the sphere of the living, "where men sit and hear each other groan." This reversal is, in effect, brought to completion in Shelley's elegy for Keats, *Adonais:*

> The One remains, the many change and pass;
> Heaven's light forever shines, Earth's shadows fly;
> Life, like a dome of many colored glass,
> Stains the white radiance of Eternity,
> Until Death tramples it to fragments.—Die,
> If thou wouldst be with that which thou dost seek!
> Follow where all is fled!—Rome's azure sky,
> Flowers, ruins, statues, music, words, are weak
> The glory they transfuse with fitting truth to speak.

Death fulfills the desire for spiritual unity, as un-Jewish a notion as one could find, given the implacably Jewish knowledge of the eternal space between the divine and the human (which results, paradoxically, in the intimacy between God and a few chosen characters in the Hebrew Scriptures, or between God and the Jew at prayer). "No more let Life divide what Death can join together," Shelley declares—a theme that resonates through the whole history of western literature, in opposition to Jewish Law.

This love affair with death continues in American poetry, despite (perhaps in defiance of) the Old Testament roots of American Protestantism. In "Out of the Cradle Endlessly Rocking," Whitman's poetic election is synonymous with the knowledge of death. Calling for the word that will open his poetic consciousness, the boy on the shore of Paumanok is answered by the sea, which

> Whisper'd me through the night, and very plainly before daybreak,
> Lisp'd to me the low and delicious word death,
> And again death, death, death, death, death . . .

For Whitman, the unending variety of life, the complex and diverse American experience that he celebrates every day, can only be articulated as the counterpart to the night, to which he must always and finally return. Thus in "The Sleepers," where death is folded into the rhythms of sleeping and waking,

> I too pass from the night,
> I stay a while away O night, but I return to you again and love you.
>
> Why should I be afraid to trust myself to you?
> I am not afraid, I have been well brought forward by you,
> I love the rich running day, but I do not desert her in whom I lay so long,
> I know not how I came of you and I know not where I go with you, but I
>   know I came well and shall go well.
>
> I will stop only a time with the night, and rise betimes,
> I will duly pass the day O my mother, and duly return to you.

As for Dickinson, the other great foundational figure of American poetry, death is perhaps the one subject she addresses more than any other. Here is one lyric, by no means the most famous, from among the hundreds she writes about death, that indicates the source of her fascination:

> The overtakelessness of those
> Who have accomplished Death
> Majestic is to me beyond
> The majesties of Earth.

The soul her "Not at Home"
Inscribes upon the flesh—
And her fair aerial gait
Beyond the hope of touch.

Dickinson's perpetual goal is selfhood, the "White Election" that no Father-God can grant her. She must seize it for herself, as in "The Soul selects her own Society" or "I'm ceded—I've stopped being Theirs," in which she appears "Crowned— Crowing—on my Father's breast." The "overtakelessness" that death grants the soul gives it tremendous appeal; the "fair aerial gait" to which the poet aspires is the speed that death can provide, so she can rush to her appointed deification. If in the English Romantics, death brings the soul to union with the One, in the American Romantics, death brings the soul to union with itself, so it may become the One.

This is why, for the woman in Stevens's "Sunday Morning," conventional Christian belief in the promise of immortality is inadequate, why "Divinity must live within herself." Likewise, we are told that

Death is the mother of beauty; hence from her,
Alone, shall come fulfillment of our dreams
And our desires.

The guarantee of death is found behind all our creative and procreative urges, and death, finally, is the fulfillment we seek above all else. Intimate knowledge of death leads us to seek divinity within ourselves, for although death "strews the leaves/Of sure obliteration on our paths," our love affair with death gives us the keenest appreciation of the things of this world. Our aesthetic appreciation of the world is a love inspired by death; our divinity will be confirmed by our certain mortality.

The relationship to death I have just attempted to define is a crucial part of the dominant paradigm for poetry in the west, and no poet, Jew or gentile, can avoid being caught up in its trajectory. In Grossman's essay on the theophoric possibilities of Jewish poetry, he speaks somewhat mysteriously of "the Jew's *great* poet whom I wish speculatively to summon to mind" (*Long Schoolroom* 163) or of an equally speculative "commission for Jewish poetry of a kind that may never yet have existed" (161). The Jew's great poet who takes on this commission is actually an impossibility, for as we observed in chapter 3, the absolute condition of holiness that God imposes on Jewish life is at odds with poetic representation; in terms of this absolute, a fully Jewish poetry cannot exist, for God's word is One. Likewise, the distinction between holiness and poetry is in direct correlation to the distinction between life and death, as Grossman's essay on holiness makes clear—and as his own poetry attempts to transact. The countertruth, as it were, to Grossman's vision, is Rothenberg's assertion in *Exiled in the Word* that *poesis,* including Jewish *poesis,* "is evolving, contradictory, not fixed or rigid" (6); that Jewish poetry, like all poetry, "is an inherently impure activity of individuals creating reality from all conditions & influences at hand" (9). Grossman argues that any negotiation between the categories of holiness and of poetic making must be conducted through the presence of the Shechinah, the sign of Presence, as opposed to a mere poetic muse—and given Rothenberg's understanding of the Shechinah, he would probably agree. For Grossman, the Shechinah is the bringer of God's Law, through which we choose life; thus "it is for knowledge of her that the people should look to the Jewish poet and the Jewish poet to his or her own nature" (*Long Schoolroom* 167). For Rothenberg, she is "earth, nature, orgy, love" (*Exiled in the Word* 5). It is out of these manifold contradictions that the Jewish poet approaches the impossible conditions of a Jewish poetry.

Grossman, it will be recalled, thinks of Objectivist poetry as an "evasion," but here is Harvey Shapiro (whose early poetry, it should be remembered, sounds very much like that of Grossman) attempting this same negotiation in a rather different register from the elevated, Romantic style:

> On Wednesday he chose life
> And went about getting breakfast
> With a light heart. He looked at people,
> Considered plants and stones,
> Wrote letters to distant friends.
> At nightfall he was back in the slough,
> Hip-deep, and the stuff
> Pulling him under. So he asked himself,
> How is it life obviously
> Does not choose you?
> And what does your choice come to then?
> Thursday he had no answer
> And the sick spirit withered.
> Friday he dropped the metaphor. (*Battle Report* 18)

In a subtle midrash, Shapiro counterpoises two crucial biblical moments. Following the commandment in Deuteronomy, he chooses life, but having heeded God's word, he still ends up in the slough. Job, tested by God through his affliction, cries out from the depths of his despair:

> Yes—
> I hoped for good, got only wrong;
> I hoped for light, got only darkness.
> My insides seethe and never stop,
> I face days of suffering,
> I go about in sunless gloom. (Scheindlin 123)

Like Job (though not quite so dramatically), Shapiro likewise questions the justice of human existence: "How is it life obviously/Does not choose you?/And what does your choice come to then?" No answer from the whirlwind comes to Shapiro; instead, ambiguously, "the sick spirit withered." Is it the spirit of despair that withers in him, or his own afflicted soul? All we are told is that "Friday he dropped the metaphor," at which point the poem ends.

Yet the dropping of the metaphor and the conclusion of the poem do not indicate the kind of finality we so often associate with the endings of literary works. In discussing the tendency toward "anti-closure" in William Carlos Williams's Objectivist poem "Between Walls," Barbara Herrnstein Smith notes that "What is interesting about this form of closure is that little supports it aside from the grammatical resolution and the fact that nothing follows. By stopping, however, the poem announces its own sufficiency, and, in compelling the reader to accept that sufficiency, gives a retrospective emphasis more or less to every element in it" (258). This strikes me as applicable to Shapiro's poem as well, and has implications that go well beyond those of form. Why, after all, is the poem called "Three Days"? Were those three days chosen arbitrarily? "He," the poet, object of his own dispassionate narration, presumably goes on living after his utterance is over; to that extent at least he chooses life, though he may still think of himself in the slough. By now it is Friday: the weekend—and the Sabbath—is approaching. On Friday night the Sabbath Queen, often associated with the Shechinah, arrives to bring the Jews a day of rest and holiness, a foretaste of Paradise. Nothing in Shapiro's poem indicates that he is anticipating the Sabbath; for that matter, by Saturday he may find himself neck-deep instead of hip-deep. We do not know. What we have is a report (and the poem comes from Shapiro's volume *Battle Report*), the poet's testimony or test of his own truth. Shapiro's old friend Zukofsky would no doubt observe the poem's sincerity.

For all its charm, its subtle structure, and its real sense of struggle, a poem like "Three Days" is a rather flimsy counterpoint to *Lycidas, Adonais,* or "Out of the Cradle Endlessly Rocking." That is, of course, one important aspect of the Objectivist project: the tentative verbal arrangements, the unassuming phenomenological probes launched at the conditions of being, are propositional and dialogic in nature. They are not declarative, and do not seek monumental status. One is reminded of Oppen's "Psalm":

> The small nouns
> Crying faith
> In this in which the wild deer
> Startle, and stare out. (78)

In these lines, "this" refers to the poem itself, that site of exchange between language and the world, where faith in the human power of naming may still be asserted, and life may still be praised.

One of the most complex sites of this sort in Jewish American poetry, composed not in the Objectivists' plain style but in an ironized version of the older high rhetoric, is Allen Mandelbaum's *Chelmaxioms*. Mandelbaum's Chelm is not the "counterfeit, usurping Chelm of Yiddish folklore," but "the *echt* Chelm, the meandering Chelm of the maxioms, which follow the non sequiturs—yet arabesque—of talk of talk and talk of text, which mime the riverlike careers of the Oral Law and the Written Law but carry a cargo of alegalities—the divagations, digressions, the discreet and indiscreet parentheses native to talmudic/midrashic exegesis" (xvi). According to Mandelbaum, the Scribes of Chelm—and if the Jew's word is One, then all Jewish writers are Scribes—

> are not content to be alive
>
> except when sabbath falls or love
> descends or ends—or names that lie
> in labyrinths awake and writhe
>
> and slough their skins and ask for light
> or—quiet, penitent—consent
> to leave the furrowed text, to die. (113)

The meaning of the scribe's existence depends on bringing the names up out of the labyrinths of death and into the world of light and life. The image of the names sloughing their skin is that of a snake regenerating itself, and in blessing the names, the scribe, in effect, blesses the Name. Mandelbaum acknowledges death as a part of life, for all that is mortal must eventually consent to the reality of death. But the poetic or scribal task, though it is always informed by the knowledge of mortality, is also akin to that of "the prayers of holiness—the *kedusha* and the Kaddish," which perform the task, according to Grossman, of "the repair of the creation under the sign of absence, the reconstruction of goodness as holiness after the loss of holiness as the primordial goodness of oneness with source" (*Long Schoolroom* 184). And so the scribe affirms the perfection of being, which the Jews know in this world through the weekly descent of the sabbath, and which all of humanity knows through the vicissitudes of love.

If Jewish poets seek to repair creation under the sign of absence—if they are, in other words, still so closely allied to the condition of holiness in the full knowledge of death—then perhaps it is time to consider the one Jewish American poem that has been a greater source of contention than any other: Allen Ginsberg's "Kaddish." In the course of this book, we have seen that the argument surrounding the meaning and value of this poem inevitably opens on the larger debate about what makes a poem Jewish. That "Kaddish" is an American poem has never been a matter of doubt: the harrowing details of Naomi Ginsberg's life that are embedded in her son's lament may or may not contribute sufficiently to the poem's Jewish dimension, but they certainly constitute an immigrant narrative of the type that is by now a standard American genre. Naomi's story is as identifiably American as the blues of Ray Charles to which the poet listens at the beginning of the poem, as he chants both the Kaddish prayer and "Adonais' last triumphant stanzas aloud" (Ginsberg 209). The intertwining sounds of the blues, the Kaddish, and Shelley's elegy signify the cultural tensions at work in the poem: the Jewish ritual of sanctification is set against one of the most passionate embraces of death in the western canon, below which is heard the ground bass of the African diaspora wrenched into a uniquely American music.

According to Ginsberg, "Death is that remedy all singers dream of, sing, remember, prophesy as in the Hebrew Anthem" (209). If by the "Hebrew Anthem" he means the Kaddish, then the critique that John Hollander has leveled against the poem (see chapter 3) has some validity, for the prayer (which is mostly in Aramaic, not Hebrew) is certainly not a song or prophecy of death, but a ritual of blessing that purifies life and renews its holiness. Ginsberg, at least at this early point in the poem, mistakenly assigns to the Kaddish (and by implication, his own text) the same task as that of "Adonais" and of the western elegiac tradition in general. But what follows in Ginsberg's poem—indeed, what it largely consists of—is peculiarly unelegiac. Sections I and II of "Kaddish," narrated by the poet, tell the story of Naomi's life and of Ginsberg's struggle to love and understand his mother. Telling Naomi's story is not meant to immortalize either her or the poet, as in the classical or Shakespearian mode; nor is it meant to celebrate the union of the soul with the One, as in the Romantic mode. In other words, Death is not the mother of beauty in "Kaddish," and beauty in any conventional sense is not to be found in the "plate of cold fish—chopped raw cabbage dript with tapwater— smelly tomatoes—week-old health food—grated beets & carrots with leaky juice, warm" that Naomi serves her son when he visits her. This gross caricature of maternal sustenance leads immediately to a much more ghastly passage, as the son actually contemplates incest with the mother at the sight of her "big slash of hair, scars of operations, pancreas, belly wounds, abortions, appendix, stitching of incisions pulling down in the fate like hideous thick zippers—ragged long lips between her legs" (219). And it is at this point, when the corporality and decay of the material world and of human relations are at their nadir, that Ginsberg suddenly breaks into the actual words of the Kaddish: "Yisborach, v'yistabach, v'yispoar, v'yisroman, v'yisnaseh, v'yishador, v'yishalleh, v'yishallol, sh'meh d'kudsho, b'rich hu." The exaltation and hallowing of the blessed Name functions here precisely as it does in the actual prayer: it "is an act of ridding the pollution of death from the world of the living" (*Long Schoolroom* 186).

Thus, when the narrative sections of the poem are ended and Ginsberg recites his "Hymmnn," the text continues to treat the Kaddish prayer in a spirit of authenticity even as it observes the salient features of Naomi's and Allen's lives:

In the world which He has created according to his will Blessed Praised
Magnified Lauded Exalted the Name of the Holy One Blessed is He!
In the house in Newark Blessed is He! In the madhouse Blessed is He!
In the house of Death Blessed is He!
Blessed be He in homosexuality! Blessed be He in Paranoia! Blessed be He
in the city! Blessed be He in the Book! (225)

Ginsberg remains true to the Kaddish even when his repetitions modulate into
"Blessed be Thee Naomi in Death! Blessed be Death! Blessed be Death!/ . . .
Blessed be Death on us All!" Death is folded into the Blessing; in the Kaddish,
notes Grossman, there is "no affirmation less than total even in the face of death"
(*Long Schoolroom* 186). By the end of the poem, God and His Creation are in
unity in a moment of restoration (*tikkun*), as "the crows shriek in the white sun
over graves stones in Long Island" and the Name is heard in what would otherwise
be understood as a cry of death: "Lord Lord Lord caw caw caw Lord Lord Lord
caw caw caw Lord" (227).

As Grossman understood long ago, "Kaddish" is a limit text, which is to say
that readers' responses to the poem continue to reflect the conditions of our
understanding at the borders of the domain of Jewish American poetry. I have
tried to further our understanding of this domain, and in doing so, I have
repeatedly found myself at one or another of its borders: between Jewish and
American traditions of literary discourse, between religious practices and secular
behaviors, between faith and skepticism, and between the cultural binaries of the
sacred and the profane out of which is generated the process of *poesis*. In the
twentieth century, this last division has become, in a certain sense, impossible.
"Gelobt seist du, Niemand," declares Paul Celan in his famous "Psalm": "Praised
be your name, no one" (175) as Michael Hamburger translates it; or, for John
Felstiner, getting closer to the Hebrew *Baruch ata,* "Blessèd art thou, No One"
(167). For Celan, the Jews after the Shoah are the *Niemandsrose* blooming against
the No One who is their dubious Creator. Even in a world visited by total death,
Jews remain an uncanny life form reaching up, in what becomes a terribly ironic
gesture, toward the source of life.

Jewish poets in America cannot bless and deny the source in quite the same
way, but here too they enter into the debate:

Through crematorium chimneys
a Jew curls toward the God of his fathers.
As soon as the smoke is gone,
upward cluster his wife and son.

Upward, toward the heavens,
sacred smoke weeps, yearns.

God—where You are—
we all disappear. (Glatshteyn 119)

*　*　*

Where did the Jewish god go?
Up the chimney flues.
Who saw him go?
Six million souls.
How did he go?
All so still
As the dew from the grass. (*Selected Poems* 39)

Whether the Jews of the Shoah disappear into God, as in Glatshteyn's "Smoke," or the Jewish God Himself disappears through the witness of the six million, as in Shapiro's "Ditty," American Jews' responses to the Holocaust gravitate toward the culture of holiness, even when the foundations of that culture have been cast into doubt. This accounts in part for Rothenberg's notion of poets, including (or perhaps especially) Jewish poets, as "technicians of the sacred," returning to the poetic origins of sacred (the sacred origins of the poetic) under the aegis of modern ethnography. In his introduction to *Khurbn,* Rothenberg observes that "Our search since then [after Auschwitz] has been for the origins of poetry, not only as a willful desire to wipe the slate clean but as a recognition of those other voices & scraps of poems they left behind them in the mud" (4). Following the Shoah, one may surely acknowledge the desire to wipe the slate clean, though Rothenberg's poem, if not the entire ethnopoetic project, attests to the impossibility of that desire. "[T]hey are the dead & want so much to speak/that all the writing in the world will not contain them" (30) cries Rothenberg from the depths of the Khurbn. Even so. Like so many others, I have considered poetry as a speaking to death founded on a love of death. But poetry is also conceived of a speaking of the dead through—and to—the living. And in the Jewish poem, even the dead choose life.

Works Cited

Adorno, Theodor W. "Cultural Criticism and Society." *Prisms.* Trans. Samuel and Shierry Weber. 1967. Cambridge, MA: MIT P, 1981. 17–34.

Ahearn, Barry, ed. *Pound/Zukofsky: Selected Letters of Ezra Pound and Louis Zukofsky.* The Correspondence of Ezra Pound. New York: New Directions, 1987.

———. *Zukofsky's "A": An Introduction.* Berkeley: U of California P, 1983.

Alter, Robert. "Charles Reznikoff: Between Present and Past." *Defenses of the Imagination.* Philadelphia: Jewish Publication Society, 1977. 119–135.

———. "Epitaph for a Jewish Magazine." *Commentary* 39.5 (May 1965): 51–55.

Althusser, Louis. "Ideology and Ideological State Apparatuses." *Lenin and Philosophy and Other Essays.* Trans. Ben Brewster. New York: Monthly Review P, 1971. 127–186.

Altieri, Charles. "The Objectivist Tradition." *Chicago Review* 30.3 (Winter 1979): 5–22.

———. "Sensibility, Rhetoric, and Will: Some Tensions in Contemporary Poetry." *Contemporary Literature* 23.4 (Fall 1982): 451–479.

Auster, Paul. "The Decisive Moment." *The Art of Hunger and Other Essays.* London: Menard, 1982. 16–31.

Bartlett, Lee. "Armand Schwerner: A Conversation." *American Poetry* 4.3 (Spring 1987): 79–90.

Benjamin, Walter. *Illuminations.* Trans. Harry Zohn. New York: Schocken Books, 1969.

———. "N [Re the Theory of Knowledge, Theory of Progress]." Trans. Leigh Hafrey and Richard Sieburth. *Benjamin: Philosophy, Aesthetics, History.* Ed. Gary Smith. Chicago: U of Chicago P, 1989. 43–83.

———. *Reflections: Essays, Aphorisms, Autobiographical Writings.* Trans. Edmund Jephcott. New York: Schocken Books, 1986.

Bernstein, Charles. "Reznikoff's Nearness." *My Way: Speeches and Poems.* Chicago: U of Chicago P, 1999. 197–228.

Bloom, Harold. *The Anxiety of Influence.* New York: Oxford UP, 1973.

———. *The Book of J.* New York: Grove Weidenfeld, 1990.

———. "The Heavy Burden of the Past." *New York Times Book Review* (Jan. 4, 1981): 5, 24.

———. *Kabbalah and Criticism.* New York: Continuum, 1975.

———. "The Sorrows of American-Jewish Poetry." *Figures of Capable Imagination.* New York: Seabury Press, 1976. 247–262.

————. *The Ringers in the Tower: Studies in Romantic Tradition.* Chicago: U of Chicago P, 1971.

The Book of Job. Trans. Raymond P. Scheindlin. New York: Norton, 1998.

Boyarin, Daniel and Boyarin, Jonathan. "Introduction/So What's New?" *Jews and Other Differences: The New Jewish Cultural Studies.* Minneapolis: U of Minnesota P, 1997.

————. "Self-Exposure as Theory: The Double Mark of the Male Jew." *Thinking in Jewish.* Chicago & London: Chicago UP, 1996. 34–62.

Boyarin, Jonathan. *Storm from Paradise: The Politics of Jewish Memory.* Minneapolis: U of Minnesota P, 1992.

————. "Voices Around the Text: The Ethnography of Reading at Mesivta Tifereth Jerusalem." *The Ethnography of Reading.* Ed. Jonathan Boyarin. Berkeley: U of California P, 1993. 212–237.

Buber, Martin. *Tales of the Hasidim: The Early Masters.* Trans. Olga Marx. New York: Schocken, 1975.

Casillo, Robert. *The Genealogy of Demons: Anti-Semitism, Fascism, and the Myths of Ezra Pound.* Evanston, IL: Northwestern UP, 1988.

Celan, Paul. *Poems of Paul Celan.* Trans. Michael Hamburger. New York: Persea Books, 1988.

Cohen, Arthur A. and Mendes-Flohr, Paul, ed. *Contemporary Jewish Religious Thought.* New York: Scribner's, 1987.

Cuddihy, John Murray. *The Ordeal of Civility: Freud, Marx, Lévi-Strauss, and the Jewish Struggle with Modernity.* New York: Basic Books, 1974.

De Man, Paul. "Literary History and Literary Modernity." *Blindness and Insight: Essays in the Rhetoric of Contemporary Criticism,* 2nd ed. Minneapolis: U of Minnesota P, 1983. 142–165.

Dembo, L. S. *The Monological Jew.* Madison: U of Wisconsin P, 1988.

———— and Pondrom, Cyrena N., eds. *The Contemporary Writer: Interviews with Sixteen Novelists and Poets.* Madison: U of Wisconsin P, 1972.

Derrida, Jacques. *Of Grammatology.* Trans. Gayatri Chakravorty Spivak. Baltimore: Johns Hopkins UP, 1976.

————. "Structure, Sign and Play in the Discourse of the Human Sciences." *Writing and Difference.* Trans. Alan Bass. Chicago: U of Chicago P, 1978. 278–293.

Donne, John. *Poetical Works.* Ed. Herbert Grierson. London: Oxford UP, 1933.

DuPlessis, Rachel Blau. "Armand Schwerner." *Sulfur* 11.2 (Fall 1991): 212.

————. "Objectivist Poetics and Political Vision: A Study of Oppen and Pound." *George Oppen: Man and Poet.* Ed. Burton Hatlen. Orono, ME: National Poetry Foundation, 1981.

Eagleton, Terry. *Criticism and Ideology.* London: Verso, 1976.

Eliot, T. S. *The Complete Poems and Plays 1909–1950.* New York: Harcourt, Brace & World, 1971.

Featherstone, Dan. "Poetic Representation: Reznikoff's *Holocaust,* Rothenberg's 'Khurbn.'" *Response* 68 (Fall 1997/Winter 1998): 129–140.

Felstiner, John. *Paul Celan: Poet, Survivor, Jew.* New Haven: Yale UP, 1995.

The Five Books of Moses. Trans. Everett Fox. New York: Schocken Books, 1997.

Foster, Edward. "An Interview with Michael Heller." *Talisman* 11 (Fall 1993): 48–64.

Fredman, Stephen. "Call Him Charles." *Sagetrieb* 13.1 & 2 (Spring & Fall 1992): 55–81.

Finkelstein, Norman. "'The Master of Turning': Walter Benjamin, Gershom Scholem, Harold Bloom, and the Writing of a Jewish Life." *People of the Book: Thirty Scholars Reflect on Their Jewish Identity.* Ed. Jeffrey Rubin-Dorsky and Shelley Fisher Fishkin. Madison, WI: U of Wisconsin P, 1996. 415–426.

———. *The Ritual of New Creation: Jewish Tradition and Contemporary Literature.* Albany, NY: SUNY P, 1992.

———. *The Utopian Moment in Contemporary American Poetry,* rev. ed. Lewisburg, PA: Bucknell UP, 1993.

Freud, Sigmund. "Family Romances." *The Freud Reader.* Ed. Peter Gay. New York: Norton, 1989. 297–300.

Gardner, Thomas. "An Interview with Michael Heller." *Contemporary Literature* 32.3 (Fall 1991): 297–311.

Gilman, Sander L. *Difference and Pathology: Stereotypes of Sexuality, Race, and Madness.* Ithaca, NY: Cornell UP, 1985.

———. *Freud, Race, and Gender.* Princeton, NJ: Princeton UP, 1993.

———. *Jewish Self-Hatred: Anti-Semitism and the Hidden Language of the Jews.* Baltimore: Johns Hopkins UP, 1986.

———. *The Jew's Body.* New York: Routledge, 1991.

Gingerich, Willard. "Armand Schwerner: An Interview." *American Poetry Review* 24.5 (September/October 1995): 27–32.

Ginsberg, Allen. *Collected Poems 1947–1980.* New York: Harper & Row, 1984.

Glatshteyn, Yankev. *Selected Poems of Yankev Glatshteyn.* Trans. Richard J. Fein. Philadelphia: Jewish Publication Society, 1987.

Glatzer, Nahum N. "Remnant of Israel." *Contemporary Jewish Religious Thought.* 779–783.

Golding, Alan. *From Outlaw to Classic: Canons in American Poetry.* Madison: U of Wisconsin P, 1995.

Grossman, Allen. *The Ether Dome and Other Poems.* New York: New Directions, 1991.

———. *A Harlot's Hire.* Cambridge, MA: Walker-de Berry, 1961.

———. *The Long Schoolroom: Lessons in the Bitter Logic of the Poetic Principle.* Ann Arbor, MI: U of Michigan P, 1997.

———. *Of the Great House.* New York: New Directions, 1982.

———. *The Sighted Singer: Two Works on Poetry for Readers and Writers.* Baltimore: Johns Hopkins UP, 1992.

Harshav, Benjamin & Barbara, ed. "Documents of Introspectivism." *American Yiddish Poetry: A Bilingual Anthology.* Berkeley: U of California P, 1986. 773–804.

Hartman, Geoffrey H. "Imagination." *Contemporary Jewish Religious Thought.* 451–472.

Heller, Michael. *Accidental Center.* Fremont, MI: Sumac P, 1972.

———. "Avant-Garde Propellants of the Machine Made of Words." *Sagetrieb* 10.1&2 (Spring/Fall 1992): 7–27.

———. *Conviction's Net of Branches.* Carbondale, IL: Southern Illinois UP, 1985.

———. *In the Builded Place.* Minneapolis: Coffee House P, 1989.

———. *Knowledge.* New York: Sun, 1979.

———. *Wordflow: New and Selected Poems.* Jersey City, NJ: Talisman House, 1997.

Hindus, Milton, ed. *Charles Reznikoff: Man and Poet.* Orono, ME: National Poetry Foundation, 1984.

Hollander, John. *Harp Lake.* New York: Knopf, 1988.

———. "The Question of American Jewish Poetry." *What Is Jewish Literature?* Ed. Hana Wirth-Nesher. Philadelphia: Jewish Publication Society, 1994. 36–52.

Holtz, Barry W. "Introduction." *Back to the Sources: Reading the Classic Jewish Texts.* Ed. Barry W. Holtz. New York: Summit Books, 1984. 11–29.

Howe, Irving. "Response to Ted Solotaroff: The End of Marginality in Jewish Literature." *The Writer in the Jewish Community.* 67–71.

Idel, Moshe. *Kabbalah: New Perspectives.* New Haven: Yale UP, 1988.

Ignatow, David. "Accents of Death and Endurance." *The New Leader* (July 31–August 7, 1961): 24–25.

Julius, Anthony. *T. S. Eliot, Anti-Semitism, and Literary Form.* New York: Cambridge UP, 1996.

Kenner, Hugh. *A Homemade World: The American Modernist Writers.* New York: Knopf, 1975.

Kumin, Maxine. "Getting the Message." *Telling and Remembering.* 183–184.

Levertov, Denise. *Poems 1960–1967.* New York: New Directions, 1983.

Mandelbaum, Allen. *Chelmaxioms: The Maxims Axioms Maxioms of Chelm.* Boston: Godine, 1977.

McHale, Brian. "Archaeologies of Knowledge: Hill's Middens, Heaney's Bogs, Schwerner's Tablets." *New Literary History* 30.1 (Winter 1999): 239–262.

Oppen, George. *Collected Poems.* New York: New Directions, 1975.

———. "Three Poets." *Poetry* 100.5 (August 1962): 329–333.

Ozick, Cynthia. *Art & Ardor.* New York: Knopf, 1983.

Pacernick, Gary. *Memory and Fire: Ten American Jewish Poets.* New York: Peter Lang, 1989.

Paul, Sherman. *In Search of the Primitive: Rereading David Antin, Jerome Rothenberg, and Gary Snyder.* Baton Rouge: Louisiana State UP, 1986.

Perloff, Marjorie. *The Dance of the Intellect: Studies in the Poetry of the Pound Tradition.* Cambridge: Cambridge UP, 1985.

———. *Poetic License: Essays on Modernist and Postmodernist Lyric.* Evanston, IL: Northwestern UP, 1990

Plaut, W. Gunther, ed. *The Torah: A Modern Commentary.* New York: Union of American Hebrew Congregations, 1981.

Rabinbach, Anson. "Between Enlightenment and Apocalypse: Benjamin, Bloch and Modern German Jewish Messianism." *New German Critique* 34 (Winter 1985): 78–123.

Ray, David. "Harvey Shapiro." *Contemporary Poets,* 4th ed. Ed. James Vinson & D. L. Kirkpatrick. New York: St. Martin's P, 1985. 771–772.

Reznikoff, Charles. *Holocaust.* Santa Barbara, CA: Black Sparrow, 1977.

———. *Poems 1918–1936: Volume I of the Complete Poems of Charles Reznikoff.* Santa Barbara: Black Sparrow, 1976.

———. *Poems 1937–1975: Volume II of the Complete Poems of Charles Reznikoff.* Santa Barbara: Black Sparrow, 1976.

Rosenberg, Joel. "Jeremiah and Ezekiel." *The Literary Guide to the Bible.* Ed. Robert Alter and Frank Kermode. Cambridge: Harvard UP. 184–206.

Roth, Philip. *The Counterlife.* New York: Penguin, 1989.

Rothenberg, Jerome. "Harold Bloom: The Critic as Exterminating Angel." *Sulfur* 1.2 (1981): 4–26.

———. *Khurbn & Other Poems.* New York: New Directions, 1989.

———. *Poland/1931.* New York: New Directions, 1974.

———. "Pre-Face." *Exiled In the Word: Poems & Other Visions of the Jews from Tribal Times to Present.* Ed. Jerome Rothenberg & Harris Lenowitz. Port Townsend, WA: Copper Canyon P, 1989. 3–14.

———. "Pre-Face." *Symposium of the Whole: A Range of Discourse Toward an Ethnopoetics.* Ed. Jerome Rothenberg & Diane Rothenberg. Berkeley: U of California P, 1983. xi–xvii.

———. *Pre-Faces & Other Writings.* New York: New Directions, 1981.

Rubin, Steven J. *Telling and Remembering: A Century of American Jewish Poetry.* Boston: Beacon P, 1997.

Rukeyser, Muriel. *Out of Silence: Selected Poems.* Ed. Kate Daniels. Evanston, IL: Tri Quarterly Press, 1992.

Schimmel, Harold. "Zuk. Yehoash David Rex." *Louis Zukofsky: Man and Poet.* Ed. Carroll F. Terrell. Orono, ME: National Poetry Foundation, 1979. 235–245.

Scholem, Gershom. *Kabbalah.* New York: New American Library, 1978.

———. *Major Trends in Jewish Mysticism.* New York: Schocken Books, 1954.

———. *The Messianic Idea in Judaism and Other Essays on Jewish Spirituality.* New York: Schocken Books, 1971.

———. *On the Mystical Shape of the Godhead: Basic Concepts in the Kabbalah.* Trans. Joachim Neugroschel. New York: Schocken Books, 1991. 140–196.

———. *On the Kabbalah and Its Symbolism.* Trans. Ralph Manheim. New York: Schocken, 1965.

Schwarzschild, Steven S. "Aesthetics." *Contemporary Jewish Religious Thought.* 1–6.

Schwartz, Howard and Rudolf, Anthony, ed. *Voices within the Ark: The Modern Jewish Poets.* New York: Avon Books, 1980.

Schwerner, Armand. *Seaweed.* Los Angeles: Black Sparrow P, 1969.

———. *sounds of the river Naranjana & The Tablets I–XXIV.* Barrytown, NY: Station Hill P, 1983.

———. *The Tablets.* Orono, ME: The National Poetry Foundation, 1999.

Seidman, Hugh. *People Live, They Have Lives.* Oxford, OH: Miami UP, 1992.

———. *Selected Poems: 1965–1995.* Oxford, OH: Miami UP, 1995.

———. *Throne/Falcon/Eye.* New York: Vintage, 1982.

Selinger, Eric Murphy. "From Bop Kabbalah to *Jews with Horns.*" Unpublished paper presented at the "Poetry of the 1950s" Conference, University of Maine, Orono, ME, June, 1996.

Shapiro, Harvey. *Battle Report: Selected Poems.* Middletown, CT: Wesleyan UP, 1966.

———. "Exalted Lament." *Midstream* (Autumn 1961): 95–98.

———. *The Eye.* Denver: Alan Swallow, 1953.

———. "I Write Out of an Uncreated Identity." *The Writer in the Jewish Community.* 21–23.

———. *Lauds & Nightsounds.* New York: Sun, 1978.

———. *The Light Holds.* Middletown, CT: Wesleyan UP, 1984.

———. *Mountain, Fire, Thornbush.* Denver: Alan Swallow, 1961.

———. "Remembering Charles Reznikoff." *Charles Reznikoff: Man and Poet.* 85–87.

———. *Selected Poems.* Hanover, NH: Wesleyan UP/UP of New England, 1997.

———. *This World.* Middletown, CT: Wesleyan UP, 1971.

Shechner, Mark. *After the Revolution: Studies in the Contemporary Jewish American Imaginaion.* Bloomington, IN: Indiana UP, 1987.

Shreiber, Maeera Y. "The End of Exile: Jewish Identity and Its Diasporic Poetics." *PMLA* 113.2 (March 1998): 273–287.

Siegal, Richard and Sofer, Tamar. *The Writer in the Jewish Community: An Israeli-North American Dialogue.* Rutherford, NJ: Fairleigh Dickinson UP, 1993.

Smith, Barbara Herrnstein. *Poetic Closure: A Study of How Poems End.* Chicago: U of Chicago P, 1968.

Sontag, Susan. *On Photography.* 1977. New York: Doubleday, 1990.

Steiner, George. "Postscript." *Language and Silence: Essays on Language, Literature and the Inhuman.* 1967. New York: Atheneum, 1982. 155–168.

Stevens, Wallace. *The Collected Poems.* 1954. New York: Vintage Books, 1990.

Tomas, John. "Portrait of the Artist as a Young Jew: Zukofsky's "Poem beginning 'The'" in Context." *Sagetrieb* 9.1 & 2 (Spring & Fall 1990): 43–64.

Van Spanckeren, Kathryn. "Moonrise in Ancient Sumer: Armand Schwerner's *The Tablets.*" *American Poetry Review* 22.4 (July/August 1993): 15–19.

Wald, Alan M. *The New York Intellectuals: The Rise and Decline of the Anti-Stalinist Left from the 1930s to the 1980s.* Chapel Hill, NC: U of North Carolina P, 1987.

Wilde, Oscar. *Complete Works of Oscar Wilde.* London: Collins, 1966.

Williams, William Carlos. *Spring and All.* 1923. *Imaginations.* Ed. Webster Schott. New York: New Directions, 1970. 88–151.

Yerushalmi, Yosef Hayim. *Zakhor: Jewish History and Jewish Memory.* Seattle: U of Washington P, 1982.

Zukofsky, Louis. *"A."* Berkeley & Los Angeles: U of California P, 1978.

———. *Complete Short Poetry.* Baltimore: Johns Hopkins UP, 1991.

———. *Prepositions: The Collected Critical Essays.* Expanded Edition. Berkeley & Los Angeles: U of California P, 1981. 12–18.

———. "Program: 'Objectivists' 1931." *Charles Reznikoff: Man and Poet.* 377–388.

———. *A Test of Poetry.* 1948. New York: C. Z. Publications, 1980.

Index